BEHIND THE LINES

THE WORLD OF DREW PEARSON

By HERMAN KLURFELD

PRENTICE-HALL, INC., ENGLEWOOD CLIFFS, N.J.

BEHIND THE LINES: THE WORLD OF DREW PEARSON

Library of Congress Catalog Card Number: 68-28377

Printed in the United States of America • *T*

Prentice-Hall International, Inc., London
Prentice-Hall of Australia, Pty. Ltd., Sydney
Prentice-Hall of Canada, Ltd., Toronto
Prentice-Hall of India Private Ltd., New Delhi
Prentice-Hall of Japan, Inc., Tokyo

AUTHOR'S ACKNOWLEDGMENTS

I am indebted to Mr. Drew Pearson for supplying me with confidential documents, manuscripts, letters, photos; for offering me access to his files and for taking time out from a crowded life to patiently answer countless questions which provided me with exclusive information and unique insights.

I am grateful to Mr. Pearson's friends, foes, colleagues, and employees for their assistance, especially the generous and gracious cooperation of Mrs. Katherine Raley, Mr. Pearson's secretary, and Ernest Cuneo, gentleman, scholar, and friend.

For both suggesting and locating sources, I wish to thank Mr. Sam Klurfeld, Miss Lucy Freeman, Miss Bernadette Monnier, and Mr. Jack Schaeffer. Special thanks to the Klurfelds who assisted in the manuscript-typing: Jim, Elaine, Ruth, Judy, Larry, and Scott.

CONTENTS

FOR JEANETTE

ST. LOUIS POST

The Only Evening Newspaper in St. Louis With the Associated Press News Service

ST. LOUIS, WEDNESDAY, NOVEMBER 7, 1928.—48 PAGES.

STATES FOR HOOVER; 444 ELECTORAL VOTE

...DSLIDE BREAKS VIRGINIA, NORTH CAROLINA, FLORIDA—PROBABLY TEXAS—FROM SOLID SOUT...

The New Political Map

G. O. P. MAJORITY

SMITH GE... ONLY E... STATES... 87 V...

Hoover Has 17... Smith 12,48...

VARIETY

BROADWAY

SCREEN

25¢

...ALL ST. LAYS AN EGG

The New York Times.

NEW YORK, TUESDAY, OCTOBER 29, 1929.

TWO CENTS

THE WEATHER

...RS RENEW ON HOOVER ...FF STAND

Roosevelt's Memory Honored In Navy Day Fete on Ships

EUROPE IS DISTURBED BY AMERICAN ACTION ON OCCUPATION DEBT

London Urges an Explanation of Move for Direct Payments by Germany.

BANK'S PRESTIGE INVOLVED

STOCK PRICES SLUMP $14,000,000,0... IN NATION-WIDE STAMPEDE TO UNLO... BANKERS TO SUPPORT MARKET T...

Sixteen Leading Issues Down $2... Tel. & Tel. and ...

The New York Times.

LATE CITY EDITION

NEW YORK, FRIDAY, JULY 29, 1932.

TWO CENTS

TROOPS DRIVE VETERANS FROM CAPITAL; FIRE CAMPS THERE AND AT ANACOSTIA; ... KILLED, SCORES HURT IN DAY OF STRIFE

Thousands Crowding Into Los Angeles For Opening of Olympic Games Tomorrow

HOOVER ORDERS EVICTION

"All the News That's Fit to Print."

The New York Times.

LATE CITY EDITION

NEW YORK, SATURDAY, SEPTEMBER 19, 1931.

TWO CENTS

...PANESE SEIZE MUKDEN ... BATTLE WITH CHINESE;

MRS. COLLINGS' STORY ATTACKED AT INQUEST AS SHE STAYS AWAY

White House Inquiry for Brewery Data Stirs Wets; For Outsider, Says Secretary

By RICHARD V. OULAHAN.

RELIEF COMPROMISE REACHED AT A... AFTER CONFERENCE LASTING TILL... ROOSEVELT'S COMMISSION PLAN A...

Three Unemployment Measures Passed by One or Both Houses

ALL DIFFEREN...

The New York Times.

LATE CITY EDITION

NEW YORK, THURSDAY, JULY 28, 1932.

TWO CENTS

$3,000,000 IS LOANED TO ILLINOIS BY R. F. C. AS FIRST RELIEF ACT

Emergency Advance Made as State's Funds for Unemployment Reach Vanishing Point.

3% INTEREST TO BE PAID

Lightning Strikes Riverside Church Tower; 5-Foot Stone Blocks Fall 400 Feet to Drive

ROOSEVELT AND ELY REACH AGREEMENT AFTER ALBANY TALK

Massachusetts Executive to Announce Results of Conference on Monday.

San Francisco to Analyze Liquor Free After Three Die

WARN CITY TO SLASH BUDGET, CUT REALTY BY $3,000,000,000

PREFACE

Drew Pearson was the son of a scholarly Quaker. As World War I was breaking out, he entered Swarthmore College, a Quaker institution, where his father had taught public speaking. Graduating from Swarthmore in 1919, Pearson worked with the American Friends Service Committee in the Balkans and returned home with the desire to enlist in the diplomatic corps. Unable to finance his diplomatic aspirations, he accepted a position teaching industrial geography at the University of Pennsylvania.

Pearson sought a suitable substitute for a diplomatic career. He decided to make himself a foreign correspondent. A friend who had lectured around the world lent him a copy of his publicity circular and, with his permission, Pearson substituted his own name. Marked "Confidential—Not for Publication," the circular, under the headline "Around the World with Drew Pearson," stated: "Asia, Africa and Europe are favorite fields to Drew Pearson. He has visited all three continents. He has an international point of view. . . . As a lecturer on international politics, Pearson is known over most of this country and in Europe."

Later, Pearson traveled around the country and sold his idea to thirty-five editors from Philadelphia to Seattle.

While Pearson was moving around the world, he received a wire from a newspaper syndicate offering high fees if he could obtain interviews with some of Europe's leaders. Pearson got the interviews. Following this coup he was offered and accepted the post of foreign editor of a new Washington paper called "The United States Daily." From this job he stepped into the Washington Bureau of the *Baltimore Sun* and was assigned to cover the State Department. While there he became acquainted with another Washington correspondent named Robert S. Allen. They wrote an anonymous book titled *Washington Merry-Go-Round,* an exposé which bared the warts of heretofore sacrosanct politicians and society leaders.

The furor created by the book attracted the attention of syndicate editors. United Features Syndicate offered Pearson and his partner a contract to write a column titled "Washington Merry-Go-Round." The starting salary was $25.00 weekly each. The first column appeared on December 12, 1932. By the end of 1933 it was published in 225 newspapers. As a pioneering effort, the column had a far-reaching influence on government and journalism.

Until the 1830's the leaders of journalism were masters of the poison pen and the political backstab. They were succeeded by the dramatic and egocentric editors of the second era, notably James Gordon Bennett and Horace Greeley, who gave way to the strong-minded businessman-publisher titans—Joseph Pulitzer, William Randolph Hearst, Colonel McCormick, and Joseph and Cissy Patterson.

The evolution of column-writing had its roots in the ferocious competition among newspapers. Publishers constantly sought to create new merchandising methods. The New York *World*'s editor Herbert Bayard Swope created the famous "op-ed" page. This was nothing more or less than printing the work of excellent writers opposite the editorial page. Since their unique personalities could not be duplicated by competitors, they gave the newspaper a special selling advantage. Thus were developed F.P.A., Heywood Broun, and many others.

The publishers found that these unique personalities could sell their papers. They realized that columnists were gaining their own followers, and then offered columns as a by-product to newspapers throughout the country, usually offering the columnist a 50-50 arrangement.

This was the early pattern. Such an arrangement not only gave the columnist far more circulation than any individual newspaper,

Drew Pearson, shortly after beginning his column. "The black cat," he told the photographer, "signifies bad luck for dishonest politicians."

Pearson meets Congressman Joseph Martin. Capitol Hill has been one of his favorite news sources and targets.

but provided a national following. And it also gave the columnist fullest financial independence. Some columnists even began to have their own radio programs.

As the popularity of columns spiraled and the Pearson column gained national recognition, the Washington image was gradually transformed.

Until Pearson and others launched their style of national reporting, there had been an aura of sanctity about the White House, the Supreme Court and the Federal Government in general. Thanks to the columnists, Washington stopped being a mystery to the American people. Affairs of state began to be available to the average citizen. He no longer had to take government policies on faith.

Of course the Old Guard fought Pearson. It used every instrument of the Establishment, from closing news sources to blacklisting. But it didn't work. Pearson was using straight reporting tactics in a field where there was more befogging incense than hard fact. He was the first Washington columnist with the nation as an audience. This straight-line reporting had the effect of debunking the old mystique. It also caused the American people to become more conscious of national politics and their role in them.

The feet of clay of the old gods were revealed. The Depression was on and Pearson reported the government in terms of the people's daily lives, at a time when their very existence was at stake. His vast readership looked to him to reach into and explore the process of government. Ultimately, government leaders went to Drew Pearson to explain the processes of government to the people.

Pearson's career has resulted in tangles with almost every president and countless politicians over the last four decades. This is his story behind, and between, the lines.

"All the News That's Fit to Print."

The New York Times

NEW YORK, FRIDAY, SEPTEMBER 1, 1939.

THREE CENTS

LXXXVIII....No. 29,805.

GERMAN ARMY ATTACKS POLAND; CITIES BOMBED, PORT BLOCKADED; DANZIG IS ACCEPTED INTO REICH

FREE CITY IS SEIZED

Hitler Acts Against Poland

HITLER GIVES WORD

In a Proclamation He Accuses Warsaw of Appeal to Arms

ROOSEVELT TOTAL GROWS

EXTRA

20 Pupils Gassed

BLUE STREAK EDITION

WEATHER: RAIN

THE CALL BULLETIN

85TH YEAR

WEDNESDAY, NOVEMBER 6, 1940

5c DAILY

40 States Go To Democ...

State Lead Now ...

WAR EXTRA

The San Francisco News

FINAL

SPORTS-FINANCIAL

PRICE FIVE CENTS

Local Forecast: Fair and mild today, tomorrow and Sunday; moderate west wind. (Full U. S. Weather Bureau report on Page 22.)

No. 197

SAN FRANCISCO, FRIDAY, AUGUST 16, 1940

Vol. 38

LONDON BOMBED

The Philadelphia Inquirer

PUBLIC LEDGER

An Independent Newspaper for All the People

LATEST WAR EXTRA

MONDAY MORNING, DECEMBER 8, 1941

Second Largest 3c Morning Circulation in America

THREE CENTS

JAP AIR TROOPS IN PHILIPPINES

Pearl Harbor Raid Kills 1...

NEW YORK, Dec. 8 (Monday) (A. P.).—Mutual Broadcasting System's correspondent in Manila reported today that Japanese parachute troops had been landed in the Philippines. The National Broadcasting Co. said the U. S. aircraft tender ... unofficially in Manila to have been damaged in action with Jap-

Pearson from San Diego, where she was toiling as a waitress. She had changed her mind about him.

In the spring of 1925, Pearson went to San Diego and they were married. The marriage was an emotional roller-coaster, zooming with months of joy and plunging into months of despair. Pearson has declared: "My mother-in-law did everything possible to bring happiness to a match which had few ingredients of success. Among other things, she offered us a fabulous income, which we refused."

Pearson's $125 weekly income did not add to marital harmony. After all, his wife had lived a jeweled existence. Countess Felicia had the world on a string; Mrs. Pearson had to live on a shoestring.

In an effort to minimize the economic problem, Pearson managed to wangle a trip to China to cover the Communist movement there. He and his wife traveled first class, all expenses paid.

From China the Pearsons headed for the Gobi desert toward Mongolia, the wedge between Red Russia and China. After some difficulty, Pearson managed to secure a passport to Mongolia by bribing an official with candy, cigarettes, and a blue-and-gold silk handkerchief. In Mongolia, Pearson got his first significant exclusive story. He was able to obtain photographs of Russian arms entering China. A caravan of Chinese-driven cars, stacked with rifles, moved from Russian to Chinese territory. In time, Pearson managed to leave Russian territory and turned over to the American military attaché in Peking the evidence of Russia's secret buildup of a Communist military machine in China.

Historically this was a momentous story. But this was 1925, and Americans were apathetic about the threat of Communism in China. As a matter of fact, anyone who stressed this peril was swiftly dismissed as an hysterical alarmist. Nobody gave a damn. Hardly anybody, at any rate. Pearson's syndicate failed to interest editors in the Communism-in-China story. The nation was enjoying the Roaring Twenties, Wall Street was flying high, and the big problem was gaining admittance to the proper speakeasies. The New York *American* was the only paper to carry Pearson's story.

In the meantime, Pearson's marriage began the agonizing process of disintegration hidden by the legal word, "incompatibility." After the Pearsons returned from China they settled in Washington and

Drew joined the staff of David Lawrence's *United States Daily*. Mrs. Pearson wrote film reviews for the Washington *Post*. A daughter was born, and Pearson's mother-in-law brimmed with delight. No grandmother could have been grander. But the happy event was only a flash of sunlight in a marriage that was dimming. Felicia Pearson later explained: "He wanted me to be too domestic. I'm not much for pressing pants."

Some time later, Pearson was covering foreign affairs for the *United States Daily*. One afternoon he was in a State Department elevator bringing him to the pressroom when he noticed a man standing next to him reading the front page of the Washington *Times*. Pearson glanced at a headline and was unable to comprehend what his eyes could see: "DREW PEARSON TO BE DIVORCED."

Strangely, the divorce seemed to intensify the warmth of the relationship between Pearson and his mother-in-law. Perhaps the togetherness was motivated by the swords-point stance between Cissy Patterson and her willful daughter. Their quarrels were prolonged and bitter. Moreover, Cissy had no son, and after the marital split the mother-in-law and son-in-law became more like mother and son. When Cissy's second husband, Elmer Schlesinger, succumbed to a coronary on a golf course in Aiken, South Carolina, Pearson accompanied Cissy on her sad mission to bring the body home.

Following the death of her husband, Cissy sought an outlet for her energies. Her interest in journalism flared. She tried to purchase Hearst's Washington *Herald*. Hearst and Cissy were good friends and his admiration for her was enormous, but he refused to sell. She did, however, impress the publisher with her journalistic enterprise—securing several exclusive stories, including an interview with underworld chief Al Capone—and Hearst offered her the editorship of the *Herald* at $10,000 a year.

Cissy quickly accepted the offer. The money was secondary, of course. She was spurred by the desire to use her paper as a weapon against Alice Roosevelt Longworth, with whom she had feuded. And feud she did.

The feline barbs Cissy tossed at Mrs. Longworth were must-reading for Washington society. As Cissy quickly learned, Washington adores reading about itself, and the more personal the better. Her personal journalism caused a steady increase in the *Herald*'s circulation. From 1930 to 1936—while Cissy functioned as editor—the paper's circulation zoomed from 60,000 to 130,000.

In 1937 she expressed opposition to Hearst's anti-FDR policies and leased the *Herald,* so that she could express her own views. Several months later she leased the evening *Times.* Shortly thereafter, she bought both properties and published them as the Washington *Times-Herald.*

Her competition was the conservative Washington *Star,* the Scripps-Howard tabloid *News,* and the liberal Washington *Post,* then published by Eugene Meyer. Cissy's *Times-Herald* outsold its competitors by a wide margin.

Through the early period of Cissy Patterson's journalistic career, everything was blue skies and sunshine with her son-in-law. His column was highlighted in her paper. She sought his editorial counsel. He often visited with her at her Long Island home and always spent summer holidays with his daughter at Cissy's Maryland estate. The sunny atmosphere extended to the new Mrs. Pearson. The columnist's bride was Luvie Moore, the Washington *Times-Herald* movie critic. The new Mrs. Pearson, a bright and beautiful young lady, was accepted by Cissy as a daughter. Her blessing represented the most treasured wedding gift for the happy Pearsons.

Drew admired and was awed by Cissy's slashing journalistic style. She was never content to dwell on a mountain top and survey the world. She wanted to be where the action was. If the action stilled, she created more. Before long her personal journalism began to grow teeth. Her victims described them as fangs.

Cissy's imperious qualities characterized her paper. Every night she passed upon the paper's banner headlines and front-page makeup. Even when she was thousands of miles away, she checked this by phone. With total authority she controlled details that most publishers delegated to the taste and judgment of editors. Through her gift for journalism, her native feeling for the dramatic, her remarkable sense of timing, she built an exciting paper. Cissy Patterson had the sharp foresight that enabled her to map out in her mind tne newspaper she desired. She knew what she wanted and what Washington readers wanted.

What air and bread are to ordinary folks, feuds and gossip are to Washington. Intrigue is a major industry there. As Pearson later wrote: "Along with the rest of Washington, I smirked and enjoyed Cissy's feuds and gossip. Little did I dream that the acid that dripped from my mother-in-law's pen later would fall on me."

Eugene Meyer's hide was among those Cissy nailed to her typewriter. At the time he resigned from the Federal Reserve Board to purchase the Washington *Post,* Eugene and his wife, Agnes, had been Cissy's friends and intimates. But as far as Cissy was concerned, friendship was one thing and business another. She was willing to sacrifice one for the other.

The Washington *Post* published several of the Chicago *Tribune* syndicated comic strips. Since the comics were born in the family's paper, Cissy was of the opinion that she should inherit them. Publisher Meyer refused to surrender his contractual rights, whereupon Cissy sued and lost. The courtroom setback failed to stop her, for Cissy never accepted defeat as final. Defeat was merely a delay of victory, and it intensified her attack. For openers, she sent Meyer a gift-wrapped pound of raw beefsteak with a card reading, "Eugene, here is your pound of flesh." Their feud raged for years.

Toward the end of the 1930's, Cissy Patterson's comic strip controversies were supplanted by deadly serious debates involving the fate of the nation. Nazism and Fascism were moving toward their sinister destination, but many Americans, including Cissy Patterson, lacked a sense of urgency. They insulated themselves from the harsh realism and believed the nation could isolate itself from catastrophe.

The isolationists were challenged by the interventionists. It was basically a journalistic clash. The isolationist case was argued by the Patterson family papers and the Hearst group. On the other side was a committee formed by William Allen White, famed editor of the Emporia *Gazette*. White came from isolationist Kansas and was widely respected by his fellow newspaper editors. He urged all aid short of war to the Allies. White's group gained the support of Drew Pearson, Walter Winchell, the Washington *Post,* and other notables in the journalistic arena. The lines were drawn.

The isolationists and interventionists each saw different worlds. At first the debate was a competitive struggle of ideas actuated by honest convictions. But somewhere, somehow, the squabble became savage, personal, and unreasoning. It was personalized by Drew Pearson and Cissy Patterson. She had supported FDR, and had once described Mrs. Roosevelt as "the noblest woman I have ever known." But in 1939 she changed her opinion. The isolationist-intervention issue made Roosevelt an anathema to her. It was an ugly fight. And it was a fight to the finish.

Pearson expressed his opposition to isolationists vehemently and almost daily. As a result his mail was littered with threats. One day the Pearson office received a package addressed to Mrs. Pearson. It was wrapped as a gift. Inside was a miniature black coffin with a paper skeleton marked "Your husband." The grisly gift indicated the black mood of the times.

Cissy's reaction to Pearson's anti-isolationist campaign is understandable on a purely emotional basis. After all, her cousin Bertie McCormick and her brother Joe Patterson were compulsive isolationists. The Chicago *Tribune* and New York *Daily News* were the most powerful isolationist voices in the land. Since Cissy considered Drew a member of the family, his maverick stance on this vital issue was equated with family disloyalty and even ingratitude. Pearson, in her view, was a defector from the family's united front which Cissy upheld with an almost mystical dedication.

The bitterness of the debate deepened after FDR won his tradition-breaking third term. The President interpreted the election result as a mandate for all-out support of Britain: "The United States must be the great arsenal of democracy."

Roosevelt's election was followed by two major Pearson scoops relating to the isolationist-interventionist conflict. He broke the destroyers-for-bases deal. At first it was categorically denied by the White House, and Cissy chided Drew about this inaccuracy. But two weeks later his story was officially confirmed. It was a horse trade whereby the United States would receive in exchange for forty destroyers a string of naval bases essential to the defense of the United States. The deal infuriated isolationists.

Another exclusive Pearson shocker concerned Senator Lundeen of Minnesota, a much-publicized isolationist leader. After Lundeen was killed in a mysterious plane crash in 1940, Drew disclosed he was enroute to deliver a pro-Nazi speech written for him by George Sylvester Viereck, a paid agent for Hitler. Isolationist Senators Wheeler and Borah delivered scathing speeches on the Senate floor and hurled the liar charge at Pearson. Later Viereck was prosecuted for being a German agent, and during the trial it developed that he had written Lundeen's speeches. He went to jail.

Although Cissy was dismayed by Pearson's opposition to her isolationist position, their personal relationship remained on an even keel until November 1941. Some of Cissy's "best friends" were interventionists. She enjoyed the black humor of inviting isolationists and interventionists to 15 Dupont Circle and then awaiting the inevitable fireworks. During one black-tie get-together her guests included interventionist Bernard Baruch and Senator Wheeler, a fanatic isolationist. The placid elegance of the evening vanished as Wheeler and Baruch engaged in a heated debate. Everyone got into the battle. As the departures were made, the battle-ruffled guests were hardly speaking to each other. Cissy at the head of the staircase was a study in mixed emotions. She was a political supporter of Wheeler, but she was tremendously fond of Baruch. On the other hand, she was fairly glowing with the enjoyment of the drama of the battle royal, and whether the glow was that of enjoyment or of contained wrath, or both, witnesses now have trouble in recalling.

In November 1941 there was a lively hubbub at the Pearson home as Cissy arrived to celebrate her birthday with Drew and his wife. Politics was unmentioned—the conversation was dominated by happy trivialities. Cissy was charming, gay, and motherly as ever. That was the last time the Pearson-Patterson friendship burned brightly.

The first signs of the dimming fire came in the form of censorship. Within a two-week period, Cissy heavily edited or deleted a half-dozen of Pearson's columns. The columns massacred by her blue pencil were concerned with Pearson's advocacy of aid to the Allies or rebuffs to isolationists. Cissy's intentions were crystal clear.

Pearson was confronted with the paradox of syndicated journalism. Having four hundred outlets means you are without a single boss, yet you may have four hundred masters. Each editor has the right to cut a column, and often the cuts are made for reasons of space. Sometimes the excisions are purely geographic—an agricultural item might be meaningful in Kansas and lack news value for New York City readers. All too often, however, the editorial cuts are motivated by political partisanship, fear of alienating local groups, or purely personal hostility. Some editors derive a certain pleasure in butchering the efforts of famous columnists. Frequently the question of whether the editing is responsible or irresponsible depends on whether you are a columnist or an editor. Possibly columnists and editors are condemned by nature, like cats and dogs, to hostility. Editors are high on the list of Pearson's pet gripes. "Those who publish my column," he observed, "often hack it up and twist it around. Hell, one editor said he likes my columns better than Lippmann's because mine are easier to cut."

Clearly, the columnist-editor relationship will never be fully reconciled. Over the years, Pearson has been quick to retaliate against what he considered censorship. In May 1937 the columnist divulged that Postmaster General Jim Farley had received a $100,000-a-year salary offer from the Hearst chain. His syndicate killed the story.

The columnist responded by sending a private letter to every editor using his column:

> To the Editor Using the Washington Merry-Go-Round:
>
> You probably have been puzzled regarding the kill of that part of the May 14th column in which Mr. Hearst was reported offering a $100,000 salary to Postmaster General Farley.
>
> The "kill" was issued by the United Feature Syndicate without our authorization and despite our vigorous protest. The accuracy of the story is not questioned. It had been confirmed by Mr. Farley and was not disputed by the Hearst organization, although there were requests from its representatives that the story be suppressed.
>
> The authors took the stand that a salary offer to so important a figure as the Postmaster General and Chairman of

> the Democratic National Committee was news, and should be published whether the offer came from a newspaper publisher, a liquor association, or anyone else.
>
> The Syndicate, in the end, took a contrary view. In fairness to you, I felt that you should be advised of the facts.

Pearson was aware of his vulnerability before the Farley incident. It became clear that his columns were run at the editor's whim when some columns he wrote about Pan-American Airways were suppressed. It shocked Pearson into the realization that he must have an alternate outlet. The obvious one was radio. Thus Pearson joined the newscasting ranks.

By the end of the 1930's radio news began to emerge from a long silence. Newspapers were no longer the originators of spot news since radio deprived them of that function. Basically, the expansion of newscasting was the consequence of the European crisis.

In September 1938, Hitler's threat of war against Czechoslovakia roused the apathetic American public to the terror of a global war. As a corollary, the war crisis expanded the efforts of radio correspondents overseas. Prior to the crisis, newscasters abroad were heard infrequently, generally reporting innocuous events. For example, when the Nazis overran Austria, Edward R. Murrow, CBS' chief European correspondent, was in Warsaw arranging a musical program featuring a children's choir.

The war changed the course of radio news. Those who reported and analyzed European events—H. V. Kaltenborn, Edward R. Murrow, William L. Shirer, and Drew Pearson—all attracted huge audiences. The power and popularity of newscasting became a fact.

For a time, Pearson used his microphone to make public news and opinion that Cissy had censored. Although Drew was irritated by the blue-penciling, he was patient for personal reasons. He believed that this was merely a passing pout on the part of his former mother-in-law and that his freedom of expression would soon be restored.

One week prior to December 7, 1941, the Washington Merry-Go-Round had reported, "The Japanese fleet has been put out to sea and might attack anywhere."

Walter Winchell speaks to Mr. & Mrs. America.

Calvin Coolidge and family.

Cissy Patterson in roundtable discussion with Postmaster-General Jim Farley and friend during 1943 AP meeting in New York.

Publisher Cissy Patterson aboard the *Ile de France* in August 1934.

Cissy dismissed such reporting as "the rantings of alarmists and warmongers." She never believed the United States would be attacked. And even the Japanese attack failed to change her isolationist stance. On the contrary, she became more fervently isolationist in the week following the Pearl Harbor attack, and her censorship of the Pearson column became more reckless and frequent.

Late in January 1942, Pearson flew to Brazil to attend a conference of Latin-American foreign ministers blueprinting the defense of the Western Hemisphere. When he returned, he learned that Eugene Meyer, publisher of the Washington *Post,* had approached Robert S. Allen, then coauthor of the column, and they had tentatively agreed to transfer the column from the *Times-Herald* to the *Post*. Drew was reluctant. He knew the move meant a battle. Newspaper publishers can cancel columns, but columns never cancel publishers. However, Pearson's coauthor was adamant and Eugene Meyer was persuasive. It fell to Pearson to write his mother-in-law on February 13, 1942, giving her six months notice of cancellation. This began a knockdown, dragout fight that left an indelible mark on Pearson. He was forever branded with Cissy's rage. Most of the time, a columnist's move from one paper to another is a routine occupational shuffle. But not in this case. There was raw emotion involved. In Cissy's judgment the switch might be compared to changing sides in the middle of a war. She was not concerned with the logical inevitability of Pearson's change as a result of her censorship. This was something personal, deeply personal. And hardly anyone was more subjective than Cissy Patterson. She translated everything in personal terms.

Pearson immediately topped her lengthy hate list. At first she called him her "headache boy," but this was a mild rebuke compared to the slugging that followed.

Pearson canceled his column in Cissy's paper. This was the equivalent of a columnist firing a publisher. Cissy regarded this as a massive insult, unforgivable and deserving of every punishment. Moreover, she was emotionally incapable of accepting Pearson's decision to leave her paper.

She lashed back with an editorial contending she had dropped

Pearson for three reasons: He was unreliable, irresponsible, and reprehensible. The columnist was understandably stunned and angered by Cissy's blast. He sought to set the record straight by buying a full page ad in the Washington *Post,* stressing that the shoe was on the other foot. The columnist had chosen to leave Cissy Patterson.

But it was not easy to place the facts on the public record. Washington *Post* publisher Meyer put his tail between his legs. He had been exposed to Cissy's heat in the past and had no desire for an encore. Pearson later commented: "I didn't blame him. He knew the lady's wrath." Besides, the Publishers' Establishment has its own unwritten code. It is practically taboo for one newspaper publisher to criticize or embarrass another. Publishers, despite their competition for news and the advertising dollar, tend to regard themselves as members of a family and generally prefer to thrash out differences behind closed doors.

Pearson then went to the vice-president of the Washington *Evening Star*, who was equally reluctant to let the demon out of the bottle. He considered the ad amusing but would not run it. "Publishers have to stick together."

The Washington *News* also rejected the ad, but recorded its text, word for word, as a news story.

As the weeks passed, Cissy's fury mounted. Her anger against Pearson was neither limited by anything specific nor bounded by any sense of discrimination. It was not one thing about Pearson that enraged her—or ten or twenty. It was everything. Everything Drew said, did, wrote; every aspect of his professional life, every corner of his personal life. It was a classic case of character assassination. Cissy, of course, deemed it justifiable homicide. As one correspondent observed, "If Drew reported that Tuesday followed Monday, that was reason enough for Cissy to lambaste him."

Generally, the Washington press enjoyed the spectacle of a columnist being thrown to a lioness. Pearson's major journalistic ally was Walter Winchell. The latter was as vigorously anti-isolationist as Pearson. In common with Drew, Winchell's column was the object of Hearst's censorship. And like Pearson, Winchell utilized his radio broadcast to report news and opinions deleted from his column. In time, Winchell tangled with Cissy and she sued him for libel.

Except for Winchell and one or two anti-isolationist papers, Pearson's struggle was a lonely one. Although the United States was engaged in a global war, the prime topic of conversation at Washington social affairs was the Pearson-Patterson War.

Cissy enlisted every ally. She assigned writers to prepare anti-Pearson diatribes for legislators who would insert them in the Congressional Record. Actually, the most vitriolic pieces were written by Cissy, a master of invective who seemingly never ran out of ammunition. Her shots echoed in magazines and other newspapers. Pearson was under siege.

One of her milder rebukes: "The Baltimore *Sun* got rid of Pearson. He found himself about as welcome as a leper in a diet kitchen. Possibly no man in Washington ever had so many doors slammed in his face. Hate began to corrode him, and former friends relate that, green around the gills, he used to roll on the floor in hysterical rages."

At first Pearson sought to counter Cissy's offensive with a calm, logical recitation of the facts that she often ignored or distorted. This was ineffective. In a knockdown brawl, logic is at a disadvantage. The only thing that counts is muscle.

Cissy had the muscle. Drew was unable to exceed the power of her vituperation. Accordingly, he was compelled to roll with the punches.

A typical Cissy Patterson flurry appeared on the editorial page of the Washington *Times-Herald* under the title "Rats Under Cover."

> We have been reading with considerable interest the dispatches by one Drew Pearson from the Paris conference. He started out with a pro-Russian patronizing attitude toward U.S. Secretary of State Byrnes and now is openly anti-Russian and pulling frantically for the American shore.
>
> On Wednesday, Pearson even had this to say. "One of the great mistakes we are making is a tendency toward Balkanization—Italo-Americans are behaving as if they were Italians, Jewish-Americans as if they were Palestinians,

Polish-Americans as if they were Poles—rather than all Americans.

"They took no oath to uphold others, and splitting our country into groups can be disastrous."

Imagine that, coming from a thing who has devoted the past five or six years of his life to fomenting more racial and religious hate and discord in America than anybody else still out of jail.

What's happened? The answer is plain enough.

When Hitler rose to power in Europe, a collection of un-American crackpot intellectuals, intrigue lovers, revolutionaries and plain crooks saw an opportunity to get rich over here and at the same time build up their apparent importance. In that general corner were Pearson, Winchell, and the New York *Post*. It is a disgustingly familiar list.

Because Hitler was attacking minorities and inflaming hatreds in Europe, these troublemakers began to work the same racket over here in their own way.

Some went after the Catholics, some after the Protestants, some after the Jews, and others after Americans only lately from Europe, to revive and play on the ancestral bigotries they had come here to escape.

Pearson is just one example, but we use him here because he worked out of Washington and we know him. And how. For years he was both undercover agent and big mouthpiece for the Anti-Defamation League, a powerful Jewish organization which, seized by war hysteria, sought by hook or by crook to force quite a number of free Americans to change their way of thinking. Pearson supplied the crook part.

He taught many a Jew and non-Jew as well to fear and hate his fellow Americans.

And he added to that his apology and special pleading for Communist Russia, an old line he had been peddling without variation from the day the United States recognized the Soviet regime in 1933.

This racket made him rich. It put in his pocket money beyond his wildest dreams. More than that, it satisfied his natural and overpowering lust for lying, intrigue, character assassination and spying. All of which, next to money, are the aims of his life.

We will say for him that he played his part with obnoxious art and success. He and Winchell screeched back and forth to one another on the radio in fine hair-raising style, and in their various columns peddled to small newspapers all through the country they planted their jolts of strychnine cleverly.

Many people were taken in and believed their guff to the effect that Russia was our Great Ally which had gone to war to save us. No mention was made of the now almost forgotten fact that actually Stalin and Hitler jointly pulled the trigger that started the war in 1939 and nobody in Russia ever lifted a finger contrariwise until Hitler attacked Russia in 1941.

It was a highly profitable racket while it lasted, but since V-J Day, it has run down. The American people have not forgotten the propaganda blared out by Pearson, Winchell, et al. And today they recognize it only as a pack of damned lies.

So the rats are beginning to grease over the side of the sinking ship. Winchell was the first to go. He started out with more and more sour cracks at his old pal, Molotov, then made a feeble attempt at reviving his pre-statesmanship style of Broadway gossip.

Pearson, since he got to Paris, has been trying the same escape trick. He is trying to pretend at last that he has always been 100 percent American, maybe because J. Stalin has proved himself for Russia first, last and all the time.

Pearson even has the consummate gall to come slithering along claiming that he, too, is an American Firster and has been all the time—after all the low down, smearing assaults he made on America First back when that organization was trying to do a patriotic job. Actually, Stalin has just kicked over the stone by his tactics since V-J Day and Pearson is one of the queer things running out into the light for the first time.

He has got over there to Paris and had a look right down the muzzle of the gun. He has seen that all the world is at last being forced to decide whether or not it wants to go

> Communist, with all the blood and horror that brings with it.
>
> But he hasn't got the guts to go through with his old routine, this time, now that he has come to enjoy the feel of money and importance harvested by setting one class of Americans against another.
>
> Also it is a familiar communistic tactic to disappear underground when things get too hot. But watch this baby. He'll pop up again.

Unquestionably, there were times when Cissy's abuse almost drove him to wild counterattack. Pearson confessed that he once gravely mulled the idea of suing his former mother-in-law. In desperation he went to his fifteen-year-old daughter and painfully informed her of his intention to take her grandmother to court. The youngster reacted with the wisdom of a Supreme Court judge. She advised: "That's exactly what grandmother wants. Don't give her that satisfaction." Father obeyed.

Pearson tried several methods of living under siege. For several weeks he sought to ignore the barrage, but thoughtful friends told him what Cissy wrote. In the end, the ghoulish fascination of her attacks drew him toward her words.

One Cissy effort covered more than a full page of closely spaced type. It was a devilish masterpiece. For the benefit of historians of vitriol, an excerpt from the introductory remarks:

> Ladies and Gentlemen and Fellow-Chautauqua Lecturers! This is the story of a Quaker Oat who became a sour mash in Washington!
>
> Gather closer, folks, because it's practically an epic. It is instructive, informative, a warning to evildoers. I'm sorry, lady, you'll have to get that boy out of here. This is strictly for adults.
>
> We present for your inspection one of the weirdest specimens of humanity since Nemo, the Turtle Boy. People on seeing him for the first time often make wagers on which way he is facing. Madame, I'm sorry, but I must be insistent. Please take the boy out of here. I don't care if he does have a dirty mind. This is no place for one of his tender years.
>
> Our principal exhibit, ladies and gentleman, is baffling.

> No one can tell how he got that way. The reason why it's difficult to tell which way he is facing is that he has two faces. Also he can talk out of both sides of his mouth at the same time, and if a word of truth comes from either, this management will seriously consider refunding your money.
>
> Don't be alarmed folks, when you first lay eyes on this oddity. But be sure to keep facing him. He has been known to do awful things to people the minute they turn their backs.
>
> This creature, folks, actually has two eyes. At first glance, you may think he only has one, like that fellow Velocipede or Cyclops. The explanation is that his eyes are so close together they overflap.
>
> Don't be frightened when he sniffs at you. . . . The sniff is a nervous habit acquired after years of reading things he wrote. It is a strange sniff, ladies and gentlemen, disconcerting to strangers.
>
> In the event we can get our exhibit to open his two faces wide enough, you will note the poison sacs. For years now we have had to keep our pet Gila monster away from him because, in a battle of fangs, it wouldn't be a fair fight.
>
> The name of this thing—this What-Is-It—is Drew Pearson. Years ago, when he first came to Washington, he was nearly all one color, having only about the normal number of spots on his escutcheon. Today, by rolling in the muck virtually all of his working hours, he has more spots than you can shake a leopard at.

Cissy's Pearsonizing was read aloud at Washington parties. It elicited loud laughter, particularly among politicians who were victims of the Pearson column.

Although Drew had the dubious distinction of leading Cissy Patterson's hate list, he was closely followed by rival publisher Eugene Meyer and by FDR. Cissy referred to Meyer's paper as "our venerable lady friend, the *Post*."

She stepped up her opposition to the President. War or no war, Cissy was utterly convinced of the rightness of her isolationist position. The Washington *Times-Herald*, in conjunction with other press isolationists, represented a formidable problem for FDR, who was realistically aware of isolationist power. When he ordered naval patrols in the Atlantic in the spring of 1941, he did it by executive action. He feared Congressional isolationists might block such authorization. The continuing strength of isolationists was clearly indicated in the summer of 1941 when the House extended the Selective Service Act by the margin of a single vote.

The isolationists included a sinister fringe of bigots, fascists, and assorted crackpots. Some apostles of hate echoed Nazi propaganda and others were not so blatant, but their campaigns of dissension obstructed the nation's war effort.

Pearson spearheaded the campaign against the troublemakers. He was joined by Walter Winchell, the New York *Herald Tribune,* and the Washington *Post*. Reporter Dillard Stokes wrote a series of exposés in the *Post* detailing the activities of the hate-mongers. This resulted in their leaders being indicted for seditious conspiracy.

The Government's efforts to prosecute the defendants were subjected to sniper fire from a group of isolationist and pro-fascist Congressmen. The *Times-Herald* extended editorial support to isolationists and slanted its news columns in their favor. It followed that *Times-Herald* editorials were quoted with approval by the enemy radio and the more vicious isolationist publications in the United States. In all fairness it should be noted that a paper cannot accept responsibility for advocates of its editorial position. Cissy probably despised the lunatic-fringers who echoed her opinions, yet she neglected to reject them. In the end her glaring journalistic sin was not one of ideology but of deliberate distortion of news.

As the war progressed, Cissy's malice alienated some members of her staff. One day the *Times-Herald* carried a photo of American war victims. The caption indicated FDR was responsible for their deaths. Cissy's managing editor, George DeWitt, pleaded with her to delete the layout. When she refused, he quit. Over the years about a dozen editors left the *Times-Herald* as a consequence of their inability to stomach the publisher's capricious methods and blind prejudice.

Cissy Patterson would have been the last to concede that her isolationist position was untenable. The fact was, however, that she was fighting a losing battle. The war's inevitable patriotic surge, coupled with the rampant extremism of many isolationists, marked the beginning of the end. The public gradually realized a policy of isolation was neither safe nor realistic.

Radio played a prime role in changing the national attitude. Newscasters Drew Pearson and Walter Winchell commanded an enormous audience. And their immense popularity armed them with unusual editorial freedom. Rating services estimated the Pearson-Winchell audience exceeded fifty million. Week after week they expressed support for FDR's war policies and hammered isolationists and their cohorts.

The enormity of their audience, the impact of the spoken word, made it realistically impossible for the isolationist forces to launch effective counterattacks. Nevertheless, they tried. Pearson and Winchell were excoriated by isolationist Congressmen, attempts were made to intimidate their sponsors, Cissy Patterson sued Winchell for libel and the case was settled out of court. In the end the tide of history was with the Pearsons.

Personal vicissitudes accelerated Cissy's decline. Her health was failing and she drank too much. She confided to friends that she was gripped by deep depression. "But," she added, "the only happy thought I have is knowing I can go down to the office and give the Administration hell."

And hell she continued to give. Her fury against Pearson was never modified. As a matter of fact, she was motivated by her spleen. Her acid burned others, but it also seared Cissy. The pattern of destruction encompassed self-destruction.

She absorbed a succession of blows. Her brother, Joe Patterson, who had always had the proud and joyous proximity of her affection, died. Cissy, who never did anything halfway, had a star-crossed love affair with a celebrated Eastern publisher who refused to divorce his wife. Her sharp words had whittled away her friends. She had alienated her daughter and communication between them had ceased. Pearson's daughter was uneasy and unhappy when she visited her grandmother.

When her only granddaughter announced her marriage, Cissy's former son-in-law sent her an invitation and a friendly note pleading for peace, or at least a truce. But, in the end, she was the ultimate isolationist. She isolated herself from most of her friends and members of her family who retained a lingering affection for her.

Cissy Patterson's will ignored her granddaughter. And she virtually disinherited her daughter. This was the final slash of an embittered woman. She left her newspaper as a trust to seven executives who promptly sold it to her cousin, Colonel McCormick of the Chicago *Tribune*—who then peddled it to Cissy's feuding partner, Eugene Meyer. In time Cissy's paper was merged and submerged, for a logical reason. The paper was Cissy Patterson. It mirrored her personality and reflected her whims. When she was gone there was no reason for the paper to exist.

Drew Pearson was among her mourners. The funeral was held at her Dupont Circle castle. There a queen reigned, an unruly queen, but still she had the touch of capricious royalty. She ruled, she commanded, she impressed. And for many years her palace was the scene of history, excitement, and gaiety.

It was difficult for Pearson to reconcile the funeral at Dupont Circle with the joyous memories that the house held. It was truly, for the columnist, a bittersweet farewell.

The next day Pearson began his column with the following:

> A great lady died the other day—a lady who caused me so much happiness and so much pain.
>
> She was my ex-mother-in-law, Eleanor Patterson, who used to write about me in such scathing terms that even the very frank *Time* magazine had to interpret them with dots and dashes. And although I never answered her, I want to write about her now, because she represented a great newspaper cycle which may be coming to an end.
>
> Cissy Patterson's one ambition was to be as great a newspaperman as her brother Joe, and though she may not have realized it, she was. She and Joe had grown up together and she worshiped him. That's how Cissy got her nickname; for Joe, as a little boy, could not pronounce "Eleanor."
>
> . . . I shall miss the personal journalism of my ex-mother-in-law, even though I did not agree with it. I shall miss her diatribes against me.
>
> Cissy was tired toward the end of her life, tired and lonesome. Her ruthless use of power had alienated some of her old friends, part of her family.

> The subway under Dupont Circle and in front of her house, which Cissy had fought so bitterly, was finally put through. The ironic fact was that as friends went to her funeral, workmen shoveled on the subway outside.
>
> And so the house on Dupont Circle now goes to the Red Cross and a great lady, representing a great age of journalism, will be troubled by "headaches" no more.

Within Pearson's personal context she was a "Great Lady." Cissy certainly had an angelic side and Drew was lucky enough to have seen it. Yet he was emotionally involved and could not be expected to make a calm appraisal. Pearson, however, was correct in noting that she "represented a great age of journalism."

Three years after Cissy's death, William Randolph Hearst died. The lone survivor of great personal journalism, the Chicago *Tribune*'s Colonel McCormick, died several years later.

In Washington, Cissy Patterson's passing left the Capital journalistic scene tranquil and dull. Even those who assailed Cissy were sorry to see her go. She was an original and unique, a true primitive. She was colorful, zestful, unpredictable as a hurricane. She had awesome vigor and was a fearless fighter. She neither dodged an issue nor feared an enemy. Nevertheless, she dissipated her assets by her inability to anchor herself to rock-like principles. For all the power of her words and the potency of her fury, she frightened more people than she influenced. Her magnificence was one of failure. In common with the mighty publishers who embodied the aura of personal journalism, she did more to entertain and excite than enlighten.

NEW YORK, WEDNESDAY, JANUARY 16, 1935. TWO CENTS

EASURY STEPS IN
DOLLAR MOUNTS
N GOLD CASE TALK

gn Exchange Gyrations
cked After Spectacular
inges by Gold Groups.

FEDERAL BONDS RISE

Hoffman Asks Income Tax And 2% Sales Tax in Jersey

Inaugurated as Governor, He Moves to Raise $35,000,000 for Relief and to Ease Real Estate Burden.

RETAILERS FAVOR JOB INSURANCE AND OLD-AGE FUND

Far-Reaching Program for Social Security Is Proposed by Nation's Merchants.

FEDERAL AIMS ENDORSED

Percy S. Straus Praises Plan as First Action of Kind Taken by a Business Group.

TWO MORE EXPERTS NAME HAUPTMANN AS WRITER OF ALL THE RANSOM NOTES

Wilentz Hopes to Close State Case in a Week

SCOUT FRAME-UP THEORY

Head of Washington Times-Herald, Member of Family Noted in Journalism

BEGAN AS EDITOR IN 1930

Director of Chicago Tribune Was Former Board Chairman of New York Daily News

DAUGHTER FIGHTS PATTERSON WILL

Asserts Mother Was Unstable, Victim of Fraud in Leaving Times-Herald to Executives

WASHINGTON, Sept. 13—Countess Felicia Gizycka, only child of the late Mrs. Eleanor Medill Patterson, attacked her mother's will today, with allegations that Mrs. Patterson was of unsound mind, and the victim of fraud, deceit, undue influence, duress and coercion.

Mrs. Patterson died July 24 at her near-by Maryland country home, leaving an estate of $16,500,000, and bequeathing The Washington Times-Herald, which she published, to seven veteran executives.

Countess Gizycka was named to receive most of Mrs. Patterson's personal effects, real estate in Port Washington, L. I., and North Dakota, and $25,000 annually. No provision was made for the Countess' daughter, and Mrs. Patterson's granddaughter, Ellen Pearson Arnold, because the will stated that a "substantial gift" had previously been made.

Countess Gizycka, who filed a protest today against probate of the Patterson will, is the former wife of Drew Pearson, newspaper columnist. The daughter of that union, Ellen Pearson, is Mrs. George L. Arnold, daughter-in-law of Thurman W. Arnold, the former Assistant Attorney General and Federal judge.

For some time there had been curiosity as to whether Countess Gizycka would permit the will to be probated without an objection. She answered the question by filing a formal paper today, making charges

...rk Times.

LATE CITY EDITION
Generally fair and colder today. Tomorrow generally fair and continued cold.

...ANUARY 6, 1940. THREE CENTS

CHAMBERLAIN SHIFTS BRITISH CABINET; HORE-BELISHA IS OUT AS WAR MINISTER; GERMAN PRESS WARNS SCANDINAVIANS

REICH CITES STAND

Nordic States Informed They Are in Danger of Being Battlefields

ALLIED PLANS STRESSED

Press Also Sees U. S. in Ranks of What It Terms 'War Prolongers'

By OTTO D. TOLISCHUS

Sweden Demands Soviet Inquiry After Submarine Shells Freighter

Fenris, Coastal Ship, Is Attacked Without Warning in Gulf of Bothnia—Scandinavia Held Growing Bolder Toward Russia

Special Cable to THE NEW YORK TIMES.

STOCKHOLM, Sweden, Jan. 5—The Swedish Foreign Office tonight asked its legation in Moscow to request an investigation by Russian authorities into the shelling of the Swedish coastal ship Fenris without warning by a submarine in the northern part of the Gulf of Bothnia today. The nationality of the submarine was officially given as "unknown," but there can be no doubt that it was Russian. It is known that Soviet submarines have wriggled through the mine field at the southern end of the Gulf of Bothnia.

The Fenris, of 464 tons, caught fire after the shelling, which took place about four miles off the Swedish shore. The crew left the ship and is safe aboard the Sydostbrotten Lightship. The wreck is drifting in flames toward the Swedish shore.

The Fenris was en route from Stockholm to the North Swedish port of Holmsund with a 200-ton cargo of miscellaneous goods. For years the ship has been engaged solely in carrying on trade between Swedish ports.

The International Situation

In a sudden shake-up last night Prime Minister Chamberlain dropped from the British Cabinet Leslie Hore-Belisha, the War Secretary, and Lord Macmillan, Minister of Information. Friction with the chiefs of the army, in which he had made many reforms, was assigned as the cause of the downfall of Mr. Hore-Belisha, who was replaced by Oliver Stanley. [Page 1.]

While the German press intensified its warnings to Sweden and Norway, declaring that they risked becoming "battlefields" if they allowed Allied aid to reach Finland through their territory [Page 1], Stockholm demanded that the Soviet Union investigate the shelling and wrecking of a Swedish steamer in the Gulf of Bothnia by a submarine.

FRICTION IS BLAMED

Secretary Said to Have Differed With Staff on Army Matters

INFORMATION CHIEF QUITS

Macmillan Had Been Widely Criticized—Stanley Takes Over the War Office

By RAYMOND DANIELL

HUGE R. A. F. BOMBS BLAST OSNABRUECK

Reich Industrial City and Rail Outlet for Ruhr Attacked by Several Hundred Planes

By DAVID ANDERSON

LONDON, Tuesday, Aug. 11—Tangled railroad tracks and smoldering ruins of German war factories lie in the wake of a heavy attack made Sunday night by the Royal Air Force at Osnabrueck, important industrial town northeast of the Ruhr and junction for Nazi shipments from that area to the North Sea and Baltic ports.

The British Air Ministry reported that a "strong force," probably 200 to 300 planes, that included a high percentage of the biggest four-motored bombers

Japanese Seek World Rule By 'Divine Appointment'

The following article, the first of a series, is from the Tokyo correspondent of THE NEW YORK TIMES, who arrived in Rio de Janeiro yesterday aboard the liner Gripsholm ... this country.

By OTTO D. TOLISCHUS

RIO DE JANEIRO, Brazil, Aug. 10—According to propaganda fed the Japanese people by the military control of the Japanese Government, Japan is prepared to wage war for a hundred years and will not stop till the United States and Britain are crushed, till Japanese troops parade down Piccadilly and the Japanese Navy holds a victory review off New York.

Continued on Page Eight

M'ARTHUR'S ... CUT AIR A...

Raids on Bases ... and Feeder ... Believed Pay...

...ALY AT WAR, READY TO ATTACK; ...AB IN BACK, SAYS ROOSEVELT; ...VERNMENT HAS LEFT PARIS

NEW YORK, TUESDAY, JUNE 11, 1940. THREE CENTS

The International Situation

On the Battle Fronts

OUR HELP PLEDGED

President Offers Our Full Material Aid to Allies' Cause

AMERICA IN DANGER

Fate Hangs on Training and Arms, He Says

Nazi Tide Laps at Paris as Italy Joins War

DUCE GIVES

2

THE ROOSEVELT SHOW

While the nation in 1932 was numbed by economic paralysis, there was a boom in Washington correspondents—over forty new ones appeared. Early in the year their attention focused on the Democratic party after Republican President Hoover announced his re-election plans. In general, the correspondents were unimpressed by Democratic front-runner Franklin Delano Roosevelt. They sought a strong man capable of reviving the nation's economy. Roosevelt was considered a deft politician who lacked the essential hubris to inspire the Depression-plagued American people.

Drew Pearson differed with a majority of his colleagues. He was an early Roosevelt supporter. Prior to the Chicago convention, Pearson and Sumner Welles, later to become Undersecretary of State, drafted the foreign affairs planks for the Roosevelt platform. Specifically, they urged the "Good Neighbor Policy" which he accepted. Behind-the-scenes another newspaperman was playing a dominant role in the selection of the Democratic candidate.

Pearson is familiar with the story. Publisher William Randolph Hearst began his President-making with a phone call to his Washington correspondent, George Rothwell Brown. Hearst's first Presidential choice was Speaker John Nance Garner. The publisher assigned Brown to interview Garner and determine his stand on domestic and international issues. Hearst was primarily interested in Garner's position on foreign entanglements. For Hearst, a rigid isolationist, the idea of United States involvement in European affairs was an anathema. Equally abhorrent was the theory of liberal government spending. He was a sound-dollar man.

Apparently Speaker Garner received high grades during his examination by correspondent Brown. Within a week after the Garner-Brown interview, Hearst used a coast-to-coast radio network to launch a drive for Garner.

"Unless we Americans are willing to go on laboring indefinitely merely to provide loot for Europe," he said, "we should personally see to it that a man is elected to the Presidency this year whose guiding light is 'America First.' "

Hearst's choice startled the political pundits. By and large, Washington correspondents considered Garner the darkest of horses. Franklin Roosevelt and Alfred E. Smith were the names that dominated their stories dealing with White House aspirants.

FDR partisans immediately established a line of communication with Hearst. They assured him privately that Roosevelt was as isolationist as Garner and that his position on monetary policies represented the ultimate in conservatism. Hearst disdained private assurances. "Tell Mr. Roosevelt to make his position public," he answered.

Hearst and his imperious order were accepted with the utmost gravity by FDR's supporters. The power of his press was an acknowledged fact. Within forty-eight hours Roosevelt publicly proclaimed his opposition to American participation in the League of Nations. But FDR's public appeasement of Hearst was not wholly convincing to the publisher. He recalled some of Roosevelt's past internationalist statements. Several days after FDR's surrender to him, Hearst assigned George Rothwell Brown to write a glowing Garner biography for his newspaper string.

When the delegates arrived at Chicago, Roosevelt was eighty votes short of nomination on the first ballot. James A. Farley, FDR's campaign manager, worked hard to persuade favorite-son candidates to withdraw, predicting that if they did not do so, the convention would deadlock and leave the Democratic Party in shambles.

The pivotal factor was the Garner bloc: the forty-two Texas votes and California's forty-four. Farley sought to communicate with the source of power. He telephoned Hearst at San Simeon. Hearst hung up on him. Roosevelt lieutenants had a private meeting with Hearst reporter Damon Runyon, who was covering the convention. They urged him to contact his boss and relay their views. Other Hearst deputies at the convention were buttonholed. The following day Hearst had a change of mind. Mainly he feared that scuttling FDR's chances would throw the nomination to Alfred E. Smith, and he hated Smith more than he distrusted Roosevelt.

Hearst went into action. He gained the hat-in-hand assurances from Roosevelt's managers that FDR would isolate himself from Europe. Thereupon Hearst conveyed his decision to Washington correspondent Brown, who went to Garner and urged him to release his delegates to Roosevelt. Garner later denied that he swapped his delegates for the Vice Presidential spot on the Democratic ticket. However, Garner presented his bloc to the FDR forces. That evening history was made at Chicago by a simple declaration. William Gibbs McAdoo, the head of the California delegation, came to the microphone and proclaimed: "California casts forty-four votes for Franklin D. Roosevelt." Hearst had utilized the immense power of his press to nominate a candidate he really did not like. In addition to Hearst, FDR's earliest journalist proponents included the New York *Daily News* and Cissy Patterson.

Most Washington correspondents were unimpressed by the Democratic party's choice. Walter Lippmann described FDR as "an amiable man who is no crusader. He is no tribune of the people. He is no enemy of entrenched privilege. He is a pleasant man who, without important qualifications for the office, would very much like to be President." Columnist Frank Kent observed: "What the people obviously want is a hero. Yet both parties are completely bereft of heroes." The San Francisco *Chronicle* and H. L. Mencken agreed that "the Democrats had nominated their weakest candidate."

Hoover was renominated by the Republicans. During his campaign he contended that world conditions were responsible for the Depression and that the United States was an innocent bystander. The Democratic platform promised a balanced budget, a cut in Federal expenditures, a sound currency, and no interference with legitimate private enterprise. At the same time it called for reform of certain business abuses.

"The frustration and anger of the American people," noted Drew Pearson, "turned the Republicans out of power." The Chicago *Tribune* pointed out that Roosevelt's "personality and his ideas pleased the people. They were impressed by his good will and good faith." The Richmond *Times-Dispatch* was more omniscient than most: "Tuesday's election has been termed a 'peaceful political revolution.' It is far more than that. It is a peaceful social revolution. Privilege rode too proudly. Then came Roosevelt with the magic phrase, 'The Forgotten Man.' "

For Drew Pearson, the election of FDR was part of the happy conspiracy of events that moved him and Roosevelt along the same road. It began when Roosevelt sketched his plans for the nomination. Sam Rosenman, one of FDR's advisers, suggested that FDR draw upon the universities for advice rather than upon businessmen and politicians. Roosevelt was enthusiastic about the suggestion. Among the names Roosevelt mentioned were Raymond Moley, professor of political science at Columbia University.

Moley had served FDR in the past. It was he who wrote Governor Roosevelt's opinion in the trial of Sheriff Farley, the Tammany chieftain removed from office by Roosevelt. Moley's eloquent opinion in that case represented a stirring declaration of a moral standard for public officials.

FDR asked Moley to form a group of experts in various fields of policy. He invited Rexford Tugwell, Lindsay Rogers, Joseph D. McGoldrick, James W. Angell, and others. All were members of Columbia's faculty. As a former member of the university's teaching staff, Pearson was acquainted with these men. He shared many of their ideals. In general they were pragmatic scholars who helped create and implement the visions of Roosevelt's "New Deal."

Of course, in 1933 extraordinary vision was essential. As Pearson recently said: "The Depression was an unbelievable horror story. Between 1929 and 1932 the national income decreased from $82 billion to $40 billion. Total industrial production dropped by almost 50 percent. More than one-quarter of the nation's labor force was jobless. In 1932 there were almost five thousand bank failures. In parts of Europe the Depression struck a fatal blow at liberalism, democracy, and even private-enterprise capitalism."

One of the more stunning transformations involved Washington journalism. In December 1932, FDR invited Pearson to visit him in Warm Springs, Georgia, and asked his advice on Washington press relations. Pearson said: "Don't worry about the publishers but make friends with the newspapermen who cover the White House. They're on the firing line, and they fire five thousand words a day as against one editorial a day written by the publishers." Shortly before Roosevelt entered the White House, the Washington correspondent for *Editor and Publisher*, the journalism trade weekly, reported that Mr. Roosevelt planned franker press relations and added, "In fairness to both Mr. Roosevelt and the press, however, it must be recorded that the new deal in press relations is hoped for rather than expected by correspondents."

The new deal in press relations more than realized the dreams of newspapermen. FDR's high-powered personality and his astute handling of the press popularized Washington journalism in general. A star of the first magnitude, he inaugurated semi-weekly press conferences and indulged in virtuoso performances. He literally dazzled reporters. After he concluded his first press conference, correspondents broke out in a burst of spontaneous applause.

Ray Clapper, then chief of the United Press Washington Bureau, wrote: "Reporters sensed that Roosevelt was a man at peace with himself and at ease with his job. He was patient in answering questions and brushed aside delicate queries with a quip. He had a remarkable sense of news. He never sent reporters away empty-handed."

Approval was the theme of a Washington *Herald* editorial: "Roosevelt is a newspaperman's President, no matter what you think of his policies."

FDR made some drastic changes. He discarded the old rules requiring written questions. He buried the Coolidge-Hoover ghostly "White House spokesman." Reporters were allowed, at first, to ask all the questions they wished. There were no rules, except the restrictions of time. Questions and answers were swapped with machine-gun rapidity. On certain occasions, FDR permitted direct quotations.

All in all, the President threw the press conferences wide open, making them festive and informative events for reporters. When the mood was upon him, the President would regale correspondents with political banter. Sometimes FDR was an editor. He would say: "If I were writing that story I would put it this way: That by no stretch of the imagination has the President ever been in the least bit concerned over the possibility of this oil lease involving the United States in any shape, matter, or form in the Ethiopian or Italian problems. And then, if you are going to write one more paragraph, I would put it this way: That this is another proof that since March 1933, dollar diplomacy is not recognized by the American government."

Further, the President functioned as a professor of journalism. While discussing tax problems he said: "It is a rather interesting fact that as these stories come out of Washington, not one statement contains any reference to the very large section of our population that doesn't have a decent standard of living. In other words, here's a national problem that apparently in these stories is only viewed from one angle." The President then urged reporters to write interpretive stories. At that time, interpretive reporting was rather novel, and many editors and publishers complained the stories coming out of Washington seemed to be dictated by the President, slanted in the New Deal's favor, and pure propaganda.

As far as the correspondents were concerned, FDR was their Pied Piper. For a time they danced to the tune of his music—and enjoyed every minute of it. FDR's news conferences were the best shows in town. Coolidge had been taciturn, Hoover had been dull. But FDR was the gay and gabby hero. Sometimes he replied to a query by saying, "'I will consider that question not asked." Answering another question, he would say, "I can give you a good tip on that if you don't say I said it."

And always overpowering the journalistic scene was Roosevelt's incandescent charm. "His charm," wrote columnist Mark Sullivan, "is not easy to describe. But it is hypnotic."

Nobody—certainly not FDR—underestimated his charm. He

was always in command of the press conference. He could flatter, cajole, impress, guide, teach. He not only gave news, he helped classify it. After explaining a certain economic issue, he told the assembled reporters: "This is not a spot-news story. It is a long-range story." More often than not, the reporters would follow his instructions. FDR's only journalistic experience had been as editor of the *Crimson* at Harvard, but he operated like a seasoned professional.

He approached correspondents as friends and allies for two reasons. He relished the give-and-take with them, and the need to communicate with the people during the monetary crisis was obviously vital.

FDR also stressed the background news conference. Previous Presidents had sporadically employed the background-only device. Roosevelt made it a regular and important branch of his Administration's news policies. Favored reporters and columnists were called in and given information pertinent to the development of major events. Within a few weeks the President had become a master of news dissemination.

Originally, several publishers and editors objected to FDR's dominant news position. Although he extended the reach and influence of reporters, at the same time he extended the reach and influence of the President. But if a few sophisticates were aware of FDR's ulterior political motives in the use of the press, they were barely heard during the first hundred days of his Administration. Press support for him was practically unanimous—and enthusiastic. Will Rogers wrote in his column that "the whole country is with him, just so he does something. If he burned down the Capitol we would cheer him and say 'Well, we at least got a fire started anyhow.' "

The New York Times editorial page joined the chorus of approbation: "The yearning of America is for action, almost any kind of action. Roosevelt makes a flying start by satisfying that long-balked appetite. . . . Roosevelt has changed the atmosphere of the capital, has raised the morale of the country. . . . No President in so short a time has inspired so much hope."

He began to ignite the government information explosion. Within three months after FDR assumed the Presidency, the number of

Federal press information officers quadrupled. Back in 1910 the Federal government hired its first public relations man at a $10 weekly salary. During the Coolidge and Hoover administrations there were about two dozen press officers on the government payroll. Roosevelt made a drastic change. Within a decade the government press information industry flourished to the point where literally thousands of public relations experts—and some not-so expert—were feeding on public money.

Radio joined the mass media in 1933. CBS launched its own news service in Washington. FDR then added an extra dimension to radio news with his warmly popular "Fireside Chats." He was delighted with the public approval of his radio comments. FDR once greeted Pearson with the query, "Did you see my latest Hooper rating?" (The Hooper was radio's popularity index.) FDR was right up there with such radio stars as Amos 'n' Andy and Jack Benny.

As FDR's popularity expanded, the writings of those who reported the Washington drama elicited greater acceptance. During the first year of the New Deal, Pearson added about two hundred subscribers to his syndicated column. Pearson operated as a hard-news reporter. He buttonholed politicians, listened to them, lunched with them, and joined them at cocktail parties. Sometimes they spilled exclusive stories between mouthfuls, especially when plied with alcohol. Pearson quickly developed an extensive network of news sources, ranging from the President to Cabinet members to major and minor officials in Federal agencies.

FDR's friendly cooperation with correspondents seeped down. Steve Early, the President's press secretary, told the departmental press assistants, "Do your job just like you were working for a newspaper." It was Early who expanded and guided the growing apparatus of public relations throughout the Federal government.

Columnists received special treatment. Roosevelt assigned his lieutenants to maintain continual contact with the syndicated specialists. They provided them with background information and inside stories, generally designed to inform the public or enhance an FDR project.

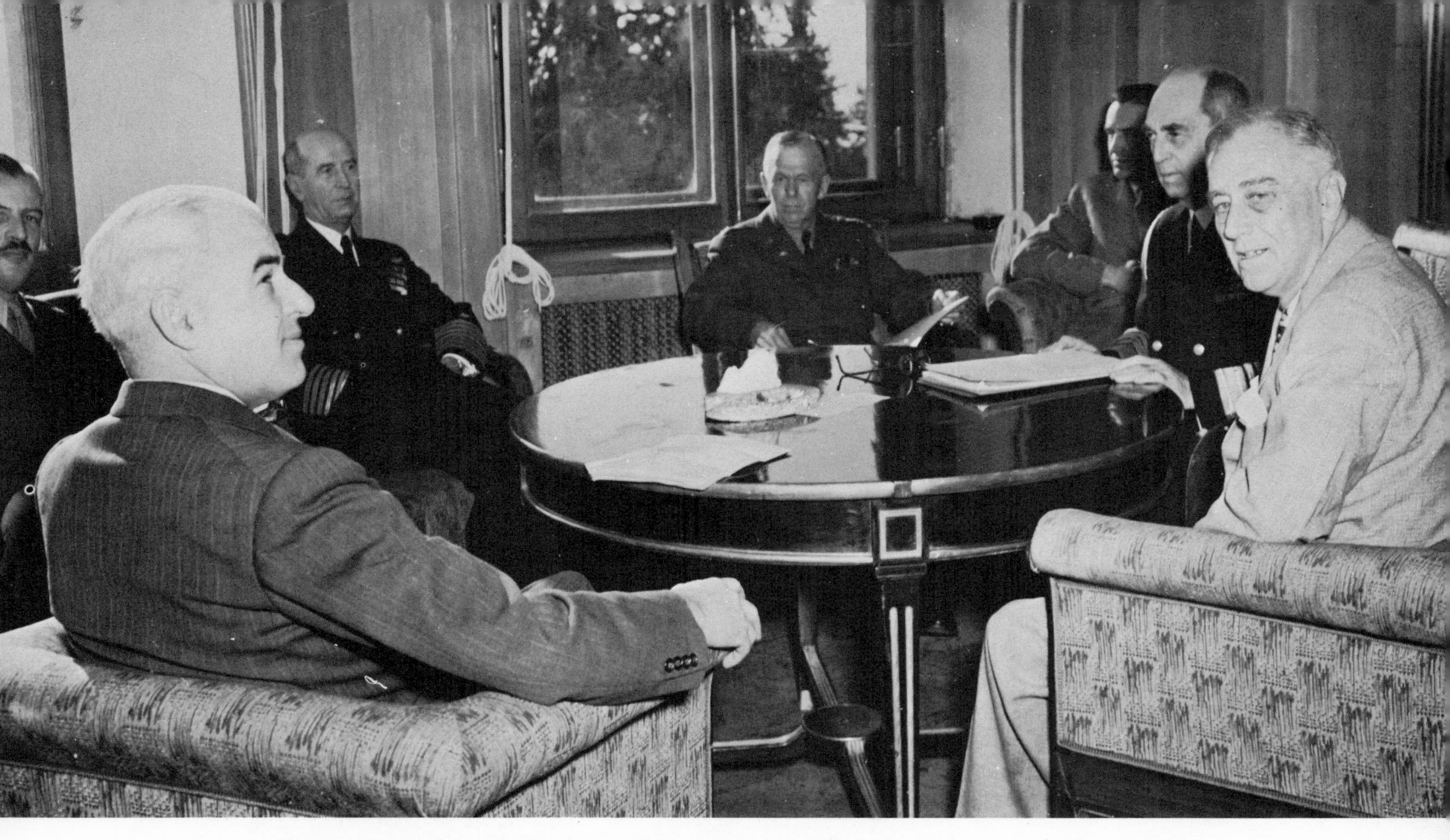

FDR surrounded by (l to r) Secretary of State Stettinius, Maj. Gen. Kuter, Admiral King, Gen. Marshall, Ambassador Harriman, and Admiral Leahy.

Churchill's V for Victory.

Hitler and henchmen.

President Hoover and President-elect Roosevelt.

Mrs. Eleanor Roosevelt Christmas shopping, 1938.

The First Lady.

The Roosevelt Administration not only made news available, but also added sundry aids and conveniences to lighten the tasks of the reporters. This was partially good standard public relations and partially essential service.

Washington was becoming a complicated beat. The old straight-news reporting encountered severe limitations. The government was becoming more complex and it required greater degrees of sophistication on the part of the press corps. For example, the New Deal banking and gold policies required monetary expertise in reporting the stories. The Administration assigned government economists to help reporters.

The expansion of news coverage provided a field day for press photographers. FDR's handsome, mobile face and his sense of the unusual and dramatic had editors clamoring for more and more pictures. He was shown fishing, eating hot dogs, munching peanuts, playing with his dog, kissing his wife. There was just one taboo: The polio-crippled President forbade the taking of pictures while he was in pain. Once he slipped and sprawled on the floor while a dozen press photographers were around him. Not a single flash bulb popped.

The growing cooperation between the Roosevelt Administration and the press gave Drew Pearson a front-row seat for witnessing the pageant of history. He broke a series of exclusive stories in 1933. Drew reported that Robert L. Vann, a Negro publisher, would be appointed a special assistant to Attorney General Cummings. No Democratic precedent could be found for this appointment. As a matter of fact, when "Green Pastures" played Washington in 1932, special Sunday performances were given for Negroes—who were barred, in the capital of the United States, from attending regular performances and witnessing actors of their own race.

Pearson was the first to indicate that FDR planned to recognize Soviet Russia, and during the Senate's investigation of munitions-makers, he broke a series of exclusives. The fantastic profits garnered by munitions-makers stunned the people. The nation was shocked to discover a fundamental fact: War fuels on blood but produces gold.

Further, Pearson was among the first to note that the New Deal was simply a continuation of the progressive movement fathered by Theodore Roosevelt and Woodrow Wilson. Its concept had the support of the people, but the Democratic party was by no means dedicated to progressive ideals. The party organization, controlled by Southern conservatives and northern machine politicians, played cat-and-mouse with farmers, middle-class reformers, and labor leaders. It was a tribute to FDR's political dexterity that he assembled this political jigsaw into a recognizable picture.

Pearson secured much newsworthy information during his private meetings with the President. He was a frequent dinner guest at the White House. He enjoyed listening to FDR's nostalgic recapture of his early days in politics. The President, a gifted storyteller, mesmerized the columnist. Pearson personally revered Roosevelt.

Yet the cordiality of the personal relationship posed professional problems for Pearson. Friendship and a reporter's allegiance to report all the news sometimes conflicted. Drew guarded his journalistic independence with tiger-like ferocity. Despite the warmth between them, Pearson reserved the right to be critical. Probably no newspaperman can maintain genuine friendship with the people he writes about. In the end, a newspaperman's best friend is his integrity. And so, many New Dealers were handled roughly in the Pearson column, especially Secretary of State Cordell Hull. Pearson comments: "Unlike Winchell, I was not a propagandist for Franklin D. Roosevelt and the New Deal. Roosevelt got sore at me over many things I wrote. I praised him when I thought he was right and panned him when I thought he was wrong."

As the months passed, friction between Pearson and some of FDR's White House team became more common. Much of the friction originated in the numerous splits within the Administration.

FDR's Cabinet was politically incongruous. It included several Southerners, notably Tennessee's Cordell Hull. The northern big city machines were represented by James A. Farley. Harold Ickes and Henry Wallace were progressive Republicans.

From the first, FDR's closest advisers were outside the party organization. Several months after Roosevelt entered the White House, his Inner Circle was dominated by a pair of whiz kids named

Tom Corcoran and Ben Cohen. They were later joined by Harry Hopkins, who was destined to be FDR's prime adviser. As a group, Corcoran-Cohen-Hopkins was a fusion of hope and energy that moved through the traditional smoke-filled rooms of politicians like a breath of spring air. The political climate was determined by the stars in their eyes. They refreshed and infuriated the Washington Establishment. And they were closest to Pearson's ear.

Within six months the Franklin-in-Wonderland euphoria among correspondents diminished markedly. The Hearst papers had originally hailed FDR's cooperation with the press, and Hearst had described the President as a great copy editor. Now a few reporters began to accuse him of suppressing or coloring the news. Bitter class conflict erupted in the wake of New Deal reforms. Many businessmen were infuriated about government interference in private enterprise. Numerous editorials grumbled about Washington's "socialistic experiments."

Power struggles began to divide New Dealers. Jealousy and envy were rampant. Ickes and Hopkins, for example, were locked in a feud. FDR stepped in and gave Hopkins power over projects costing up to $250,000; Ickes was detailed to command those costing more. The Pearson column observed: "For Ickes, canals; for Hopkins, ditches. For Ickes, highways; for Hopkins, sidewalks. For Ickes, water systems; for Hopkins, reservoirs. For Ickes, public buildings; for Hopkins, landscaping. For Ickes, big dams; for Hopkins, little dams."

Although the paragraph gave Washington a chuckle, it reflected the deepening cracks within the New Deal structure. The power struggles among New Dealers and the inevitable jealousies proved a mixed blessing for Pearson. One side or the other came to him with information designed to enhance themselves or damage those who impeded their upward movement.

The moral ambiguities of the problem invited some soul-searching. Is it proper to publish news motivated by malice? How meaningful are the news-gathering circumstances? Is allegiance to truth a journalist's sole obligation? In brief, does the news end justify the means? Pearson sees his responsibility in terms of a policing chore. "It is the job of a newspaperman," he has written, "to spur the lazy, watch the weak, expose the corrupt. He must be the eyes, ears, and nose of the American people. Yes, the nose is important. For no matter how much stench a newspaperman is exposed to, he must never lose his sense of smell."

In the case of the fragmented New Dealers, Drew's policing consisted of picking up the pieces and making them public in his column. He quoted the conversations of White House insiders and needled some of the feudists, thus intensifying the behind-the-scenes bickering.

At first, FDR accepted with philosophic resignation Pearson's reports of the squabbles within his political family. But as news of the vendettas expanded—and were picked up by other members of the Washington press corps—his irritation mounted. Hopkins privately described the rifts in the White House as "a fight in a harem."

The President was miffed when Pearson reported that Britain's Lord Beaverbrook had given Mrs. Hopkins a magnificent emerald necklace. The Hopkinses denied receiving any emeralds. Drew printed the story and reported that the denial was accurate—the gift was a $4,000 *diamond* necklace, not an emerald one. The correction was as damaging as the original report, and FDR fumed.

As a journalist building columns on New Deal events, Pearson soon found that he was unable to drive a nail without bruising the President. He also exposed the injudicious activities of Roosevelt's sons, who utilized the aura of the Roosevelt name in order to feather their nests in private business deals. After the Pearson columns appeared, the White House was inundated with critical mail. FDR, of course, refused to accept this cheerfully. He was irate, to say the least, and he made clear his indignation in private comments.

Another irritation was almost traditional in Washington. The President was annoyed by "leaks" to the press. As has happened to other Chief Executives, the leakage stemmed from White House insiders. FDR sought to stop the flood. He bluntly ordered his official family to clamp the lid on subordinates. Roosevelt was determined not to tolerate the leaks, especially on a government reorganization proposal that he was anxious to put through Congress.

Secretaries Wallace and Roper informed their lieutenants that a rigid "gag" was in force on the reorganization plan. They demanded a hush-hush policy on and off the record. Secretary Ickes was more severe. He called in his assistants and told them that "a sure and quick way to commit hara-kari would be to attempt to knife the reorganization proposal. There must be no talking and no lobbying."

There was just one thing wrong with FDR's blockade. The attempts to stop the leaks were leaked to Pearson, and he published the details. As a matter of fact, the leakage that poured into Pearson's column once inspired Secretary of State Hull to begin a meeting by looking around the table and glaring: "Are we talking for this room or for Pearson?" (The remark was later attributed to Secretary Forrestal, who may have repeated it under similar circumstances.)

Actually, it is impossible to make the government leak-proof. Realists in Washington—both in politics and the press—accept the leak as standard journalistic procedure. Smart operators will leak to newspapermen when it is to their advantage, and politics is crammed with smart operators. Such are the simple facts of political expediency and political maneuver.

FDR himself was not above the use of a leaked story. At one point he felt Vice President Garner was blocking some New Deal legislation. Roosevelt used a Cabinet member to leak the story to Pearson, a move calculated to embarrass the Vice President. Of course, the President wanted to be certain the story could not be traced back to him. After the item appeared, Garner stormed into Roosevelt's office and loudly challenged Pearson's veracity. Mr. President just sat there, listened, and smiled his enigmatic smile.

The secrecy game heightened the friction between Drew and the President. On the face of it, the battle of secrets was rather trivial, yet neither FDR nor Pearson considered it a petty issue. Pearson viewed it in the larger context of a threat to the responsibilities of a free press.

The President adored secrets and wanted the pleasure of springing them. Some members of his Administration first heard about their appointments from radio announcements. Sometimes FDR was stubborn and vain and eager to demonstrate he was better informed—or more quickly informed—than others in the Administration.

For the President it was a game. Often he loved to surprise the State Department by unexpectedly making public certain information he had gained from private sources. Of course, his private sources were occasionally inaccurate. The result was a dunking in hot editorials.

Part of the reason for Roosevelt's desire to hoard secrets was the delight he derived in surprising the person directly involved. He truly enjoyed seeing the shocked look when he divulged the news. He never told Harold Ickes that he was to be Public Works Administrator until the moment of the appointment. When Ickes heard the news he just stood there transfixed for several moments without uttering a word. His reaction was manna to the President. He gazed at Ickes's bewildered expression, tossed back his head, and roared with laughter.

As far as Pearson was concerned, Washington secrets were the heartbeats of his column. In the capital a secret is anything told in a whisper—generally to a newspaperman.

In retrospect, the points of friction between FDR and Pearson appear insignificant. In the heat of the times, however, they were accepted with the utmost gravity on both sides. As a matter of fact, Pearson's rift with FDR can be traced directly to his critical comments about FDR's assistants.

Despite the tension, the ambivalence of the FDR-Pearson relationship remained constant. The columnist continued as a conscientious devotee of the major New Deal policies, although the President regarded Drew's needling of his assistants as a flirtation with the enemy.

As the White House irritation with Pearson's reporting mounted, the columnist was stunned to learn that a man he revered was privately damning him. At one time, FDR was so annoyed that he seriously considered legal action to put Pearson out of business. Several members of the Cabinet informed the columnist of the President's anger. While Pearson was slightly dismayed, he continued to function as the Administration's guardian angel, gadfly, and watchdog. Despite the White House tantrums evoked by Pearson's reporting, the President sought Drew's assistance in the 1938 primary campaign when FDR attempted to purge Senator Millard

Tydings of Maryland. Behind-the-scenes Pearson functioned as campaign manager for Representative David Lewis who opposed Tydings. Pearson wrote most of the speeches for Lewis, raised his campaign funds, and contributed to the Labor Day speech Roosevelt delivered at Denton, Maryland. The site of the speech, a rural area on the Eastern Shore, was not of Pearson's choosing. He urged that the Labor Day speech should be given in Baltimore, a labor union stronghold. But FDR wanted the excuse to cruise down the Potomac, then across the Chesapeake to the Eastern Shore. There was little enthusiasm for the speech and the political effects were disastrous. Tydings was a landslide victor. Later, however, FDR cleared every Federal appointment in Maryland with Pearson before it was made.

The human factor in Pearson's relationship with FDR was graphically illustrated by an incident that began with an item in the March 31, 1938, Pearson column. Under the heading "Roosevelt's Breakfast Rolls," the column noted:

> When the President departed for Warm Springs last week, he left behind a surplus supply of Danish twisted buns. This is the President's favorite breakfast bread. When the President left the other day, someone forgot to cancel the order, and there were Danish buns to spare.
>
> They are large, flat buns made of long strips of Danish pastry wound and twisted into circular shape and sprinkled with cinnamon and sugar. Each bun is about four inches across. Price—forty cents a dozen. Another delicacy which the President orders constantly is nut butter crisp. This is a flat candy made by a coating of a brittle base with chocolate and sprinkling chopped nuts on top and bottom. It is a very rich candy and he buys it for sixty-five cents a pound.
>
> Note: Baker Taylor has a substantial White House trade but doesn't want to be interviewed about it. "It's a matter of principle," he says, "not to talk about what I make for the President."

This represents amusing trivia. The delicacies were described in detail, right down to the fact that the bon-bons were enveloped—top and bottom—with chopped nuts. Clear, complete, factual, touching all the bases of proper journalism. And most people evidently enjoy reading peripheral or even irrelevant information about luminaries. The human simplicities of the famous helped popularize Broadway-Hollywood columns. To a larger extent, every aspect of a President's life has a public attraction. In the White House fishbowl, the fish and the bowl and the water are news.

Pearson published the paragraph with the utmost equanimity. As a matter of fact, it was considered "filler" material, generally used to flesh out a column on a dull news day.

Several days after the Danish pastry exposé appeared, Cissy Patterson called on FDR. The publisher and the President had planned a private discussion on domestic and international issues. But soon after she entered the President's office, his natural jauntiness vanished. At first, FDR grimly explained to Cissy—whose paper carried the Pearson column—that he was annoyed with the Danish pastry story. Then, as he warmed to his objections, his voice became harsher and his temper exploded. The President spent about fifteen minutes verbally flogging Pearson in particular, and the press in general, using the Danish pastry squib as a glaring example of journalistic irresponsibility.

"I simply do not like Danish pastry," FDR stormed.

That was not the end of it by any means. Several days later, Jim Farley informed Pearson: "The President is mad as hell. He doesn't like Danish pastry."

L'Affaire Danish pastry may have been the sheerest nonsense, but at the time, it was the talk of the town. For a while, it was uppermost in the minds of FDR's chief aides. Harry Hopkins chided Drew for running the item. Mrs. Roosevelt, appearing on a coast-to-coast radio program with Pearson, gently reproached, "I know that you didn't mean to make a mistake, but my husband just doesn't like Danish pastry."

Eventually, for the benefit of future historians, Pearson sought to set the record straight. It marked the one and only time the columnist disclosed a news source.

> The item came from the Taylor Bakerette Shop on Wisconsin Avenue, which had suggested to my sister-in-law

> that she buy some Danish pastry because the White House had forgotten to countermand its order with the departure of the President.
>
> It may be that FDR called it "breakfast rolls" and Mr. Taylor called it pastry. Anyway, I saw the Taylor delivery truck on various occasions afterward backed up at the White House kitchen door unloading something—for the sake of accuracy we will call it a baked product of wheat flour with sugar on the top.

The Roosevelt-Pearson estrangement was indicative of a gradual alienation of affection between the White House and columnists. During press conferences, FDR complained about the inaccuracy of columnists, pointedly hailed the educational value of radio, labeled two columnists as dunces and ordered them to stand in a corner. Although columnists were the prime targets of his waspish comments, his relations with other White House reporters remained cordial. Washington columnist Raymond Clapper reported in 1938 that while more than 40 percent of the White House press corps was critical of the New Deal, at least 90 percent retained their personal admiration for FDR.

Roosevelt's irritation with columnists was aggravated by domestic problems that beset the nation during the mid-1930's. Georgia and South Carolina were torn by striking cotton workers; police engaged in pitched battles with rioting silk workers in New Jersey; rival coal mine unionists were killing each other in Illinois; disgruntled farmers, angered by slipping commodity prices, were threatening to embroil the Midwest in an agricultural strike. As a matter of fact, one objective of FDR's announced intention to recognize the Soviet Union was to drive domestic problems off the front pages.

From the White House perspective of world and national problems, it is easy to understand the causes of FDR's impatience and scorn when he read the efforts of his columnist critics.

The personal coolness between Pearson and Roosevelt resulted in a form of accommodation that can roughly be described as peaceful coexistence. Realism dictated the détente. After all, Pearson still had a job to do, and the President remained Chief Executive. As far as the columnist was concerned, he continued to maintain his many New Deal pipelines. There was no secret about Pearson's close relationship with Secretary Ickes, Undersecretary of State Sumner Welles, Vice President Wallace, Harry Hopkins, and J. Edgar Hoover. They frequently joined Pearson for lunch in the Mayflower Hotel's Presidential Room.

Although the pitch of FDR's indignation reached a feverish peak when he discussed Pearson in private, it did not prevent him from making use of Pearson's national audience when the occasion demanded. When the President's son, Elliott, was editorially thrashed for using an Air Force plane to transport his dog, FDR's press secretary phoned Pearson and urged him to soften the editorial blows. In this case the columnist believed FDR's son was being used as a scapegoat by the President's journalistic foes and came to his defense.

The glacial relations between the President and Pearson failed to cool the columnist's affection for Mrs. Roosevelt. Time and again he came to the First Lady's defense when she was subjected to critical press comment.

But Pearson's valentines to the First Lady did not ease the tension with the President which was partly rooted in the inevitable conflict between political expediency and journalistic responsibility. The following incident is a striking case in point: During the Spanish Civil War, Pearson published a list of Cabinet members opposed to the United States embargo on shipment of arms to Spain. The list included the name of Attorney General Frank Murphy, Pearson's source for the story. Nevertheless, after the report appeared, various high Catholic leaders were critical of officials who opposed the embargo. Murphy's reaction was determined by Washington's survival code. He denied it. An accurate story factually, it was imprudent in terms of political expediency.*

Within the context of political reality, only the naive would damn expediency as an insensitive and reckless political instrument. After

* After leaking a news story to three correspondents, President Theodore Roosevelt told them, "If you even hint where you got it, I'll say you're a damned liar."

all, practical necessity demands the transmission of official views to the people.

FDR took full advantage of the press. He enlarged its importance and simultaneously extended the dimensions of his own image. During his first term, Roosevelt held about four hundred press conferences—more than the total number of press conferences held by all of his White House predecessors.

The growth of this technique was both a blessing and an evil. It offered newspapermen easier access to White House news, but it gave the White House easier access to newspapermen as an instrument of persuasion. The disadvantages caused New York *Times*-man Arthur Krock to write that the Roosevelt Administration used "more ruthlessness, intelligence, and subtlety in trying to suppress legitimate news and unfavorable comment than any I know."

The subtlety was primarily FDR's personal charm and the trick of dominating the news conference with a soliloquy, which left reporters little time for embarrassing questions.

Every rational Washington newspaperman must be aware that since the President is not obliged to hold press conferences or engage in private discussions with reporters, the simple facts of political life almost makes it necessary for a President to use the mediums of communication for personal or political advantage. This in itself is not bad, since no newspaperman is required to accept as truth every Presidential utterance.

The Chief Executive has another advantage in his give-and-take with Washington reporters. The press corps, in common with most Americans, has a profound respect for the Presidency. Very few journalists participating in the forum will sharply disagree with the President or demand detailed explanations when he is evasive. In their relations with the President, the majority of reporters are generally on the defensive. It is all part of the game.

Pearson accepted the President's personal animosity without whining. This is not to say he was impervious to wretched feelings, but he still sought to maintain a balance. Aware of the President's burdens, he could understand his edginess on occasion. Roosevelt publicly berated and damaged the reputations of critical reporters, and competing journalists eagerly quoted the President's wrathful outbursts, especially when they applied to Drew Pearson, who was leading the league in scoops.

In retrospect, Pearson has no desire to make amends for much of the reporting that resulted in FDR's implacable coldness. If he had the opportunity to do it over again, he probably would write and say the same things. The columnist is not apologetic, but he is regretful because a cherished friendship was ruptured.

Yet as the column he wrote ten years after FDR's death illustrated, his devotion to FDR remained intact. He never stopped battling for many of the New Deal principles. His oldest and closest friends in Washington are men who played major roles in the New Deal. Although the columnist does not adhere to hero-worship or halo-worship, the fact is that Drew Pearson misses FDR. To Pearson, those who have followed Roosevelt into the White House appear to be lesser players in a series of anticlimactic epilogues.

The Providence Journal

VOLUME CXVI. NO. 135 TWENTY PAGES

PROVIDENCE, TUESDAY, JUNE 6, 1944

Founded as a semi-weekly in 1820; as a daily in 1829

PRICE THREE CENTS

INVASION STARTS

General Eisenhower Announces Allied Landings In Northern France Under Aerial and Navy Cover

ROOSEVELT SAYS REICH WAR HABIT MUST BE HALTED

Asks Germany Be Driven to Point Where She Cannot Start New Conquest

HAILS CAPTURE OF ROME

ALLIED AIRPLANES BATTER GERMANS OUTSIDE OF ROME

Nazi Wounded, Dead, Blazing Trucks Litter Highways to North of Seized Capital

BOMBERS BLAST RAILWAYS

Points Where Europe's Invasion Starts

GERMAN AGENCIES FLASH FIRST NEWS OF ALLIED ATTACK

Three Nazi Sources Disclose Parachute Troop Landings on Normandy Peninsula

DEFENSE FORCES IN ACTION

MONTGOMERY HEADS TROOPS IN ASSAULT ON CHANNEL COAST

Germans Say Main Blow Struck in Le Havre Area; British, U.S., Canadians in First Wave

Supreme Headquarters, Allied Expeditionary Force, June 6.—(AP)—General Dwight D. Eisenhower's headquarters announced today that Allied troops began landing on the northern coast of France this morning strongly supported by Naval and Air Forces.

Text of the communique:

Under command of Gen. Eisenhower, Allied Naval forces supported by strong air forces began landing Allied armies this morning on the northern coast of France.

The Germans said the ...

...E MAKIN, GAIN ON TA...

...NE OF WORLD'S MOST DESTRUCTIVE AERIAL BOMBARDMENT

...Force planes showered 2,300 tons of bombs on ...industrial suburbs Monday night. The suburbs hit ...u and Siemensstadt (A), Wilmersdorf (B), Neu...tenberg (D) and Pankow (E). In the heart of the ...aiser Wilhelm Gedaechtniskirche (1) was reported ...re the Hungarian Legation (2) and the Swedish Legation (3). The Potsdam railroad station (4) was said to have been destroyed and the British Embassy (5) and the French Embassy (6) were declared to have been razed. Other places reported damaged were the Finnish Legation (7), the Danish Legation (8), the State University (9) and the Foreign Office (10). Vast fires were set and casualties were estimated at 10,000 killed and wounded.

...EES CHINA ...'S NEMESIS

...feat of Foe Will ...ungking's Area ...en, Airfields

Patton Struck Ailing Soldier, Apologized to Him and Army

By MILTON BRACKER

By Wireless to The New York Times.

ALGIERS, Nov. 23—Lieut. Gen. George S. Patton Jr. struck and insulted a shell-shocked American soldier in an evacuation hospital in Sicily last August and ordered the patient to return to the front lines, it was officially revealed today. Gen. Dwight D. Eisenhower denounced the conduct of the commander of the American Seventh Army as "despicable" and threatened to break him unless he made amends at once. General Patton thereupon apologized to the soldier, to the officers and patients who had witnessed the incident and to the Seventh Army.

Although there were at least fifteen witnesses to the incident, none was a professional reporter. The first two reporters to check on the episode arrived at the hospital ...

'DOOMSDAY' SCENE IN BERLIN PAINTED

Swedish Traveler Reports Fires Created Almost a Summer Temperature

By GEORGE AXELSSON

By Cable to The New York Times.

STOCKHOLM, Sweden, Nov. 23—An eyewitness from Berlin ... the British bombing attack last night told the writer here today that the French Embassy on the Pariser Platz and the British Embassy on Wilhelmstrasse were razed by explosives and incendiaries.

Reich Foreign Minister Joachim von Ribbentrop's official residence on Wilhelmstrasse was destroyed ... The top stories of the Foreign Office building and of Adolf Hitler's Wilhelmstrasse residence were ...

RUSSIANS RETREAT TOWARD KIEV AGAIN

Germans Win Several Towns at High Cost, but Red Army Gains on Other Fronts

By The United Press

...CAPTURE PORTS; ...AN STEEL CENTE...

...IANS RETURN TO DIEPPE

...mphal march of the Dominion fighters through the streets of this "Cana...

BRITISH SMAS...

Swarm Over Alber... as Foe Fights t... Flanking of L...

CANADIANS IN ...

Patton Wins Th... Moselle Brid... in Costly ...

By DREW ...

SUPREME HE... Allied Expedition...

...NA ...NESE

Allies 10 Miles From Belfort Start Battle for Gap to Reich

By The Associated Press.

AT THE FRENCH-SWISS FRONTIER, Sept. 6.—The battle for the Belfort Gap began today with a preliminary Allied artillery barrage and an all-day series of air attacks. Three Allied motorized columns were approaching, with the most advanced within ten miles of the city of Belfort.

Allied artillery opened up at ... and continued to fire fairly regularly during the morning and ... afternoon.

Fighter planes searched out German positions, using dive-bombing tactics.

Montbeliard still was in German hands this morning. Belfort was bombed during the day ...

BELGIAN LEADERS BACK IN BRUSSELS

Populace Cheers Government Chiefs—Future of King One of the Main Problems

3

THE THUNDER OF A SLAP

Long before World War II, Drew Pearson clashed with generals and diplomats. His critical attitude toward General Douglas MacArthur resulted in a libel suit. And his coverage of the State Department sketched a pattern of acrimony. After all, Pearson inaugurated his Washington journalistic career as a State Department reporter, and the subsequent pipelines he established were both numerous and authoritative.

When war came, the diplomatic and military forces merged in many areas. Their influence was reciprocal. Military strategy and diplomatic tactics became part of a similar general policy. Nevertheless, since the people had the right to know, no journalist worth his salt could surrender his duty to find out and report.

One side of the problem has been explained by Washington columnist James Reston: "Journalism and foreign policy in America are hard to reconcile. The Secretary of State must think in generations and continents, but the reporter thinks in 'stories' and 'minutes' and often in 'fragments.' One profession is quiet, the other noisy; one slow, the other fast; one precise, the other imprecise. What makes their relationship even more difficult is that they are stuck with one another."

There are other complications in this sensitive area. Diplomats often speak in terms of psychological warfare. Then again, they will attempt to communicate a message indirectly to other nations through press channels. And there are times when diplomats will leak stories to journalists in an effort to influence the White House or government agencies.

Since diplomats are rarely candid and Machiavellian tricks are their stock-in-trade, the function of a reporter requires a gift for delicacy, a touch of extrasensory perception, and just plain gall. These three requisites are Drew Pearson's standard equipment when dealing with diplomatic news. Moreover, he is aware of the constant attempts of military and diplomatic leaders to cover up stupidity or wrongdoing under the heading of "Top Secret."

There is another meaningful factor in Pearson's diplomatic news coverage. A Washington correspondent once cracked: "Pearson has more pipelines than Standard Oil." His contacts with foreign diplomats are hardly a secret in Washington. Ambassadors dominate the guest list at Pearson's dinner parties.

Soon after the war began, Pearson expanded his coverage of military and diplomatic events. American and British intelligence agents added to his news sources. Unexpectedly, another rich news source developed: He was flooded with tips from ordinary soldiers. All were checked and some turned out to be good exclusive stories.

Most stories from GI's concerned military waste and tragic loss of lives. Thousands of letters poured in to report on such cases as the four hundred American paratroopers shot down by United States and British naval vessels during the invasion of Sicily. He disclosed that an Admiral flew a cow up to the Aleutian Islands, but forgot that a cow will not give milk for long without a bull. Pearson reported that twelve carloads of leather jackets at the Philadelphia Navy Yard were purposely damaged so they could be condemned.

As he checked the tips, Pearson was confronted with denials, dodges, and lies. Moreover, he was constantly shadowed by military intelligence agents and his phones were tapped.

All this was not calculated to endear Pearson to the Military Establishment. Defense Department officials discussed ways to block Pearson's news sources. Some suggested retaliation—gag Pearson in the name of military security. Fortunately, Chief of Staff George C. Marshall spurned such tactics. He publicly hailed Pearson as "one of my best inspector-generals."

Other government officials were not as sanguine as General Marshall. As the war progressed, Pearson's reporting was the source of considerable irritation in the White House and the State Department. For instance, Pearson once secured copies of Churchill's secret cables, both in Greece and India. This infuriated Churchill. He phoned FDR and raged about Pearson's disclosure of Ambassador Phillips' cables from India. FDR explained to the bristling Prime Minister that twenty-one top-secret copies had been distributed and he would have them back in two hours. The President issued orders for return of the copies. Within one hour, *twenty-six* were returned to the White House. This being war, British Intelligence utilized every instrument at their command to discover the leak. It turned out to be an Indian military attaché who was ordered returned to his country, was put in the front lines, and was shot.

Another time, Churchill simply went wild when Pearson published Churchill's attempt to save the remaining crowns of Europe. This was a hush-hush British operation. The Prime Minister failed to save the crown of Italy, but he did rescue the Crown of Greece. He refused even to discuss the latter with FDR. When Greece fell, Churchill promised the King he would be returned if he fought on as head of the government-in-exile. The King of Greece agreed, provided Churchill would make the promise in the presence of the British King. Churchill stuck by his word. Nevertheless, the King was unpopular. Accordingly, when Greece was liberated Pearson threw the fat in the fire by revealing Churchill's secret order to the British Command: "Treat Athens like a conquered city."

Pearson's inside diplomatic-military reporting aroused the ire of FDR as well as Churchill. The climactic moment was reached when the Second Front debate raged.

The President's advisers split into two camps in regard to the conduct of the war. The Harry Hopkins-General Marshall side was convinced that Russia had to be the favored ally. The Cordell Hull-Admiral Leahy camp did not fully subscribe to this concept, advocating a policy that was London-oriented. This resulted in a tremendous crisis over the question of the Second Front, and produced the only great tensions of the war between 10 Downing Street and the White House.

The British wanted to delay the second front, to thrust up through the Balkans as the primary offensive and not strike across the Channel. It was perfectly obvious what Churchill had in mind, to crush the German right flank and at the same time put the Allied Army across the path of the Red Army, thus saving Middle Europe from the Russians.

Naturally, this was bitterly opposed by Stalin. He wanted Middle Europe. Further, Russia was drowning in the blood of its own staggering casualties. He urged the winter invasion across the Channel. In addition, Stalin was anxious to relieve the pressure on the Red Army. He privately believed the Allies were quite happy about the Nazis and Reds hammering each other to death.

The American press as well as White House advisers were split on the second front. Mail on the subject poured into 1600 Pennsylvania Avenue. FDR watched current trends closely. He studied his mail, scrutinized public opinion polls, assigned government specialists in opinion research to examine the public pulse. Always the astute politician, he was sensitive to public opinion.

In the end, a Drew Pearson story exerted a major influence on the second-front debate. The background of the story is complicated by political antagonism and personal animosities. Pearson was a close friend of Undersecretary of State Sumner Welles. The President often dealt with Welles directly, which made Secretary of State Hull fume. But this was a normal method of operation with FDR. He pitted men against each other: Hopkins vs. Ickes, Wallace vs. Jones, Jones vs. Morgenthau, and many others. The outstanding feud, the most bitter, was Hull vs. Welles.

Pearson was an incessant Hull critic. He needled and ridiculed him. His Hull-baiting covered major as well as inconsequential matters. For example, Pearson was critical of such minor State Department matters as the promotions of young diplomats and the locations of Negro messengers' desks.

Again and again, Hull blamed Welles for leaking information to Pearson. That the men had many conversations and that Welles spoke freely to Pearson is acknowledged. But Welles was professionally distant. His confidences were probably sparingly given, since all trained diplomats are cautious. Actually, Pearson had other contacts in the State Department. Moreover, Drew had better contacts with the embassies, in many cases better than the State Department.

But the Welles-Hull bitterness could not be cooled by fact or reason. The burning intensity of the feeling between the men was exemplified by Hull's private comment: "Everybody has a son-of-a-bitch in his life. But I've got the All-American son-of-a-bitch Welles." Finally, Hull provoked Welles' resignation. An ugly personal rumor about Welles was spread in Washington and Hull helped to circulate the melancholy story. As a consequence of the rumor, Welles resigned.

Pearson retaliated against Hull's State Department. The columnist was merciless, his anger intensified by the State Department's friendship for Spain's Dictator Franco as well as its tolerance for the rising dictatorships in Latin America.

FDR shared Pearson's annoyance with the State Department's ultra-caution. It may have been one of the reasons he bypassed Hull to deal with Welles. At any rate, the President was acidly reminded by Pearson and other correspondents that in the midst of a great World War, his State Department had continued to remain neutral.

Pearson's war with the State Department reached an explosive peak at a time when the Russians were openly expressing their distrust of British and Americans, particularly over the delay in establishing a second front. The columnist let loose a bombshell that shook Washington, London, and Moscow. He reported that Secretary Hull wanted to see "Russia bled white." The President was furious. He hastily called a press conference and bluntly called Pearson a liar.*

Ernest Cuneo, then OSS Chief Donovan's liaison with the FBI and British Intelligence, has stated: "Drew's story may well have

* Shortly after the President lashed the columnist, Washington's National Press Club scheduled Churchill to deliver an address. An advance copy of the Prime Minister's speech came to the attention of Barnet Nover of the Washington *Post*. It included a blast at Pearson as part of Churchill's defense of FDR. Eugene Meyer, publisher of the *Post,* learned of the proposed criticism. He promptly contacted Churchill's press aide and succeeded in having the anti-Pearson comment deleted.

been a decisive factor in the second-front decision. To allay Russian fears, the President definitely committed the United States to a Channel crossing."

The story was an historic example of the people's right to know vs. national security. In this case, Pearson believed his story was important news. But FDR considered it detrimental to his conduct of military-diplomatic affairs, so he called Pearson a liar.

In time of war it is no small thing to be accused by the President of being a liar. Many of Drew's friends felt that he deserved better from the President, and that in a showdown, Pearson was worth a half-dozen Hulls to the President. One of the columnist's friends stormed over to the White House to protest the severity of FDR's castigation of so useful a journalistic ally. Harry Hopkins, one of FDR's chief aides, expressed some sympathy, but observed that Pearson could take care of himself. He refused to issue any statement to soften FDR's heavy blow.

Several days after the President branded Pearson a liar, the author dined at the Stork Club with two New York newspapermen and one of Drew's old friends. Of course, the prime topic of conversation was FDR's blast. One newspaperman was certain the attack would destroy Pearson as a journalist of consequence; the other argued "Drew must apologize and explain to the President." Pearson's friend was more pragmatic. He contended the affair was just a passing thing that would soon be dismissed from the public mind.

As the lengthy talk progressed, Sherman Billingsley, the Stork's host, joined the table, listened to the talk, and exclaimed: "What's the excitement about? The fact that the President thought he was important enough to rap isn't a bad thing."

At any rate, before the dinner ended it was agreed that a diversion was the proper strategy. If Pearson broke a big story the public would forget the conflict with the President. Several days later, Drew ignited a page-one firecracker. It involved General George S. Patton, and it illustrated again the insoluble journalism vs. military issue.

As a professional soldier, General Patton was an impressive

figure: ramrod-straight, a flash of lightning in his eyes, a weather-beaten face—the look of a finely trained athlete. There was a swagger in his speech and in his writings. Resplendent in his beribboned uniform, he was the arch-military specimen right down to the pearl-handled revolver he loved to brandish.

Shortly after the United States became embroiled in World War II, he quickly became one of the legendary American commanders. Only Eisenhower inspired more newsprint. Patton's words were quotable and his exploits reportable. He once swam across a stream in icy weather to demonstrate to his men that it could be done. One war correspondent described him as a man "crazy with courage." He had a natural flair for verbal flamboyance, which he often demonstrated. Once, before going into battle, he declared: "In forty hours I shall be in battle, with little information, and on the spur of the moment will have to make momentous decisions. But I believe one's spirit enlarges with responsibility and that, with God's help, I shall make them and make them right. It seems that my whole life has been pointed to this moment."

During the Battle of the Bulge—perhaps the most desperate battle ever faced by a United States Army—Patton called a conference of correspondents. The room was heavy with gloom until Patton strode in confidently. The atmosphere changed immediately. He roared: "What the hell is all this mourning about? This is the end of the beginning. We've been batting our brains out trying to get the Hun out in the open. Now he is out. And with the help of God we'll finish him off this time—and for good."

Patton's appeal to God, his propensity for prayer, was well-known. On the eve of one offensive he bowed his head and proclaimed: "Sir, this is Patton talking. Rain, snow, and more rain, more snow—and I am beginning to wonder if they actually are in Thy headquarters. You must decide for Yourself on which side you are standing." Several days later he prayed again: "Sir, this is Patton again, and I beg to report complete progress. Sir, it seems to me that You have been much better informed about the situation than I was, because it was that awful weather which I cursed so much which made it possible for the German army to commit suicide.

That, Sir, was a brilliant military move, and I bow humbly to a supreme military genius."

His fellow officers called him "Georgie," and GI's nicknamed him "Blood and Guts," although some soldiers sardonically remarked, "Our blood and his guts." Patton was a master of profanity and could be as raucous as a beer party at a logger's camp. He often went into battle riding atop his tank, daring all the fates.

Some of his critics considered him insensitive and arrogant, yet these characteristics made him a formidable military commander and a leader of men in that brutal business known as war. "For certain types of action," said Eisenhower, "he was the outstanding soldier our country has produced."

Patton's weakness was within his emotional machinery. One balance wheel was misweighed, some gear was out of ratio. This flaw was his tragic one.

One of the author's friends served as an officer under Patton and remembers him as a "terrific guy. He was like something out of a Hollywood script. He was an exciting man and he seemed to communicate his excitement. When he was in a room, nobody talked but Patton. And everybody listened to everything he said. He was a great storyteller and a damned good dirty-joke teller. He was the kind of General who won the respect of his men by trying to be one of them in the sense that he spent more time in the front-line foxholes than any other General. Some dirty GI would look up from his grimy hole and see Patton jumping in beside him to congratulate him or encourage him. You don't know how important that was to soldiers in the line. That did more for their morale than a whole boatload of entertainers. Oh, a lot of us thought he was a showboat and a big ham. But you couldn't deny his guts. I think he is one of the few people I know who enjoyed war. Nothing else was as fascinating to him. I think there are some people who are just naturals for certain types of jobs. Like Joe DiMaggio as a ball player. Well, Patton was just made for soldiering and war. Sure he was an emotional man, as emotional as hell. I thought it was a lot better to be that way than to be cold and stuffy. So many general officers were unapproachable, it was a refreshing relief to have someone like Patton around. A lot of the men around him cursed him privately when he chewed them out, but I didn't know one who really didn't respect him. As I said, he was emotional. I remember him doing something that startled me and everyone else during a visit to a military hospital. He walked up to the bed of one badly mangled soldier and looked at him for a moment, then dropped to his knees, buried his head in the blanket, and prayed for the wounded soldier. It was a spur of the moment thing and I'll never forget it."

But two incidents proved Patton's undoing. The first took place at a military hospital in Italy and was hushed. The official report of the affair was written by Major Charles Barton Etter.

> On Monday afternoon, August 10, 1943, at approximately 1330, General Patton entered the Receiving Ward of the 93rd Evacuation Hospital and started interviews and visiting the patients who were there. There were some ten or fifteen casualties in the tent at the time. The first five or six that he talked to were battle casualties. He asked each what the trouble was, commended them for their excellent fighting, told them they were doing a good job, and wished them a speedy recovery.
>
> He came to one patient who, upon inquiry, stated that he was sick with a high fever. The general dismissed him without comment. The next patient was sitting huddled up and shivering. When asked what the trouble was, the man replied, "It's my nerves," and began to sob. The General then screamed at him, "What did you say?" He replied, "It's my nerves. I can't stand the shelling any more." He was still sobbing.
>
> The General then yelled at him, "Your nerves hell, you are just a goddamn coward, you yellow son of a bitch." He then slapped the man and said, "Shut up that goddamned crying. I won't have these brave men here who have been shot seeing a yellow bastard sitting here crying." He then struck at the man again, knocking his helmet liner off and into the next tent. He then turned to the Receiving Officer and yelled, "Don't you admit this yellow bastard, there's nothing wrong with him. I won't have the hospitals cluttered up with these sons of bitches who haven't the guts to fight."

> He turned to the man again, who was managing to "sit at attention" though shaking all over, and said, "You're going back to the front lines and you may get shot and killed, but you're going to fight. If you don't, I'll stand you up against a wall and have a firing squad kill you on purpose. In fact," he said, reaching for his pistol, "I ought to shoot you myself, you goddamned whimpering coward." As he went out of the ward he was still yelling back at the Receiving Officer to send that yellow son of a bitch to the front lines.
>
> All this was in such a loud voice that nurses and patients in adjoining wards had come outside to see what the disturbance was.

Thus ended the graphic report that was buried in the files by military censors. The Big Brass considered it "a family affair."

The second incident involved Pvt. Paul G. Bennett of South Carolina. He had enlisted in the regular Army prior to Pearl Harbor and served with distinction in North Africa and Sicily. After he learned that his wife gave birth, he developed severe anxiety. He feared he would die before seeing his child. The condition was aggravated when his best friend was killed in a massive bombardment. Anxiety wrecked Private Bennett. A medical officer ordered him evacuated to a hospital, although Bennett pleaded that he wanted to remain with his unit.

General Patton arrived as Private Bennett was being processed in the admission tent. Patton erupted when he learned Bennett was being hospitalized because the soldier was "nervous." He slapped Bennett and walked out.

The first face-slapping incident had been effectively hushed, but the second came to the attention of American war correspondents. Among newspapermen who investigated the incident were CBS' John Daly and Quentin Reynolds. The latter gravely opined that there were at least fifty thousand American soldiers who would shoot Patton if they had the slightest chance. Daly submitted a detailed report to General Eisenhower's press aide. He believed Patton was a victim of temporary insanity. Meanwhile, General Eisenhower ordered Surgeon General Blesse to investigate the incident, and wrote a sharply critical letter to General Patton.

Lt. Gen. George S. Patton.

Field Marshal Montgomery and Patton in Sicily.

Generals Eisenhower, Patton, Bradley, and Hodges.

At Teheran in March 1943, Roosevelt, Churchill, and Stalin plan the death of Nazism.

Secretary of State Cordell Hull.

When Patton heard the rumors concerning the GI's reaction to him, he was characteristically forthright. He addressed several thousand American troops in Palermo, and his first words were: "I just thought I'd stand up here and let you soldiers see if I'm as big an s.o.b. as you think I am."

The soldiers cheered him. General Patton hoped the cheers would silence the whispers about the face-slapping incident. General Eisenhower never formally asked correspondents to ignore the Patton story, but the newspapermen shared Eisenhower's belief that Patton's impressive military accomplishments made him valuable enough to protect.

Capt. Harry C. Butcher, General Eisenhower's naval aide, later wrote: "General Eisenhower spent several sleepless nights trying to determine how to save the best Allied ground gainer and still prevent repetition of his actions. He had written Patton a stern rebuke and then had personally ordered Patton to apologize to each soldier individually, and collectively to the assembled officers of each division. The action had been explained by Eisenhower to several press and radio men, and they, in turn, spread the word to other correspondents that disciplinary action had been taken. They voluntarily cooperated beautifully in not sending stories home about the deplorable affair."

The fact was that the correspondents had surrendered en masse to military censorship.

Pearson's source for the Patton face-slapping story was OSS official Ernest Cuneo, a long-time Pearson friend. The columnist checked the story, verified it, and made it public. "I decided it was time to let loose on him," he said.

On Sunday evening, November 21, 1943, Pearson reported the story to his radio audience. General Eisenhower's press aides then made a major tactical mistake: They denied Pearson's story. The denial heightened its news value. Within twenty-four hours, American correspondents covering the Italian campaign broke their self-imposed silence and confirmed Pearson's story. Confronted with the facts, the military propagandists beat a hasty retreat and denied their denial.

The story caused an editorial storm. A few editorials reprimanded

Pearson for talking out of turn, but the vast majority praised him.

Typical of pro-Pearson editorials was the Cleveland *News* comment: "The confidence of the country in the honesty and integrity of Army official spokesmen has been shaken sharply by the revelations of the General Patton incident. The Army erred twice, first in keeping it a Mediterranean secret for three months, second for lying about it when it finally was exposed. To Columnist Drew Pearson, our congratulations for prying out a story which never should have been hidden. We hope it teaches the brass hats a worthwhile lesson in public relations."

The St. Louis *Star-Times:* "After months of rumors that magnified the Patton incident, Drew Pearson told the truth over the air. He did the correspondents' job for them. He exposed the shabby incompetence and autocracy of our censorship. Even then, the military authorities were not through with their policy of concealment. They denied that any such incident had ever occurred. For twenty-four hours, they permitted the denial to stand, making Pearson appear a liar before the nation."

Louisville *Courier:* "Now Patton has received, thanks to Mr. Pearson, what probably to him is the worst punishment of all, a public airing of his behavior. His record on the whole is that of a soldier of extraordinary courage and competence, in spite of all his theatricalism, and there can be no satisfaction in belaboring him further. It is possible to hope he has learned a lesson."

Mobile, Alabama, *Register:* "Thanks to the usual accuracy of Drew Pearson, his story not only stood up but has been verified in even more shocking scope and detail than he told it. It is nothing out of the ordinary for somebody to say or imply that Drew Pearson is a liar. But there is a vast difference between calling a man a liar and proving him a liar. The customary experience has been that those who have implied that Pearson is a liar have not come forward with the proof of it. We offer in evidence, as the most recent exhibit, Allied headquarters in Algiers."

The minority dissent was represented by Sack Alexander in the *Saturday Evening Post:* "Pearson's disclosure of the slapping was scarcely an act of courage, in the normal meaning of the word. There was no danger involved in it, except that of adding more readers and listeners to an array of followers already counted in the millions. Nor was the Pearson story 'a scoop' which is what reporters—at least those of the screen—call a news story which is published before rivals are aware of its existence. For several months, some sixty-odd war correspondents had knowledge of the slapping, but none had tried to send it back home. It was likewise known to many newspapers and magazines in this country. All, except Pearson, voluntarily refrained from making it public."

Alexander then went on to reprimand Pearson for his excessive "theatricality." This section of his critical report was on firmer ground. The fact is, on occasion, Pearson has overdramatized the news.

As a case in point, there was the breathless announcement he made to his radio audience: "Attention all Americans along the Atlantic, the Pacific, and the Canadian border: The Air Force will soon start building a radar wall completely around the United States to detect enemy airplanes. The location of these radar sites *must be kept secret*. So, if the government has bought land for a secret project in your neighborhood, pay no attention to what goes on. And above all, *please don't talk about it!*"

Among reactions to the Patton story was a demand for a court-martial for Patton. The demand was made by Florida's Senator Pepper. Some legislators, however, failed to join the parade in Pearson's honor. One of the exceptions to the general hurrah was Texas' Congressman Nat Patton, no kin to the General.

While the Patton controversy churned, Pearson had lunch with several legislators in the House restaurant. Throughout lunch, the columnist was aware that Congressman Patton downed beer after beer while he glared in Pearson's direction. Finally, Patton shakily got on his feet, went over to Pearson's table, pulled a knife out of his pocket and waved it under Drew's nose. Shocked lawmakers in the room immediately interceded, disarmed the knife-waver, and eased Pearson out of the room.

After Pearson lambasted Patton there was also a widely circulated story about Robert S. Allen, who had been Drew's columnar associate and had joined the army at the outbreak of World War II. Rumor said Allen was made General Patton's public relations officer, presumably as a hostage against further attacks by Pearson. Only one thing was wrong with the Allen-hostage story: It just was not true.

As a consequence of the public outrage, General Eisenhower called in Patton and severely reprimanded him, although he retained him on active duty. Patton publicly apologized to the entire Army. But the damage was done. The Patton image was tarnished, his heroic stature diminished. The man who was ready to fight all evil with bare fists, if necessary, defeated himself with a single slap.

Pearson continued his campaign against Patton. He made public additional illustrations of Patton's eccentric behavior. He had ordered an Italian peasant's mule shot when it went over a military bridge. He fired his pearl-handled revolver in the air when dressing down a fellow officer. During his early army days Patton shot a horse after it failed to perform satisfactorily in a polo match.

Pearson continued to write that the Senate Military Affairs Committee "is not as interested in General Patton as in the broader question of army procedure. They are wondering about the Army's buck-passing between Washington and Eisenhower's headquarters, and about who was really responsible for keeping Patton on.

"They are also skeptical about all army promotions from now on. Inasmuch as Patton's behavior in the hospital was so studiously kept off the record and his name sent up for promotion regardless, they are wondering how extensive this cover-up system is. Unfortunately, one result of the Patton incident may be to work a hardship on other well-deserving officers."

The public uproar over the Patton incident and the subsequent Congressional probe left the secrecy-security problem unaltered. But the issue remained a debatable topic. Veteran reporter Jack Alexander wrote: "The continued presence of a leak can have a seriously hamstringing effect on the government. Early in 1941, for instance, when it appeared likely that America would be drawn into the war, one department head was charged with organizing a confidential study which had a direct bearing on preparedness. The subordinate in charge of the section to which the task would normally be assigned happened to be a Pearson leak. The department head was caught in a dilemma. If he went ahead and assigne the secret study to the section, it might become the property of the "Merry-Go-Round." If he bypassed the section and assigned it to another section, he felt confident that the distrusted subordinate, angry at being bypassed, would dribble out whatever fragments of the secret study he was able to obtain by reason of his presence in the office. He did the only thing possible under the circumstances—he pigeonholed the study."

On the other hand, *Time* magazine reported that Pearson practices "the kind of journalistic vigilance that keeps small men honest, and forces bigger men to work in an atmosphere of caution that frequently cramps their style. Many an official lives in constant fear of having the more delicate operations of diplomacy upset by Pearson's premature or partial disclosures."

Those critical about the disclosure of secret information to reporters generally ignore the reality of Washington. On occasion, such disclosures are motivated by vengeance and vanity. More often, they are the consequence of a perpetual clash. There is constant conflict between the various branches of the armed services, between Executive agencies, and between the White House and Capitol Hill. By and large these are not minor disputes. They represent a clash of major issues and ideas. And the life or death of these major concepts depends on public support. Thus the benefits to be gained by publicity encourages the partisans on both sides to disclose secrets or to reveal behind-the-scenes maneuvers.

The perplexing problem often gets down to the equally complex definition of news. Rarely have reporters and officials agreed on what should and should not be published. In the end, the definition ultimately depends on the individual judgments of reporters, editors, and publishers. Of course, their judgments are subject to myriad influences.

There are many cases where officials and reporters are simply not able to agree about what should and should not be published. In his excellent book *The Artillery of the Press,* Washington columnist James Reston of *The New York Times,* recalls an incident during the Eisenhower Administration. The United States formally charged the Soviet Union with installing "a miniature radio transmitting device back of the Great Seal of the United States in the

Embassy in Moscow. Later, the United States was caught tapping the telephones of the Dominican Republic's Embassy in Washington. This was discovered by Drew Pearson and *The New York Times,* and the facts were published. In this case, the newspapers believed the secret use of these devices was getting out of hand, but the State Department's top officials felt that the papers not only interfered with the collection of important security information, but, by disclosing the truth in the Dominican case, made every other foreign embassy in Washington suspicious that its phones were tapped as well."

Mr. Reston goes on to illustrate the other side of the picture: Failure on the part of reporters to publish private government information "about what is being discussed and decided inside the government can often damage the national interest. The reporters knew all about the Kennedy Administration's plans to help mount an invasion against Cuba at the Bay of Pigs. Some papers reported what was afoot, others did not; but after the invasion failed, President Kennedy told Turner Catledge, then managing editor of *The New York Times,* that he wished the press had disclosed much more information than it did. 'In that event,' he remarked, 'the American people might have forced cancellation of one of the most embarrassing American military and diplomatic adventures of the century.' "

Over the years there have been attempts to solve the insolvable. During World War II, Admiral King and George Marshall arranged background conferences for Washington correspondents. The meetings were informative and frequently useful. In time, however, the Army and Navy leaders sought to use the conferences to leak information designed to bolster a particular point of view. The assembled reporters were faced with the old perplexing problem of striving to separate news from propaganda.

When James V. Forrestal was Secretary of Defense he gave serious consideration to setting up a government advisory committee that might curtail the excesses of secrecy in the government and the irresponsibilities in the press. The idea of such an agency in peacetime exercising any form of control over the press was repulsive to any reporter worth his salt. The Forrestal idea never was implemented.

Every attempted solution of the problem has provoked additional problems. Now and then, Congressmen become allies of journalists. The lawmakers have frustrated officials who impeded the flow of information. They have investigated and exposed officials who imposed excessive security arrangements. Yet Congressmen and Congressional committees have sought to suppress news unfavorable to themselves.

The security-secrecy dilemma is compounded by the flexible definition of the word secret. On occasion, officials have stamped documents secret to heighten the news impact when the alleged secret is leaked to a newspaperman. Some Washington secrets are not secret—and some Washington secrets are not news.

Correspondent William S. White wrote: "Often reporters handle a leaked story with a solemn incriticalness. The documents, or whatever, are ceremoniously produced for the public—which at times must scratch its head in perplexity as to what the devil they are all about. The motivation for the leak usually is not mentioned, although that may be the most significant part of the story."

Here again, the problem is rooted in the discrimination of the individual reporter. He must determine whether he is being used as a propaganda instrument or is truly fulfilling his obligation as a dispenser of news.

Merely stating the importance of a reporter's discriminatory sense is far simpler than its daily application in the workaday world. He is caught and intimately involved in the perpetual Washington struggle. He is a part of the ceaseless battle of intelligence and counterintelligence. He is called upon to make quick decisions about what is proper or improper. And he is not always certain that in the massive Washington echo chamber of whispered and shouted voices there is the sound of truth.

The complexity of the problem facing reporters was once posed by historian Arthur M. Schlesinger, Jr.: "What is the responsibility of a newspaperman when he discovers that some rumored development of policy is really only a psychological warfare trick? Should he print the truth at the risk of wrecking the plans of the Secretary of State? Or should he suppress the truth, betray himself, and deceive the American people?"

Mr. Schlesinger's troublesome questions are relevant to the problem. Yet the relevancy has little relation to the realism of Washington journalism. The reporter cannot adopt an absolutist position. He cannot determine accuracy of motivation with scientific certitude. Often his decision depends on his instincts, experience, sophistication—or the prime exigencies of the situation. As a responsible journalist he may engage in fruitful inquiry, or have confidence in his news sources. He cannot impose too many restrictions on his production of news without negating his role as a reporter.

As previously noted, the final responsibility rests with the individual journalist. It is up to him to draw the fine line between the deceitful and diplomatic, between military expediency and military suppression, between political information and political propaganda, between attempts to inform the public and attempts to manipulate public opinion. Granted that the choices are difficult for the newspaperman. But the alternative is a government-imposed choice and that, of course, would represent the surrender of the free press.

Pearson has written: "What is hidden from the public is usually what the public is most entitled to know about, and the job of a good newspaperman is to report. . . . It is the job of a newspaperman to probe deeper than a handout or an official statement. Frequently, the best part of the story is after the spot-news cream has been skimmed."

There can be no rigid rules or hard codes of ethics for reporters. At all times they must be flexible. Their daily work must be governed by their own judgments. In dealing with the massive and ever growing military, diplomatic, and political establishment, reporters must be equipped with enterprise as well as courage.

Journalists who cover the government scene must accept the harsh fact that they are engaged in a ceaseless struggle. Victory is their own estimate of the truth.

Herald Tribune — New York

Vol. CV No. 35,943

FRIDAY, APRIL 13, 1945

LATE EDITION

President Roosevelt Is Dead; Truman Sworn In as Successor

9th Army Crosses Elbe, 50 Miles From Berlin

Roosevelt, 63, Dies of Stroke In 2½ Hours

'A Terrific Headache,' He Said at Warm Springs, Sitting for a Portrait

In Coma Quickly; Not to Lie in State

Funeral in White House Tomorrow and Burial in Hyde Park Sunday

By Merriman Smith

"All the News That's Fit to Print"

The New York Times.

LATE CITY EDITION

VOL. XCIV... No. 31,972. NEW YORK, TUESDAY, AUGUST 7, 1945. THREE CENTS

FIRST ATOMIC BOMB DROPPED ON JAPAN; MISSILE IS EQUAL TO 20,000 TONS OF TNT; TRUMAN WARNS FOE OF A 'RAIN OF RUIN'

HIRAM W. JOHNSON, REPUBLICAN DEAN IN THE SENATE, DIES

Isolationist Helped Prevent U. S. Entry Into League—Opposed World Charter

Jet Plane Explosion Kills Major Bong, Top U. S. Ace

Flier Who Downed 40 Japanese Craft, Sent Home to Be 'Safe,' Was Flying New 'Shooting Star' as a Test Pilot

KYUSHU CITY RAZED

Kenney's Planes Blast Tarumizu in Record Blow From Okinawa

REPORT BY BRITAIN

'By God's Mercy' We Beat Nazis to Bomb, Churchill Says

Steel Tower 'Vaporized' In Trial of Mighty Bomb

Scientists Awe-Struck as Blinding Flash Lighted New Mexico Desert and Great Cloud Bore 40,000 Feet Into Sky

NEW AGE USHERED

Day of Atomic Energy Hailed by President, Revealing Weapon

HIROSHIMA IS TARGET

'Impenetrable' Cloud of Dust Hides City After Single Bomb Strikes

---

The New York Times.

LATE CITY EDITION

NEW YORK, WEDNESDAY, AUGUST 15, 1945. THREE CENTS

JAPAN SURRENDERS, END OF WAR! EMPEROR ACCEPTS ALLIED RULE; M'ARTHUR SUPREME COMMANDER; OUR MANPOWER CURBS VOIDED

Third Fleet Fells 5 Planes Since End

ALL CITY 'LETS GO'

Hundreds of Thousands Roar Joy After Victory Flash Is Received

TIMES SQ. IS JAMMED

Police Estimate Crowd in Area at 2,000,000—Din Overwhelming

By ALEXANDER FEINBERG

PRESIDENT ANNOUNCING SURRENDER OF JAPAN

YIELDING UNQUALIFIED, TRUMAN SAYS

Japan Is Told to Order End of Hostilities, Notify Allied Supreme Commander and Send Emissaries to Him

MACARTHUR TO RECEIVE SURRENDER

Formal Proclamation of V-J Day Awaits Signing of Those Articles—Cease-Fire Order Given to the Allied Forces

By ARTHUR KROCK

SECRETS OF RADAR GIVEN TO WORLD

PETAIN CONVICTED, SENTENCED TO DIE

Jurors Recommend Clemency Because of His Age—Long Indictment Upheld

Terms Will Reduce Japan To Kingdom Perry Visited

Orders Given to the Japanese

TREATY WITH CHINA SIGNED IN MOSCOW

Complete Agreement Reached With Chungking on All Points at Issue, Russians Say

World News Summarized

WEDNESDAY, AUGUST 15, 1945

Two-Day Holiday Is Proclaimed; Stores, Banks Close Here Today

Cruiser Sunk, 1,196 Casualties; Took Atom Bomb Cargo to Guam

MacArthur Begins Orders to Hirohito

THE NEW YORK TIMES, SATURDAY, JULY 30, 1949

VAUGHAN ADMITS DEEP-FREEZE GIFTS AND DEFENDS THEM

He Names Himself, President's Missouri Home, Vinson, Snyder and 2 White House Aides

DENIES ANY IMPROPRIETY

Says 'Ad' Man Suggested Units for General and Friends and Told of Valueless Models

By HAROLD B. HINTON

WASHINGTON, Aug. 13—Maj. Gen. Harry H. Vaughan, President Truman's military aide, assumed full responsibility today for the gifts of deep-freeze units to himself and other persons close to the Chief Executive. He issued a statement to the press giving his side of the controversy and denying any impropriety.

Recipients of the refrigeration apparatus in 1945, the statement said, were, in addition to General Vaughan, the Little White House, President Truman's home at Independence, Mo.; the staff members' lunchroom at the White House, Chief Justice Fred M. Vinson, then Director of the Office of War Mobilization and Reconversion; John W. Snyder, Secretary of the Treasury; James K. Vardaman, now a governor of the Federal Reserve System, but then President Truman's naval aide, and Matthew J. Connelly, a White House secretary.

The gifts were brought to light in testimony this week by Albert J. Gross of Milwaukee, former head of Gross & Co., which in 1945 manufactured deep freeze units, before the Senate subcommittee investigating the activities of "five per centers" in selling alleged influence to seekers after Government contracts.

Decided Not to Wait

Secretary Snyder said today that the apparatus intended for him was never delivered. He said he had no knowledge of it supposed to...

General Vaughan said that he...

CALLING COLUMNIST IN 5% STUDY URGED

Maragon Says Senate Group Should Make Pearson Supply Evidence for Accusations

WASHINGTON, July 29 (AP)—John Maragon, a former bootblack who once had a White House pass and auto parking privileges, demanded today that Drew Pearson, a columnist, be called to testify in the Senate investigation of "5 per centers."

Mr. Maragon said that Mr. Pearson accused him in a July 20 column of being "not only a 5 per center but a 50 percenter."

The "jack of many trades"—he will not say what he is now—emerged beaming from a closed-door session of the Senate's special investigation subcommittee headed by Senator Clyde R. Hoey, Democrat, of North Carolina.

The Senators are looking into allegations that persons claiming to have influence with government officials have been telling business men they could get lucrative government contracts in return for a percentage fee.

Mr. Maragon, who used to ply his shoe-shine trade in Kansas City and met President Truman there, talked to reporters after being questioned for the second time in less than twenty-four hours by Senate investigators.

"I am happy, and I am not mad at anybody," he said. "We just talked about my personal affairs. I am happy to be here. When you have been accused of being a 5 per center or a 50 per center you want to straighten it out."

Specific Evidence Asked

He asserted that he had asked the Senators to hale Mr. Pearson before the subcommittee and demanded that the columnist be required to furnish specific evidence of his accusations against Mr. Maragon.

"What did they say?" a reporter asked.

"That," he replied, "is for them to say."

Asked if he had given the committee any clues about "5 per centers" operating here, Mr. Maragon said:

"How could I give them any ideas when I am not in a position to ascertain any?"

Mr. Maragon, 56 years old and a native of the British Isle of Malta in the Mediterranean, radiated cheer, but parried questions about what went on in the closed-door session.

"There's nothing, nothing," he said. "We just went over what I said yesterday."

He expressed doubt that the committee would recall him and said only a few hours later he was back before the committee for a third time.

4

LIFE WITH HARRY

On April 12, 1945, in the CBS Newsroom, a warning bell rang on the INS teletype which relayed that wire service to the network. Lee Otis, assistant news editor, dashed to the teletype to read the shortest news flash in the history of journalism. He stripped the yellow paper from its reel and handed it to John Daly, CBS newscaster. Daly glanced at the message: "FDR DEAD."

Daly raced into the main news studio and signaled the technician in charge to cut off the regularly scheduled program and give him the entire CBS network. Within a minute Daly was on the air. "We interrupt this program to bring you a special news bulletin from CBS World News. A press association has just announced that President Roosevelt is dead. All that has been received is that bare announcement. There are no further details as yet, but CBS World News will return to the air in just a few moments with more information as it is received in our New York headquarters. We return you now to our regularly scheduled program. . . ."

That was the first word the American people had of Franklin Delano Roosevelt's death. Seconds later, radio stations flashed the news around the world.

Drew Pearson was writing his column when he learned of the President's death. His initial reaction was inevitable shock and a surge of grief. He left his office and roamed the streets of Washington. The news of FDR's death was on everybody's face. Melancholy disbelief was rampant. Emptiness in the eyes of people. An unnatural quiet in the city. Hushed words.

Within an hour, Pearson returned to his office. As a dutiful newspaperman should, he inscribed his thoughts on paper. He began by writing: "The town seems empty today—and a little numb. Actually Franklin Roosevelt hasn't been here much this winter, and things are really no different. . . . But people always felt that he was here, that he had his hands on things, and so the town seems empty. Even the guards around public buildings, the folks who sit on the park benches,the elevator operators, the taxi drivers, seem a little lost. More than any other man, Roosevelt was their President. They felt he was working for them. And he was. They know it will be hard for them to get another such friend."

Pearson went on to recall some of FDR's triumphs and defeats and expressed his own profound sense of personal loss.

The New York Times editorial page stated in part: "A great and gallant wartime leader has died almost in the very hour of victory to which he led the way. It is a cruel and bitter irony that Franklin D. Roosevelt should not have lived to see the Allied armies march into Berlin. It is a hard and stunning blow to lose the genius and the inspiration of his leadership in this decisive moment of the war."

The Philadelphia *Inquirer* said: "He gave his life for his country as truly as the soldier who is slain on the firing line. He died in the path of duty. He could have wished for no better epitaph."

The Baltimore *Sun* reminded: "We all understand that his death lays upon us as a people and upon his successor responsibilities so grave that they can be approached only in the spirit of deepest humility."

The Washington *Post* noted: "His sudden passing will force us to meet many new problems. But that is the way of democracy. Under our system the success of great national projects is not contingent upon the fate of any one individual. The loss of a great leader may temporarily shake our confidence, but there is always a new President to take over the helm. There is always confidence in our constitutional system."

The Los Angeles *Times* observed: "It is for us to pick up where he left off and continue on, not only to the goal he had set in the war, but also for the sound reconstruction of the nation in the post-war years."

Walter Lippmann wrote: "The nation has received the news of Roosevelt's death with profound sorrow but without dismay. Surely he would have wanted it to be this way. For the final test of a leader is that he leaves behind him in other men the conviction and the will to carry on. The man must die in his appointed time. He must carry away with him the magic of his presence and the personal mastery of affairs which no man, however gifted by nature, can acquire except in the relentless struggle with evil and blind chance. . . . Roosevelt knew what were the questions that had to be answered, even though he himself did not always find the full answer. It was to this that our people and the world responded, preferring him instinctively to those who did not know what the real questions were. Here was the secret of the sympathy which never ceased to flow back to him from the masses of mankind, and the reason why they discounted his mistakes. For they knew that he was asking the right questions, and if he did not always find the right answers, someone, who had learned what to look for, eventually would."

Although Pearson was stunned by the President's death, he had been aware of his failing health. In November 1943, for example, an ominous rumor circulated in Washington. Drew received inquiries from editors along the syndicate and decided to run it down. It was rumored that FDR had secretly undergone serious surgery. Pearson learned that such an operation was considered, but was deemed too risky in view of his weakened heart. The columnist learned also that the doctors attending the President agreed that his health was failing. However, few believed the end would come so soon. The majority medical judgment was that he would at least live out his fourth term. During FDR's last Cabinet meeting, Pearson learned, the President was listless and remote. The night before FDR had been up late attending the White House correspondents' dinner.

The next day the President had every symptom of a man fatigued to the bone. He was snappish, groggy, and unable to articulate clearly. Naturally, the Cabinet members were dismayed by the President's obvious evidence of severe illness. When they filed out of the room, they were silent, grim, and white-faced. Among them were the men who, only a few years before, had upheld the necessity of running for a third term.

These were the same stunned Cabinet members who stood on April 12, 1945, in the Cabinet Room as officials searched for a Bible for the new President to hold while Chief Justice Stone administered the oath of office. A Bible was found. When Harry Truman became President of the United States, the clock beneath Woodrow Wilson's portrait marked exactly 7:09 P.M. The entire ceremony required 68 seconds. Several hours later, Truman called his initial Cabinet meeting. At that time the new President learned, for the first time, that the United States had developed an atomic bomb. Secretary Stimson told him the story. Later, Vannevar Bush, chief of the Office of Scientific Research and Development, briefed the President on scientific details relating to the weapon.

Twenty-four hours later, Truman held his first press conference and solemnly informed the assembled correspondents: "Boys, if you ever pray, pray for me now. I don't know whether you fellows ever had a load of hay fall on you, but when they told me yesterday what had happened, I felt like the moon, the stars, and all the planets had fallen on me. I've got the most terribly responsible job a man ever had."

"Good luck, Mr. President," one reporter sang out.

"I wish you didn't have to call me that," Truman responded.

The American press in general called for unified support for the new Chief Executive. Yet the feelings of Washington correspondents were mixed. Their sympathy for Truman's humble acceptance of the massive responsibility conflicted with their disdain—even contempt—for his ability to handle the obligations of the Presidency. One White House correspondent privately commented: "A pygmy has replaced a giant." Their attitude was understandable. Correspondents resented the idea of a "peasant" supplanting a "prince." At the time, Truman's lackluster personality when contrasted with FDR's enormous personal magic dismayed the correspondents. Besides, their grief over FDR's death was still raw and his hesitant, uncertain successor intensified their sense of loss.

A Washington columnist later wrote that "Truman appeared to be an intruder in the White House."

Although most Washington correspondents were skeptical about Truman's Presidential stature, the fact was that as a Senator and Vice President, Truman and the Washington press had been on an amiable, first-name basis. By and large he had received a friendly press. Drew Pearson, in particular, had publicly supported and aided the investigative efforts of the Truman committee during the war years.

As a matter of fact, Truman has a sharp remembrance of Pearson's support. This was demonstrated in 1944, several weeks after Truman was nominated for the Vice Presidency, when he met Pearson at a cocktail party. In mock severity Truman groaned: "You're responsible for all this. You've got me into a lot of trouble. I don't know whether I'll ever be able to forgive you." Truman's comment puzzled the columnist. Uncertain about whether he was kidding or not, Pearson half smiled and appeared dazed. Noticing the columnist's befuddlement, Truman promptly explained: "You're the one who first suggested that I be Vice President." At that moment, Pearson recalled that his column several months before had contained an effusive tribute to Truman's work as chairman of the Truman investigating committee and had suggested he might be good Vice Presidential timber.

Truman was a most reluctant Vice Presidential candidate. Unassuming, modest, in love with his job as Senator from Missouri, he never wanted to be Vice President. After he was elected, he dreaded the thought that something might happen to President Roosevelt. Once, during the campaign, he woke up in a cold sweat. He had dreamed that Roosevelt had died and he was called upon to assume his mantle. Truman said he never had such a terrible dream before.

The genesis of Truman's emergence as a Vice Presidential candidate was more fantasy than nightmare. Like Calvin Coolidge, he had been the product of political miracles. The first occurred when Boss Pendergast of Kansas City picked him, a totally unknown country judge, to run for the Senate; the second, when he was tapped for the Democratic Vice Presidential nomination during the summer of 1944 in Chicago. The fateful hour found Truman emotionally disturbed, reluctant, totally unprepared.

The story is rooted in the attitude of an ailing, weary President who handled the problem of the Vice President with careless indifference. FDR encouraged Secretary Hull, and several others, to believe they were strong contenders. Always reluctant to harm anyone's feelings, he neglected to say "no" to a small army of hopefuls. That was FDR's way of doing things. Mrs. Roosevelt could never get him to dismiss incompetent household employees.

At any rate, the Democratic pros, including National Committee Chairman Robert E. Hannegan, were in charge of the convention. Shortly before the convention met, FDR wrote to Hannegan that "either Bill Douglas or Harry Truman" were his VP choices. Pearson unearthed evidence, later confirmed officially, that Hannegan, who was close to Truman, altered the President's instructions to read, "Harry Truman or Bill Douglas," without Truman's knowledge, on the theory that the name mentioned first was the stronger candidate.

As for Harry Truman, he came to Chicago with the earnest intention of supporting Jimmy Byrnes as FDR's running mate. Truman later wrote: "Bess, Margie, and I got in a car and I drove to Chicago. When we arrived I found that I was a member of the resolutions committee, which committee writes the platform. I worked diligently on the platform and went to see all the leaders I knew, labor and others, to try to get them for Byrnes for Vice President. Each time I saw a leader he told me he was for Henry Wallace first and for me second. I told all of them that I was not a candidate. I reported all these interviews to Mr. Byrnes. He told me each time that Roosevelt would publicly say he was for him for Vice President."

It has never before been revealed, but Truman's first inkling that Roosevelt wanted him came while he was sitting in his room at the Blackstone Hotel. The phone rang. Someone answered it, told Truman that Hopkins was on the phone. "Hopkins," he exclaimed, then remarked that it must be Hopkins, a Kansas City friend. He picked up the phone. It was Harry Hopkins telling Truman that Roosevelt wanted him as his running mate. Truman appeared dazed. But recovering, he said: "I don't want the job. I don't think they're serious. I'll wait until I hear from the Chief himself."

Late that night, with the convention on the verge of a three-cornered deadlock, Truman was again back in his room when he received another call—this time from the President.

"Hello, Mr. President," Truman said, "how are you?" There was a pause. Truman continued: "What should I do, Mr. President? I don't know what to say."

FDR replied: "Stay in there and pitch, Harry. Everything is going to be OK."

"Fine," answered Truman, "if you say so. I'll stay in there."

Next day, when the Vice Presidential ballot was finished, Truman was seated on a box behind the rostrum eating a hot dog and drinking a bottle of pop as a voice came over the microphone. "Will the next Vice President of the United States please come to the rostrum?" The voice had to boom out several times before Harry Truman, the man who did not want to be Vice President, laid down his pop bottle and reluctantly came to the microphone.

Truman's nomination was accepted by most newspapers with a paucity of editorial comment. The St. Louis *Post-Dispatch*, a critic of Truman's patron, Boss Pendergast, editorially noted on October 24, 1944: "Hating his political origin as it does, this newspaper is among those which freely pays tribute to the Senator for his accomplishments. We hold that as candidate for the Vice Presidency he has outlived his unwholesome past and now stands as a public servant who has served the public with exceptional courage, integrity, and ability."

FDR defeated Thomas E. Dewey and inaugurated his fourth term. On another level, Inauguration Day marked a turning point in the relationship between Drew Pearson and Harry Truman. Until that day, it had been warmly chummy.

Describing the event, Pearson wrote: "Mrs. Truman has a lot to learn about official receptions. The new Vice President's wife looked like she was going to pass out after shaking only a thousand hands in the early part of the day. She received the three thousand guests with Mrs. Roosevelt at the front entrance to the White House, but couldn't keep the long line moving, complained that her right hand hurt."

Pearson considered the report a slight descriptive item. Truman accepted it as a monumental affront. Pearson should have been aware of the consequences. His long experience in Washington taught him that the mildest rebuke to a politician's wife results in explosive reverberations. He conceded as much, "It is axiomatic in Washington that you can criticize almost anything you want about a politician's policies, but if you write about his womenfolk or the details of his private life, you are in trouble."

Trouble was not long in coming. Within two weeks, Pearson had his response. The Vice President participated in a private meeting of senators' administrative assistants. It was a routine affair, until someone, perhaps innocently, asked him about Mrs. Truman's experiences as a hostess in Washington. Truman's lips tightened, his fist pounded the table, and he said, "That Drew Pearson is a ——!"

Cissy Patterson's *Times-Herald* quoted Truman: "There is one columnist in Washington who wouldn't have room on his breast if he got a ribbon every time he's been called a liar. In Missouri we have a four-letter word for those who knowingly make false statements."

Pearson was understandably upset by Truman's scathing commentary. He remembered the recent Truman euphoria when he expressed his gratitude to him. Nevertheless, Pearson accepted the barbed words as an inevitable occupational hazard. The columnist later noted: "The Vice President who blasted me was the real Truman. Tough, cocky, and candid. During his early days as President, Harry Truman was apprehensive, meek, and pleaded for press support. It wasn't long, however, before the genuine Truman emerged again."

In common with his predecessors, President Truman had his own methods of handling the press. He was willful, forthright, and given to rash outbursts. He radiated a down-to-earth informality. Truman often allowed reporters to join him on his early morning walks across Pennsylvania Avenue. Some correspondents admired Truman's frankness and contended it reflected his unquestioned integrity, but the majority were appalled by what they considered "the Truman crudity." They compared the Truman method with FDR's artful sophistication, sorely missed Roosevelt's ringing phrases and intellectual challenges, and contrasted Truman's flat Midwestern twang with FDR's voice. Besides, White House correspondents bask in the vicarious glory of the Presidency and are jealous of that dignity. They tend to be critical of anyone who sullies the aura.

On Truman's part, he viewed tact as a form of hypocrisy. While this was a refreshing attitude, it also resulted in reckless, off-the-cuff comments that were politically corrosive. When a reporter asked Truman what the public should do about soaring meat prices, he snapped, "Eat less." A correspondent who asked for comment about Truman's conference with the Secretary of State, was bluntly informed, "It's none of your business." On another occasion, when a reporter questioned the President about a Cabinet meeting, Truman responded: "There are lots of things you don't know about Cabinet meetings. I don't have to tell you about Cabinet meetings." Perhaps Truman's abrasive approach to the press merely masked his underlying sense of inadequacy in meeting the challenge of the Presidency. At any rate, when the press complained, Truman flippantly observed that he had not asked to be Vice President and he had not asked to be President.

Neither the Truman flippancy nor his candor stemmed the growing storm of criticism less than a year after he entered the White House. During that period, *Life* magazine reported: "Washington has begun to turn against him. Harry Truman betrayed himself. Instead of fighting back, he began to complain before various audiences that he had never asked to be President and everyone ought to pitch in and help him. This was the worst thing that Truman could have done, for pressure groups, like wolves, respond to any sign of weakness or hesitancy by closing in for the kill."

Truman's incompatibility with the press was actuated and aggravated by postwar problems. The United States emerged from the war endowed with power and prestige unparalleled in all history. Americans had a bellyful of war and wartime controls. Many clamored for overnight transformations. Everybody wanted to get back to "normal." Yet the wholly human desire for drastic change from war to peace was realistically impossible. Moreover, a sudden stripping of American military power could be diplomatically perilous. It would deprive the United States of the one thing Communist Russia respected—muscle.

Into this complex and delicate area moved Drew Pearson. The columnist was a pushover for the anguished stream of letters he received from wives and mothers of overseas soldiers urging the return of their husbands and sons. The letters were literally buttressed by hundreds of long distance phone calls pleading for his support. Unfortunately, the government had neglected to enlighten the public about the hard practical necessity of our continuing obligations overseas. Few politicians were courageous enough to challenge the public's emotion on this issue. In addition, many GI's were aware that their superior officers sailed for home while they remained. So they wrote to Pearson. Soon the columnist became chief mouthpiece for griping soldiers and their disgruntled kin. The stream of mail became a Niagara. One day he received a petition with thirty thousand signatures from soldiers in the Philippines. Several members of Pearson's staff urged him to take the signatures to the White House. At first, Pearson was reluctant to make the move, but associates convinced him it was his duty to carry out the wishes of so many soldiers and their families.

The columnist's decision to go to the White House represented a journalistic innovation. He appointed himself as a special ambassador with direct access to the White House. This role appealed to Pearson. He had often depicted himself as the voice of the so-called Little Man, and frequently fought his battle against the inequities of Big Government. Additional attractive factors were the possibilities of a personal coup and a subsequent sensational story. Like it or not, sensationalism represents a significant factor in Washington journalism. Whereas news from the capital frequently has a life-and-death gravity, the sharp competition for news induces sensationalism. Editors, who are also in competition, demand "hot" news, which often means something superficially exciting. Too, competing columnists are anxious to attract attention—a form of exploitation that helps sell their column. Consequently, there is often much surface excitement in Washington that tends to devalue more significant news.

It is fair to state that some—or all—of the foregoing considerations inspired Pearson to call an old friend who had become Truman's press secretary, explain his mission, and arrange a meeting. Shortly before his date with the President, the columnist reported that Mrs. Truman had traveled in a special car from St. Louis to Washington while American soldiers were left at the station. His story was inaccurate. Pearson corrected the blunder and publicly apologized. Drew's second mistake was believing that a retraction and an apology would mollify the quick-tempered President.

While waiting to enter the President's office, the columnist was filled with the profound apprehension of a man about to enter a plea of innocence in a court when he darn well knows the judge will order him shot. Pearson's fear was fully justified. As soon as he stepped in front of Truman's desk, the President became a one-man firing squad. Throughout the verbal assault, the ashen-faced columnist stood with the bundle of thirty thousand signatures under his arm. He sought desperately to maintain a mask of bland resignation, he shrugged slightly and endeavored to adjust his face into some sort of a smile. Nothing stopped the Truman barrage.

As the columnist later wrote: "Harry Truman's womenfolk are sacred to him, and he bore down heavily at this point. Then he went on to another complaint. He stormed that I was undermining his foreign policy and pointed out that the United States must have those troops abroad, since Russia was not demobilizing."

Pearson suffered in silence while Truman continued blasting. Finally the columnist managed to murmur something about "letting the boys know what the score was." When the sounds of battle subsided, Pearson hastily dropped the petition on the President's desk and literally ran from his office. To this day, Drew is unhappy about the incident. "It is true," he recalls, "that the Army and Navy had bungled the demobilization program miserably. They had let officers with pull go home, while men and officers with no pull stayed overseas. They had failed to explain the reasons for keeping a reasonably large force overseas. Still, Mr. Truman was right in saying he needed United States troops abroad to strengthen his bargaining position with the Kremlin."

Nevertheless, his embarrassing confrontation with Truman and Pearson's previous clashes with the President failed to pervert his essential objectivity. He never joined those who clawed at the President's major policies. A careful reading of the Pearson columns and broadcasts during the early years of the Truman Administration reveals he was a vigorous supporter of its major policies—Truman's position during the railroad strike, and his critical battle against inflation, which threatened the nation's stability after wartime controls were loosened. When Truman's Kansas City political friends were being mentioned in connection with the killing of two racketeers, Pearson reported that Truman had ordered a grand jury investigation and that the investigation was a thorough one. "Let's be fair," he pleaded.

Nevertheless, Pearson trained his sights on some of Truman's subordinates. Early in 1946 the columnist's close friend, Harold L. Ickes, resigned as Secretary of the Interior with a belligerent public letter denouncing the President for recommending the appointment of Edwin Pauley, California oil producer, as Under Secretary of the Navy. Further, Ickes blasted Pauley before the Senate Committee considering his nomination. In the face of ignominious defeat, the President withdrew his nomination. Truman was stubborn, however. He defied Pearson and other press critics of Pauley and appointed the oil man as a special assistant in the reorganization of the War and Navy Departments.

Several months later, Washington correspondents began a series of disclosures. Attorney General Clark lashed out against speculation in commodity markets and alleged that men "high in the government" were involved. Truman publicly condemned those who were speculating in the "human misery" of high prices. Because of the journalistic uproar, the Senate Appropriations Committee launched an investigation. The probe disclosed that Edwin Pauley had profited by more than $900,000 in commodity market operations while in the government. It was never proved that Pauley's profits were the result of inside, confidential government information, but one thing was undeniable. Pauley was exposed as a speculator. In addition, Dr. Wallace K. Graham, Truman's personal physician, was likewise involved in the commodities market. Pauley soon resigned from the War Department. Dr. Graham was allowed to remain as White House physician.

Washington scandals pyramided as Pearson disclosed that some of Truman's intimate friends and aides accepted mink coats and deep freezers from lobbyists and others, in exchange for favors. Republican speakers began to talk about "the mess in Washington," and editorial criticism mounted. The main body of Pearson's attack was concentrated on John Maragon, an ex-Kansas City bootblack who had special White House privileges, and General Harry Vaughan, Truman's military aide and friend, who functioned as one of Washington's chief power brokers.

General Vaughan was a little too loud, a little too hearty, and given to raw statements when he was angry, which was not infrequently. Thus he left himself open for wide misquotation. He also incurred the enmity of the Washington press. For example, when he went to some small Central American country, he was assailed as being the guest of the dictator. He berated the press publicly for this, telling them undiplomatically that he was "the guy they had to see when they wanted favors."

Although Truman was straight as a string, he resented attacks against friends who were not. His loyalty to them was as fierce as it was misguided. For example, FDR wrecked the Pendergast machine and sent Boss Pendergast to jail. But when Truman became President, almost his first act was to fire the U.S. Prosecutor who had convicted Pendergast. He marched behind Pendergast's casket when he was buried. It was the same type of unreasoning loyalty that embittered the quarrel between Truman and Pearson.

The columnist disclosed Maragon and Vaughan teamed to raise campaign contributions, influenced Greek policies, and thwarted building regulations to rebuild racetracks. Further, Pearson revealed that Maragon was able to demote Generals, get plane priorities to Europe, escape a conviction for smuggling, ride on the President's special trains, and stand beside Truman as he reviewed the fleet. Drew's revelations were front-paged around the country, generally without credit to him.

Caisson bearing body of Franklin Roosevelt proceeds on Constitution Avenue.

Harry Truman, a new President facing old problems.

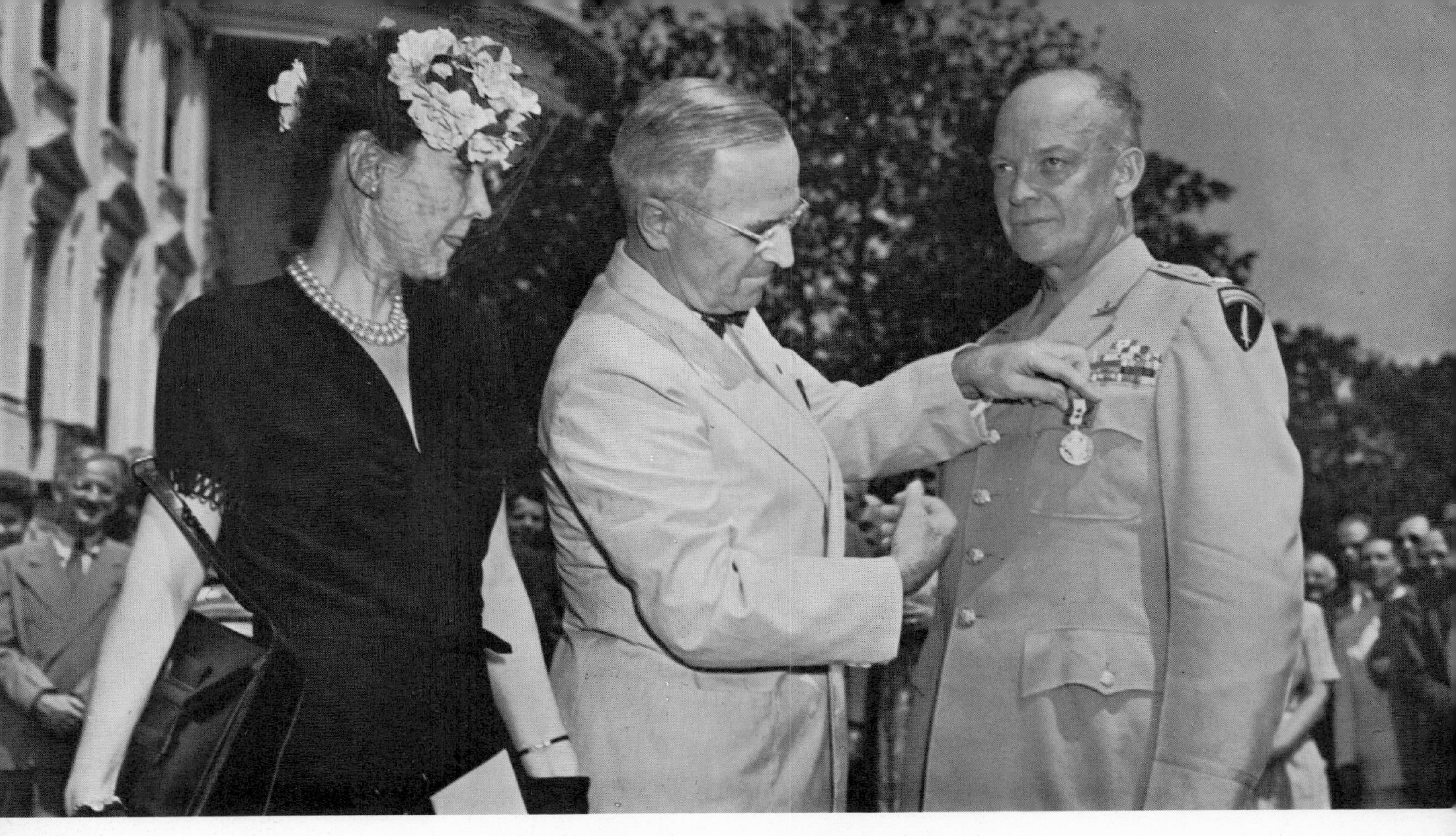

Mamie, Harry, and Ike on January 20, 1947.

Atomic Age opens with burst of fire and fear.

Generals Ridgway and MacArthur in Korea.

As the scandals mounted, Maragon and Vaughan retaliated against Pearson, evidently with the President's tacit consent. Maragon was powerful enough to coerce the FBI into working all night to check a wild rumor that a member of Pearson's staff had been a World War II draft-dodger. The FBI probed and the rumor turned out to be pure nonsense. In addition, Maragon publicly demanded the indictment of Pearson for criminal libel. At that time, the District of Columbia's criminal libel statute had not been enforced for seventy-five years. But after Pearson reported that Maragon had pleaded guilty to illegally transporting liquor in 1920, both Maragon and General Vaughan called the Justice Department and urged the columnist's criminal prosecution.

As Pearson remembers it:

> General Vaughan, it seemed, was irked because I had reported various things about Maragon, many of which the Senate Committee has since brought out under oath. Among other things, I stated that he once pleaded guilty to transporting liquor illegally, was three times arrested for disorderly conduct but never prosecuted.
>
> General Vaughan, appearing before the District Attorney, claimed this was not true. His "lovable" friend, he said, had been maligned and he demanded prosecution of the guilty columnist. Mr. Morris Fay, the District Attorney, was a little flabbergasted at seeing the top military aide to the President of the United States turn up on an errand of this kind, but he replied that he would be glad to talk to Mr. Maragon. However, he subsequently made it clear that there had been no criminal libel case brought in the District of Columbia since about the time of the Civil War, and that he had instructions from the Justice Department to bring none without prior consultation.
>
> This was because, in a criminal libel case, the Government of the United States becomes the prosecutor and undertakes to convict and jail the offending editor or newspaperman without any expense or effort on the part of the party supposedly libeled—in this case Maragon. This explanation, conveyed to General Vaughan, did not dampen his persistency. It merely increased his efforts on behalf of

his "lovable" friend. With the question of prosecuting Pearson referred by the District Attorney to the Justice Department, the good General transferred his pressure higher up, and tried to bulldoze J. Edgar Hoover. "I thought when orders were given in this Government, they were carried out," he stormed.

Hoover told him that his job was to investigate, not to prosecute, and that if orders were given him by the Attorney General to investigate the Pearson charges against Maragon, he would certainly do so. Shortly before this, Vaughan had lifted no audible voice of protest when Maragon violated the Customs Law by smuggling perfume into the U.S.A. In fact, Vaughan had continued to give him White House credentials, even though Maragon had used them in attempted smuggling and had wantonly violated their use. Nevertheless, Vaughan now demanded the prosecution of one who had exposed Maragon's lawbreaking. And, thanks to Vaughan's persistency, the Justice Department did order the FBI to investigate. The investigation cost the taxpayers a few extra dollars, plus the time of busy FBI agents needed for loyalty tests.

Maragon had claimed that the man guilty of bootlegging on July 17, 1920, was a "John F. Margon," not the "lovable" friend of General Vaughan, "John F. Maragon." So after a lot of work, including a search for fingerprints which were not taken at that time, the FBI finally located the handwriting on the Bondsman's records back in 1920. This handwriting of "John F. Margon" they found to be the very same handwriting of "John F. Maragon," the "lovable" friend.

Eventually, Maragon's past caught up with him and he was jailed for perjury.* The conviction drove Vaughan to wild fury. He continued battling Pearson. It began with Vaughan's tapping of Pearson's wires. The unsophisticated may be horrified to hear about this tactic. Unhappily, it was—and is—standard procedure in

* The day after Maragon was released from jail, he came to Pearson and asked for help in finding a job. Pearson got Maragon a job is the House of Representatives where he remained for many years.

Washington. Pearson accepts the ugly reality of the situation as one of the hazards of his job, wryly commenting, "My phone has so many listeners that a member of my staff suggested that we sell commercials." The columnist counters the tapping by employing code names while discussing news sources on the phone.

Vaughan's phone tapping was a minor problem for Pearson until he learned that Vaughan was funneling tapped information to columnist Westbrook Pegler, who amplified, savaged, and perverted the fragmented information in a manner calculated to send Pearson to jail. Or, at the very least, rubble his reputation. The columnist absorbed Pegler's scabrous sketches and Vaughan's grotesque attempts to put him behind bars. He waited for an opening. It came when the Argentine Embassy in Washington announced the award of a medal from Dictator Perón to General Harry Vaughan. Pearson bided his time. He waited for Vaughan or the State Department to reject the trophy, accompanied by the customary diplomatic poetry, otherwise known as double-talk. After all, the Perón dictatorship was Hitlerian in style. It seemed incomprehensible to Pearson that the State Department and White House would permit the medal-pinning.

When Vaughan's acceptance of the Perón medal was clearly indicated, Pearson publicly called on George Washington as his initial witness. President Washington had set a precedent, later embodied in the Constitution, that no official of the United States Government could receive a gift or decoration from a foreign government.

The Case of the Perón Medal ignited a legislative controversy, sparked editorial fires, and caused many of Pearson's fellow columnists to rush forward as associate torch-carriers. It was a fight Pearson truly relished. All the angels were on his side.

Congress debated the affair and considered an act permitting General Vaughan to receive a medal from the Argentine Government, but failed to pass it. Vaughan, whose favorite exercise consisted of putting his foot in his mouth, continued to proclaim that he would accept the medal.

Drew Pearson then issued a proclamation to his army of radio listeners: "The Ambassador of Argentine has issued specially engraved invitations to the Truman Cabinet and Washington society to see General Harry Vaughan, the President's military aide, receive his special decoration from Dictator Perón—at the very same time we are supposed to be discouraging dictators in Latin America. Next Friday, when this ceremony takes place, I am going to be at the door of the Argentine Embassy and will publish the names of those who go to see Harry Vaughan receive his dictatorial decoration."

The gauntlet was thrown. Several hours after the broadcast, in the cool and quiet of his home, Pearson had second thoughts. The idea of his playing straight man to a malevolent incident appeared foolish. The picture of himself laying siege to the Argentine Embassy seemed ridiculous. The entire proposal, he was almost ready to admit to himself, was motivated by rashness. For a few moments his aplomb almost deserted him, and he was not at all certain that he would carry out his threat. In the end, with a heavy sigh, Pearson dispelled all doubts. "I was stuck with my promise," he says, "I decided I must go ahead with it."

On the night of the Great Picketing, rain was bucketing down. Yet Drew Pearson made his appointed rounds. His drenched hat was curled, rivelets ran down his back and beaded his moustache. Despite the storm, Pearson remained at his post, grandly jotting down the names of guests who scurried through the storm into the bright warmth of the Embassy. After a while the columnist's soggy notebook gave him the impression he was writing on soft cheese. A colleague who remembers the incident described the soaked Pearson as "looking like an election bet loser, or the subject for a fraternity initiation." But few American officials dared to cross the Pearson picket line. Those who entered by the front door were mainly foreign diplomats. Americans were smuggled in via the back door.

All in all, Pearson confided later, "I made something of an ass of myself."

Congress eventually forbade Vaughan to retain his Perón decoration. A Senate investigating committee criticized Vaughan for influence-peddling, including giving priority to racetrack construction at a time when veterans' housing was desperately needed, handing out favors in return for deep freezers, demoting army officers who tangled with his friend John Maragon, and endeavoring to increase grain quotas for whiskey distillers at a time when grain was essential to feed a devastated Europe.

During the Senate inquiry, Vaughan made one last desperate clutch at his prime adversary.

Pearson was in Santa Barbara, California, enjoying an overdue holiday. He and Mrs. Pearson had decided on an unplanned vacation. They rented a car and drove through California—their destinations to be determined by their whims. Sitting on a beach at Santa Barbara, the Pearsons were suddenly hailed by a man who ran down the beach. He turned out to be from the Santa Barbara *News-Press*. Pearson beamed at the idea of being recognized while traveling incognito, but his wife failed to share his delight. She realized it meant the finish of any easygoing holiday. She was right. Several hours later one of the columnist's assistants called. The White House, it seemed, had ordered a complete check of Pearson's income tax returns.

The battle had descended to the additions and subtractions on tax returns. For Pearson there was another obvious equation: General Vaughan believed Pearson was feeding evidence to the Senate probers investigating him, and he wanted to even the score. All Vaughan had to do was add one plus one. It was even easier for Pearson to add up the obvious facts that motivated the Internal Revenuers.

After a long and almost microscopic investigation of Pearson's tax returns, one deductible item was disallowed. A dinner that Pearson had given for Chief Justice Vinson was not deductible as an entertainment expense, the agents ruled, since no one is supposed to influence or secure news from the High Court. Pearson accepted the decision without complaint. In the end, however, the columnist paid an additional $25 tax.

As the Pearson-Vaughan dispute escalated in 1948, the President's hostility toward the columnist was indicative of the tense relationship between Truman and the press in general. It was an election year and the great majority of papers were sharply anti-Truman. His defeat was considered a certainty. The polls forecast a landslide victory for Republican candidate Thomas E. Dewey. Pearson and other Washington journalists shared the pollsters' judgment. Further, Truman's predilection for outbursts made him an object of widespread ridicule, particularly after the Washington *Post*'s music critic panned Margaret Truman's singing. The President wrote to the critic: "I have never met you. But if I do you'll need a new nose and plenty of beefsteak." An avalanche of biting humor and scathing editorials followed the incident. Not only Margaret's singing but the President's manner of speaking was criticized. Washington correspondent Alistair Cooke noted, "Truman doesn't know when to pause, when to paragraph, when to go slow and easy, and when to lift into the big sentences."

As the President's press relations deteriorated, some of Truman's friends sought to reverse the trend. For example, Chief Justice Fred Vinson attempted to mediate the dispute between the President and Pearson. Truman was adamant. Although the High Court was empowered to hand down decisions on perplexing and significant issues, the Chief Justice was unable to resolve the Truman-Pearson pouting contest. Nevertheless, as the body creates supplementary canals for the blood when one artery is blocked, Pearson maintained his friendship with most of Truman's Cabinet members. After all, access to exclusive White House news is the heart of a Washington column. Survival alone dictated the continuance of the news flow.

As the news filtered into Pearson's column by way of White House "leaks," the President's fury mounted.* Truman countered by being contrary. The victim of a Pearson rap inevitably attracted a Truman rave.

Many of Truman's predecessors at 1600 Pennsylvania Avenue utilized one gambit or another in this traditional cat-and-mouse skirmish. President George Washington sought to manage and censor news that might damage the overseas reputation of the United States; he advised the Secretary of War: "Orders or advertisements,

* Some years ago a President victimized by a news leak stormed into his press secretary's office and raged: "Who leaked on me?" As soon as he blurted out the words, both the President and his news secretary roared with laughter over the unintentional ribaldry. This was probably the only news leak to elicit Presidential laughter.

which are intended to be put into the public gazettes, ought to be well weighed and digested before they are inserted, as they will not only appear in all parts of Europe, but may be handed to the enemy. To publish beyond the limits of the army, or the vicinity of it, the dastardly behavior of one's own Troops, is not a very pleasant thing." Thomas Jefferson established his own paper and it functioned as his mouthpiece. During Andrew Jackson's Administration the President's friends set up the Washington *Globe,* which was subsidized via government printing contracts. Theodore Roosevelt and Joseph Pulitzer's New York *World* were involved in continual strife. The President sued Pulitzer for criminal libel and lost. When Woodrow Wilson was elected, he declared himself in favor of "pitiless publicity for public business." Six months later, Wilson wrote to a friend: "Do not believe anything you read in the newspapers. If you read the papers I see, they are utterly untrustworthy. They represent the obstacles as existing which they wish to have exist, whether they are actual or not. Read the editorial page and you will know what you will find in the news columns. For unless they are grossly careless the two always support one another. The lying is shameless and colossal."

In one form or another, every President has echoed Wilson's bitter reprimand of the press. And every Chief Executive since George Washington has been blasted by some proportion of the press. Ineffectual Presidents have generally incurred the least criticism. The stronger the President, the more excessive the criticism. On that basis, Truman must be classified as one of the stronger Chiefs of State. The degree of anti-Trumanism in the press reached a crescendo before and during the 1948 campaign.

The criticism was coupled with confident anticipation of Truman's defeat. Twenty-four hours before Election Day, cocksure Pearson wrote a column naming Dewey's probable Cabinet and distributed it to his editors for publication the day after election. He also wrote a second column scheduled to be released the day after election. In that one he described some problems confronting President Dewey. After writing the columns, Pearson went to New York to cover the election story for the American Broadcasting Company. He arrived at the studio with the assurance of a man who expects to see sand on the Sahara. By 7:30 on election night, as the returns trickled into the studio, Pearson took one look at the numbers and his eyes glazed. There were clear indications that Truman was on his way to a phenomenal upset. Pearson started what was to become a national crow-eating binge. He did an immediate about-face and was the first newscaster to announce Truman's certain victory.

Drew returned to Washington weary and shaken. It was too late to stop the first embarrassing column. Some editors were so delighted with Pearson's predicament that they also published the second column, although he spent $2,000 in wiring a substitute column.

Truman had the last laugh, and his inauguration in January 1949 reflected the President's jubilant mood. Washington had a carnival air. Bunting curled around Pennsylvania Avenue lampposts from the White House to Capitol Hill. Over a million visitors came to make the four-day show the biggest, most expensive Presidential inaugural in history. As Harry Truman rode up Pennsylvania Avenue, he noticed a sign on the facade of the Washington *Post* building: "Mister President, we are ready to eat crow whenever you are ready to serve it."

For the President, the inaugural represented a happy island surrounded by national and international problems. "At that time," recalls Pearson, "China was in Communist hands, the Russians were dangling the atomic bomb over American heads, the Hiss case terrified the American people with the fear that the government might be overrun by Reds, the Taft Republicans were attacking the Administration for spending too much money and extending economic controls which might bankrupt the United States. Moreover, there was a fear that the Soviet-controlled Communist world might choose to attack at every point of contact between East and West."

Further, the nation's front pages were dominated by a troubling question: Was it true that Alger Hiss was Assistant Secretary of State Acheson's right-hand man during the period when, according to Congressional spy probers, Hiss was active in Communist espionage?

The question provoked a major press conference blunder. A reporter inquired, "Mr. President, do you think the Capitol Hill spy scare is a red herring to divert public attention from inflation?" Truman's affirmative response was destined to haunt him for years. It provided prime propaganda fodder for anti-Administration newspapers and politicians. Truman's Missouri-mule rigidity helped instigate the blunder. He viewed the Hiss scandal as a political maneuver—which it was, in part. He neglected, or refused to see, the larger issue. Consequently, he handled it as a political embarrassment and employed the propaganda power of his high office to dismiss the Hiss evidence as nothing more than "a red herring." It turned out to be more like a dragon.

Privately, Truman's attitude sharply contrasted with his public red herring comment. When a member of the Justice Department showed Truman copies of the documents stolen by Hiss, the President thumbed through page after page of the evidence and exclaimed, "Why, the son of a bitch—he betrayed his country!" This was later confirmed by Richard Nixon's statement: "When a friend asked the President how he could possibly make such a statement in the light of the evidence, his reply was: 'Of course Hiss is guilty. But that damn Committee isn't interested in that. All it cares about is politics, and as long as they try to make politics out of this Communist issue, I am going to label their activities for what they are—a red herring.' "

The journalistic uproar over Truman's "red herring" comment was followed by a press attack directed at Truman's Secretary of Defense, James Forrestal. The attackers included the New York *Post*, the weekly *The Nation*, and Walter Winchell; Drew Pearson spearheaded the offense. He hit the Secretary of Defense with allegations involving unethical conduct, especially the relationship between Forrestal's former Wall Street firm and the German cartel tycoons. The Secretary of Defense made little effort to counter the attacks. Behind the scenes, Cabinet members were aware of Forrestal's grave psychological problems. He brooded about being a failure and often spoke about plots to destroy him.

Pearson reported Truman planned to accept Forrestal's resignation and replace him with Louis A. Johnson, in return for the latter's campaign services. However, Forrestal's resignation was delayed by Truman's resentment of the "advice" he was receiving from Pearson. The President privately vowed to friends that after he left the White House he intended to devote himself to evening the score with Pearson. The threat was relayed to Pearson, who responded in a broadcast: "The important aspect of this incident is the fact that Mr. Truman should let important decisions of state be made or reversed by a radio commentator, no matter who he is. It's probably going to make some of us think twice about criticizing inefficient public officials for fear Mr. Truman will then decide to continue them in office." *

Pearson's campaign against Forrestal was coupled with continuing assaults against Presidential aide Harry Vaughan. After a Senate committee's investigation confirmed many of the columnist's charges, Vaughan offered to resign. The President turned him down with a brisk wave of his hand. "No," he snapped, "we came to the White House together and we're going to leave together." Nevertheless, during press conferences, reporters frequently peppered the President with questions about whether he intended firing Vaughan. Truman denied it and added: "There isn't anything crooked about Vaughan. He is being viciously abused. They are trying to get at the man in the White House. Vaughan is my military aide and that's all. He has nothing to do with running the government."

Several days after Truman defended Vaughan, Pearson directed another barrage at the military aide. The following evening, late in February 1949, Truman rose to speak at a banquet. The President did not smile as he spoke about his friend. With bitter deliberation he informed the banqueters: "I am as fond and just as loyal to my military aide as I am to the high brass, and I want it distinctly understood that any s.o.b. who thinks he can cause any of these people to be discharged by me, by some smart aleck over the air or in the paper, has another think coming."

Pearson has a clear recollection of that day. It was one of those

* In March 1949, Forrestal was succeeded by Louis Johnson. A month later, Forrestal entered Bethesda Naval Hospital and his illness was officially described as "occupational fatigue." The truth was that he was suffering from a severe psychosis with suicidal tendencies. On Sunday morning, May 22, Forrestal sat in his hospital room and copied Sophocles' melancholy "Chorus Ajax." After copying the poem, he walked out into the hospital corridor, opened a window, and plunged to his death.

beautiful days Washington occasionally mints, with aspens and willows frosted with winter's ice, yet touched with a hint of spring. On such a rare day, Drew drove from the airport to his 200-acre Maryland farm seventeen miles up the Potomac.

As the columnist remembers it: "While driving I made a lot of promises to myself, about spending more time at home, seeing more of my family, and after taking a good rest on the farm I would take Mrs. P. away for the little vacation we'd always talked about but somehow never seemed to manage."

Mrs. Pearson was dubious at first. After all, it was an echo of numerous past unfulfilled vows. This time, Pearson's promises to put some tranquil space between himself and the rest of the world appeared genuine. He made his intentions emphatic by a revolutionary decision. He turned off the phone. A columnist muting a phone is akin to Willie Mays burning his bats. In years past, Mrs. Pearson had toyed with the idea of isolating her husband from a phone; her down-to-earth contention was simply that "nothing would happen at all. The world would go on just as usual, and nobody would miss you, nor you them."

The Pearsons settled down to a long, languorous evening. Whether by accident or design, Pearson had neglected to turn off the kitchen phone. With the phone turned off upstairs, the kitchen phone emits only a muffled ring. For the next sixty minutes the Pearsons shared serenity. The repose was interrupted when the kitchen phone began its muffled cry. He ignored it. Thirty minutes later it rang again. Pearson succumbed to temptation. United Press was calling. Pearson was informed: "President Truman's temper was off the leash. During a dinner at the Reserve Officers Association he called Pearson an 's.o.b.' " The U.P. requested the columnist's comment. Stunned but calm, he responded: "I am spending a quiet evening with my wife. If Harry Truman wants to spend the evenings away from his wife making speeches about other people, that is his privilege. I don't see why I should comment."

Then came the phone deluge—the A.P., the news magazines, reporters from dozens of newspapers. The Pearson holiday? Forgotten, naturally. The columnist's first thought was that his wife would never again speak to him. However, with husbandly logic he argued: "Of course, it's all your fault. You elected him. You were the one who was rooting for him. And if he disrupts our evening and our vacation, then it's your fault, not mine. After all, you were the one who put him in the White House."

Pearson's response to Truman's epithet was characteristic:

> I don't see any reason why the initials s.o.b. should necessarily stand for what Mr. Truman meant them to mean. The meaning of any word is what's in people's minds. Some English words are fighting terms in England though they may have an innocent meaning here. When I was in Australia some years ago I was shocked to hear an Australian girl use a word that never would be tolerated in polite society here. But it meant nothing there.
>
> So words and their abbreviations are all a matter of education, custom and general usage. And I am sure Mr. Truman is a good enough sport to join me in putting a new interpretation on the initials "s.o.b."—which can much better mean "Servants of Brotherhood."
>
> When Harry Truman was a farm boy driving mules in Missouri, I don't doubt that he needed some pretty strong language. I have never driven mules in Missouri, but I had one hundred Missouri mules and one hundred Albanian muledrivers under my command in Yugoslavia once, and since the Albanians couldn't understand Missourian and the mules couldn't understand Albanian, and since the Serbian corporal couldn't understand either, I had to act as interpreter.
>
> So, along with Harry Truman, I am familiar with muledrivers' language.
>
> However, neither Harry nor I are muledrivers any more. We have graduated, I hope, to bigger and better things. Therefore, I am getting up an engraved "Servants of Brotherhood" membership certificate, and perhaps some other folks will join me in picking out people in their neighborhood or anyplace else who have really sacrificed for their fellow men.
>
> There are all sorts of people in this country who are working hard at democracy, and at being good neighbors and at doing things for others—not necessarily big shots,

> just ordinary folks. I'd like to write about some of them, tell what they're doing, and spread the word about the Servants of Brotherhood.

As was to be expected, President Truman privately scorned Pearson's appeal to salvation. The Chief Executive confided to a White House adviser: "Some people should learn the alphabet. S.O.B. is as simple as ABC."

Typical of the editorial reaction was the Indianapolis *Star*'s comment: "Mr. Drew Pearson, at whom Mr. Truman's barrack's-language remarks were directed, needs no defense from us. He can take care of himself in his own inimitable way. But we are inclined to agree with him in his estimate of Harry Vaughan, the President's Military Aide. General Vaughan accepted a military decoration from Dictator Perón of Argentina. . . . Mr. Truman made a point of saying 'I never go back on a friend.' That is obvious. But a man is known by the company he keeps as well as the language he uses. Remember Mr. Truman's great and good friend the vote stealer, income-tax dodger and penitentiary occupant, Tom Pendergast? Mr. Truman certainly never went back on him. He fired the man who put Pendergast in jail."

The Kingston, N.C., *Free Press* stated in part: "The *Free Press* has no hesitancy in saying that right or wrong Mr. Pearson has the Constitutional privilege to criticize the President of the United States or his aides. Deplorable, indeed, would it be if that privilege were not inherent in American citizenship. The President may be acclaimed by the average poolroom loafer for his intemperate language, but decent people will not condone it."

The silence between Truman and Pearson was deep and prolonged. The two men did not communicate for eight years after that day in 1945 when Pearson suffered the President's censure.

In 1953, Senator McCarthy's irresponsible lightning was striking. Shortly after Harry Truman had relinquished the White House —in the winter of 1953—Senator McCarthy quietly launched an investigation of the ex-President. Pearson, who learned of the Senator's plans, is a tough fighter but an easy forgiver. The columnist decided to call Truman and apprise him of McCarthy's intentions.

He was slightly apprehensive about the former President's reaction when he heard his voice. At the risk of being cut dead, scorned, or insulted, Pearson put the call through. Truman came to the phone all warmth and sunshine. He greeted the columnist with a friendly, "Hello, Drew," and inquired about Pearson's health. It was like a college reunion.

Pearson informed Truman that Senator McCarthy intended to accuse him of stealing $10,000 worth of steel cabinets from the White House. Truman replied: "Let him investigate. But let him get his facts straight. I paid for those filing cabinets. And I have the receipts to prove it. If he goes ahead with the investigation, he'll wind up with his ass in a sling." Pearson chuckled as he cradled the phone and expelled a sigh of relief that was truly monumental. A five-minute phone call had dispelled eight years of acrimony.

Two months later, Truman came to Washington. A mutual friend suggested that Pearson drop in on him in his Mayflower Hotel suite. Drew did just that. In the first face-to-face meeting since the lamented White House confrontation, cordiality flowed on both sides. They laughed and chatted and exchanged political gossip. The battle had truly ended.

The Pearson-Truman story is part of the unending saga of President-press relations. Basically, the relationship is determined by the personality and politics of the Chief Executive. In Truman's case, he alienated some correspondents with his abrasive attitude, fuzzy thinking, and quick-on-the-trigger judgments. At one time his hasty comment resulted in a major international crisis. In November 1951, Truman informed correspondents that the United States intended to maintain its position during the Korean War, despite the intervention of the Chinese Communists. During the question period a reporter searching for a "hot" lead or a striking headline asked the President whether the atomic bomb might be used if necessary. Truman's offhand reply: "The use of the atomic bomb in emergencies is always under consideration."

The headlined stories stressed that the President was considering use of the atomic bomb in Korea. It caused shudders around the world. Britain's Prime Minister Attlee flew to Washington for reassurance. The reassurances were given and clarifications were made, but the damage was done. In this case both the President and the press were guilty, for both had been slipshod and irresponsible. The foregoing case, and numerous others, illustrate the problems of relations between the press and President. Solutions are more complex and subtle.

The perplexing issue that defies simple solutions is rooted in the awkward relationship between the two powers. They need each other—indeed there is a mutual fascination between the press and the President—but they must remain independent. It is, in effect, a shotgun marriage wherein both parties are aware of the inevitable divorce. Nevertheless, until the Chief Executive leaves the White House he must accommodate himself to the demands of the press, which includes incessant inroads on his privacy.

Franklin Roosevelt handled the undisciplined ritual of working with the press with artistic flair and immense command of the situation, despite occasional failure and conflicts. By and large, FDR had a remarkable élan, and his relations with the press were made of silk. On the other hand, Truman was granite. He frequently was rough and unyielding. Yet it was this rough quality that endeared him to the people. However, it should be mentioned that press criticism occasionally eroded Truman's confidence, and he once pleaded with reporters, "I wish you would do a little soul searching and see if at great intervals the President may be right." Pugnacious Harry Truman's touch of humility was probably occasioned by expediency. For the very nature of modern American government makes publicity essential to the orderly functioning of government.

A President cannot carry out his duties without cultivating public opinion. And he cannot cultivate public opinion without dealing with the press. The press as a group may be regarded by the Chief Executive as ridiculous, irresponsible, suspect, even contemptible. Nevertheless, those on both sides of the fence share a similar objective: communication with the people. And so both sides adapt its objectives to flexible restrictions. Frequently this process is one of constant struggle. The struggle is an integral feature of a free government. As a matter of fact, the President's relationship with the press often provides the measure of his leadership. And the candid reporting of the Pearsons represents the yardstick of power of unfettered journalism.

Publisher J. David Stern's book, *Memoirs of A Maverick Publisher,* offers some thoughtful words on the subject: "Granted our old-fashioned partisan press smelled to high heaven, but it was the stimulating stench of human emotion. It roused the nation to brave deeds and great accomplishments. A newspaper was established to express a point of view. Publishers of the nineteenth century were concerned with public problems and they made their readers share this concern. Political zeal frequently exceeded the bounds of reason and decency, but it was an antidote to complacency, which is the Achilles heel of a nation grown rich and prosperous."

Drew Pearson is one of the few newspapermen who expresses a point of view, is concerned with public problems, and—most meaningful—makes readers share this concern. During the Truman years the simmering relationship between the President and the press in general—and Pearson in particular—was partially in the man and partially in the times. Much of the tension stemmed from Americans' obsessive fear of Communism. It provoked hatreds, irrational conflicts, as well as remarkable accomplishments by individual journalists.

"All the News That's Fit to Print"

The New York

XCV ... No. 32,169.

Entered as Second-Class Matter. Postoffice, New York, N. Y.

Copyright, 1946, by The New York Times Company.

NEW YORK, WEDNESDAY, FEBRUARY 20, 19

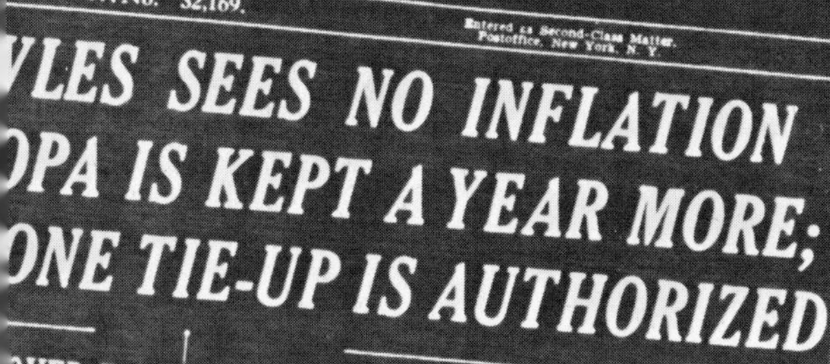

VLES SEES NO INFLATION OPA IS KEPT A YEAR MORE; ONE TIE-UP IS AUTHORIZED

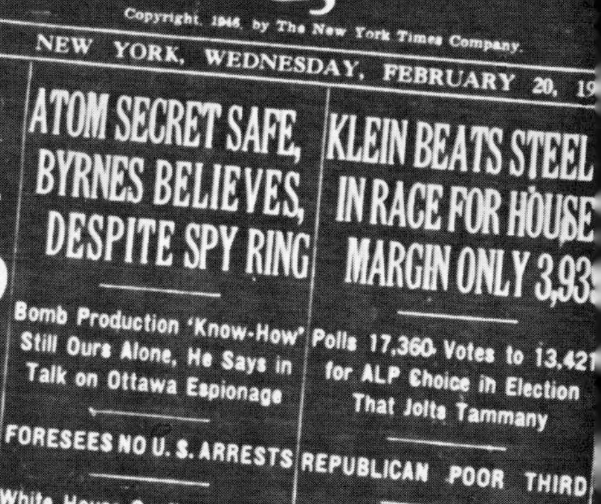

ATOM SECRET SAFE, BYRNES BELIEVES, DESPITE SPY RING

Bomb Production 'Know-How' Still Ours Alone, He Says in Talk on Ottawa Espionage

FORESEES NO U. S. ARRESTS

White House Confirms That a Civilian Body Will Assay Results of Bikini Test

By W. H. LAWRENCE

Special to THE NEW YORK TIMES.

WASHINGTON, Feb. 19—Secretary of State James F. Byrnes declared today that he did not anticipate any arrests of American citizens or other residents of the United States for espionage, and added that so far as he knew the secret "know-how" of atomic bomb production still was held exclusively by this Government.

His comments were made at a press conference where a long series of unusually direct questions were propounded with relation ... the Canadian Gover... closure in ...

KLEIN BEATS STEEL IN RACE FOR HOUSE MARGIN ONLY 3,93

Polls 17,360 Votes to 13,421 for ALP Choice in Election That Jolts Tammany

REPUBLICAN POOR THIRD

Democratic Power on Wane, Say Labor Leaders Who Charge Fraud and Thievery

By WARREN MOSCOW

Arthur G. Klein, the Democratic nominee, was elected yesterday to Congress from the Nineteenth New York district over Johannes Steel, candidate of the American Labor party, who received active Communist support, with William S. Shea, Republican, running a poor third.

But the victory was a dubious one for Tammany Hall in the ... it once ruled undis... tan's lower ...

OVER FORD

Says Auto ...d Asked ...ice Rise

HE ASSERTS

... as Example ...f What Would ...ngs End

...WAGGONER

Phone Unions Vote 4 to 1 To Back a National Strike

Memphis Meeting Decides 121,997 to 30,761 to Let NFTW Issue Call if Talks Fail —Philadelphia Strike Ends

Special to THE NEW YORK TIMES.

MEMPHIS, Tenn., Feb. 19—The National Federation of Telephone Workers' assembly empowered its executive board late today to call a coast-to-coast strike "at such time as the executive board considers proper and with due consideration to the circumstances of the several affiliates." The NFTW is trying to settle wage-hour grievances with a number of branches or affiliates of the American Telephone and Telegraph Company. ... president of the ...

they will last is something I would hesitate to even guess."

[In Washington Secretary Schwellenbach said Mr. Beirne had assured him that Federal conciliation would be used to the full before any strike call.]

Voting on a per-capita basis, leaders of the NFTW affiliates, representing 250,000 telephone workers, were 121,997 in favor of adopting the strike resolution and 30,762 against. The rest of the members are not represented by delegates at the meeting.

The "not voting" membership ...

...SSIA CONDEMNS ...ZENKO AS THIEF

Says Spy Witness in ... Faces Trial if He ...urns to U. S. S. R.

...J. PHILIP

Paris 'Bluebeard' Is Sentenced to Die; Dr. Petiot Asks Brother to Avenge Him

PARIS, April 4 (AP)—Dr. Marcel Petiot, "the monster of the Rue le Sueur," charged with killing twenty-seven persons, was found guilty of murder tonight and condemned to death. ...

THE NEW YORK TIMES, MONDAY, FEBRUAR...

CANADA ROUNDS UP ALL SPY SUSPECTS

One Man Reported Picked Up in London—More FBI Men Are Sent Into Country

15 PERSONS IN DETENTION

Ottawa Officials Keep Secrecy on Details but Note Free Information Given Russia

By P. J. PHILIP

OTTAWA, Feb. 17— ...

Newspaper Lecture Course to Begin To... With Editors of The Times as the Spea...

Edwin L. James, managing editor of THE NEW YORK TIMES, will discuss "How News Gets Printed," and Charles Merz, editor of THE TIMES, will speak on "The Function of the Editorial Page" at 4:15 o'clock this afternoon, opening an eight-week lecture course on "The Newspaper—Day by Day" ...

8 VESSELS ASSIGNED TO AID U. S. STRANDED

In compliance with a Presidential directive, the War Shipping Administration disclosed yesterday ...

NEGOTIATING GROUP STARTS FOR HOLLAND

BATAVIA, Java, April 4 ...

GERMAN PW ESCAPES AND HOLDS JOB HERE

5

WORLD OF SHADOWS

From 1938 to 1946 the major news source for Communist activities in the United States was the House Committee on Un-American Activities, dominated by flamboyant chairman Martin Dies. On the whole, the committee was motivated by personal vanity, partisan antagonism, and circus showmanship. Sensational charges overshadowed hard evidence. Congressman Dies, the Grand Inquisitor, was moved by the prospect of headlines and consequent political rewards. The committee hearings were little more than sideshows, and its circus nonsense reached a climax when Congressman Dies suggested that Shirley Temple, then a six-year-old child star, was a Communist agent. The press generally rebuked and ridiculed Dies for the Shirley Temple fiasco, and some of his friends on the Hearst press joined in the scolding. However, the general press reaction to the committee's investigation was exemplified by Washington papers. Cissy Patterson's Washington *Times-Herald* supported Dies, the Washington *Post* was generally critical. This was the rigid journalistic attitude that inevitably resulted in overreactions and exaggerations on both sides. While the liberal dailies editorially depicted the Dies Committee as a fascist advocate intent on destroying the Bill of Rights, the other side had visions of Americans being subverted and enslaved by Communist propaganda. Until 1946 there was a scarcity of news about Communist espionage. The Red exposés were directed against actors, several labor leaders, college radical organizations, and a cluster of picketing and protesting groups described as "fellow travelers." In general, Americans were complacent about the exposés. The wartime Russo-American alliance compounded the complacency.

The courage of the Red Army captured the imagination of Americans. This was coupled with hopeful American-British-Soviet displays of diplomatic unity at Casablanca, Cairo, and Teheran. Besides, public approval of the Soviet Union was expressed by some of our leading officials. In June 1942, Harry Hopkins was the main speaker at the Russian war relief rally at Madison Square Garden. Among other accolades, Hopkins hailed "the unconquerable power of the Russian people." Hopkins' attitude toward Russia was echoed by numerous papers, magazines, movies, and newscasters. The emphasis was on the virtues of our temporary allies. Their shortcomings were overlooked. Additionally, the end of military hostilities and the organization of the United Nations inspired peace-hungry Americans with a craving for international friendship in general, and friendship with Russia in particular.

The euphoria of American-Russian friendship disappeared on February 18, 1946, when Drew Pearson broke the spy story of the century. It was the first revelation of a super-espionage network in the Western Hemisphere. The story began in World War II when British Intelligence put Pearson under surveillance after he disclosed one of the great British naval blunders—the loss of fifty-nine out of sixty-six ships in the Murmansk run. Pearson's shadow was a Royal Air Force officer, Wing Commander Roald Dahl, who later distinguished himself as a film writer and is now married to actress Patricia Neal.

After several days of shadowing, Pearson wearied of the sport. He proposed a working arrangement. The columnist would give Dahl advance notice of major British news he planned publishing and Dahl would return the compliment by keeping Drew informed about British developments. In time, Pearson and his shadow became good friends. Dahl was a frequent guest at the columnist's home. After the war, he informed Pearson that he was being transferred to a highly secret assignment in Canada. The information was cryptic, but Pearson gathered it was fraught with momentous possibilities.

The columnist began his own investigation. He contacted British, American, and Canadian sources. Some clues led to dead ends. But he continued speaking to numerous Intelligence agents, diplomats, and police officials in the United States, Canada, and Great Britain. Pearson worked on the story for more than four months. Eventually, he amassed fragments of information that were spliced into a clear picture.

On February 18, 1946, his column carried a bombshell: "Secret revelations are stirring in Canada. They will make people hold their hats and run for the diplomatic storm cellars. The biggest story of espionage and intrigue is about to break. The Canadians have taken over a Russian agent, who has given the names of about 1,700 Russian agents; also has put the finger on certain officials inside the American and Canadian governments cooperating with the Soviets. Photostats showing payments to U.S. and Canadian officials have come to light."

For the column's purposes, that was the core of the exposé. However, as Pearson carried on his long and intensive investigation, the details of the fascinating story developed. The development of the story—as uncovered by the columnist—has never before been published in detail. This is the story . . .

It began when Captain Gorshakov, chauffeur to the Russian military attaché, dented the rear fender of an Embassy car one cold, rainy spring afternoon in Ottawa, and thereby instigated a life-and-death battle of wits between four major powers. His boss, Colonel Zabotin, told the chauffeur to get the thing repaired at his own expense and he would cover him, that no report would be made. Gorshakov did this immediately. However, within that very week, Colonel Zabotin got a coded telegram from Moscow bitterly reprimanding him for not reporting the negligence of his driver. Colonel Zabotin, being in the business himself, could have been little mystified by the mechanics of Moscow's action. In fact, it was routine action. As he very well knew, members of his own staff were members of the Secret Police of the Soviet Union, the NKVD. They reported on him daily to the Second Secretary, Vatali Pavlov, who was in charge of the NKVD in Canada. In disciplining the colonel, they gave mortal and lasting fright to his code clerk, Igor Gouzenko.

One late May morning in 1945, Gouzenko entered the cipher room and found one of Pavlov's men and the charwoman waiting for him. The Moscow charwoman, specially trained for just these purposes, had found a few sheets of paper lying half hidden under the desk.* Code Clerk Gouzenko's heart pounded when he saw the penciled notes. He knew they contained evidence that Colonel Zabotin was actually the head of a large and brilliantly organized espionage network throughout Canada and the United States. Gouzenko pleaded that the offense be overlooked, pointing out that though they were not in the safe which was locked and sealed each night, the steel doors of the cipher room had been locked and barred, and therefore no damage could have been done. He begged for leniency, but the NKVD gave him no assurances. Well, Gouzenko had a wife and child and another child coming. In addition, he was a young man of idealism. He believed in peace, freedom, and justice, and the stuff he was decoding was certainly far from these targets.

The NKVD did not mince around. Gouzenko's successor and the orders relieving him came in the next diplomatic pouch. Colonel Zabotin insisted, however, that Gouzenko thoroughly ground his successor in the delicate work, and it was not until the end of August that Gouzenko was ordered to turn over the safe and seals on September 6.

But Gouzenko had no intention of returning to his homeland. He had been carefully noting very important papers he could pick up at a moment's notice. The documents were a cross section of dossiers, reports, and recent top-secret directives—in short, the

* As a minor historical legend, ever since the Congress of Vienna in 1814, wastebaskets have been of special interest of Intelligence Services. At that conference, Prince Talleyrand noted that his opponents were passing notes between themselves and depositing them in the wastebaskets. He had charwomen empty them regularly and turn them over to his Intelligence in another room, which kept sending in résumés of the stuff in the wastebaskets. Obviously, it is of great advantage in any game to know the cards in your opponent's hand; Talleyrand found it of marvelous assistance. At any rate, in every Intelligence Service today all wastebasket material must be burned daily, in the presence of a rank not lower than major.

skeleton of a vast and effective espionage system that had penetrated the very top circles of the Canadian and American governments. This was horrifying enough, but there were also secret atomic formulas, which was diplomatically cataclysmic.

On the night of September 5, Gouzenko worked late, but not at Soviet business. He abstracted the papers, tucked them under his coat, and crossed the Rubicon by putting the seal in his pocket as he walked out into the late night, the only thing certain in his life being that if he ever re-entered the doors of that Embassy it would be to face torture and death. It is safe to say that if the NKVD regarded a dented fender as something requiring a reprimand to a Colonel, its view of a cipher clerk walking out with key documents would make a rattlesnake shudder.

Apparently, Igor Gouzenko's observation of the freedom of the press convinced him that it was the main bulwark of safety, because he headed straight for the Ottawa *Journal*. Since it was late at night there was only one reporter on duty, a woman who advised him to go to the Department of Justice at the earliest possible moment. It was a wise and honorable thing to advise. Had an American reporter turned away one of the greatest spy stories of the war, his editor undoubtedly would have died of apoplexy or hara-kiri. At any rate, the guards opened the doors of the Secretary to the Minister of Justice on the morning of September 6 and found Gouzenko, his wife, Anna, who was seven months pregnant, and his eighteen-month-old son, Igor. Gouzenko had hardly launched into his story before he was referred to the Royal Canadian Mounted Police (RCMP) on the ground floor. Because the difficulty he had in expressing himself, he was not taken to the Intelligence Branch. Gouzenko volunteered that he wished to become a Canadian citizen at once under the belief, apparently, that his application would protect him from Pavlov and the NKVD, and he was directed to the City Court. He had no success. He spoke to a journalist there, but he turned down the "story" as too hot to handle. Thus late in the afternoon he was walking the streets with his wife and child in mortal fear, but the RCMP had him and his family under heavy protective surveillance.

RCMP's Intelligence Branch, notified by the Inspector, had immediately asked the Under Secretary of State for External Affairs for instructions in the case of a Russian employee who wished to furnish information. External Affairs at once requested instructions from Prime Minister Mackenzie King, who ordered that nothing be done for the time being for fear of diplomatic repercussions that might follow a false step. The RCMP, of course, was keeping close watch on their Russian visitor. Gouzenko's feelings must have been awful as he made his way back to his apartment, the only place he could take his pregnant wife and the very place Pavlov would look for him. But many eyes were peering at the apartment house on Somerset Street West; RCMP had covered it like a tent. In fact, an RCMP man was standing at the Sergeant's desk when the City police received a call saying that a Russian, his wife, and a child had taken refuge with their neighbor since their lives were in danger. At nine o'clock City Police visited the neighbor's apartment, routinely said they would keep an eye on the place, noted that Gouzenko's own apartment was empty and locked, and departing walked by the plainclothes RCMP in the street as if they never saw them.

But something else was happening too. Flying north in a military courier plane was Sir William Stephenson.* A high-ranking World War I flying ace, he was Churchill's ace in the grimmer, if less sporting, Intelligence game. A lot of water had gone over the dam and a lot more blood had soaked into the fields since he had won his first battlefield medal at agonized Paschendaele Ridge. But the mustard gas he withstood then without a gas mask was scarcely less searing and certainly not less deadly than the atmosphere into which he was now heading.

The Canadian Government was faced with nothing less than acceptance of an Intelligence War with Soviet Russia, which was certain to have the widest diplomatic repercussions. And no one could predict the results of this War. The Government of Canada knew that and Sir William Stephenson knew it, even as he stepped from the plane into the car that whisked him to the secret late-hour

* Stephenson was called "Silent Bill" by the British Combined Chiefs. The American Joint Chiefs Command called him "Little Bill" to distinguish him from "Big Bill" Donovan.

Cabinet meeting. For the very few people who knew him, there could be absolutely no doubt whatsoever of Sir William's decision. Like Admiral Cunningham of the Mediterranean Squadron, he instinctively accepted action, indeed more often sought it, without slightest inquiry of the odds. He would urge, and successfully, that the Prime Minister reverse the order and throw in the full resources of RCMP Intelligence. By the time the action was over, Prime Minister Mackenzie would not be the only Chief of State involved: The British Prime Minister and the American President would have equally grave decisions to make.

The RCMP men outside of the apartment on Somerset West watched the City Police leave and settled down to wait. Their wait, as expected, was not long. Shortly after 11 P.M. a Soviet Embassy car arrived. Four men got out and entered the apartment house. They were given sufficient time to be caught *in flagrante delicto.* Then an Ottawa City police car drew up and two constables followed them inside. This obviously was a brilliant move: The Russians did not know where Gouzenko was or they would not be looking for him. They could not know if the RCMP knew, because the City Police were acting legitimately. The Russians had used a three-foot steel bar jimmy, necessarily noisy, in prying open the door.

The Second Secretary of the Soviet Embassy, Pavlov, the Assistant Military Attaché Vassili Rogov, in uniform no less, and Pavel Angelov, the Air Attaché, were in view as the constables entered. NKVD Alexandre Farafontov was searching the bedroom. Pavlov, perceiving that the constables were city patrolmen, seemed to have been taken in. He informed them that they were interfering with the Russian Embassy, a serious offense which they would hear about from their own superiors. He denied breaking an entrance and stated that he had permission from the owner, who had merely lost his key. The key, a three-foot steel bar, was plainly in view. The Canadian officers, murmuring that they would have to take their chances with their own government, told the Russians to leave. In the meantime, Sir William's view prevailed: City Police were ordered to deliver Gouzenko to RCMP for questioning the next day.

He and his family were kept under heavy guard all night; Gouzenko himself appeared at RCMP Headquarters the following morning at 10:30.

Gouzenko's first statements were so fantastic that they exceeded the bounds of credulity—until he produced the documents to prove them. A first glance at them proved that a huge Soviet network was operating inside the Canadian Government, including the Department of External Affairs and the High Commissioner of the United Kingdom, and that this was being run by Colonel Zabotin as chief, with the assistance of Lieutenant Colonel Motinov, Chief Assistant Military Attaché, along with Major Sokolov of the office of Commercial Counselor.

Safety gained, Gouzenko was at the point of nervous collapse. Further questioning was unwise. Under heavy protective guard, the Gouzenko family was taken out of Ottawa to a place beyond Pavlov's knowledge or reach. One of the chief worries now was that Gouzenko might kill his wife and commit suicide—he was in a state of great mental shock. Guards never left him. When questioning was resumed, Gouzenko revealed that both British and American security, as well as Canadian, had been seriously invaded. The British High Commission and the FBI were immediately notified. Since there was evidence that the Canadian ciphers might have been compromised, a special telekrypton wire was rigged to New York headquarters of British Security. Not even top secretaries were allowed to transcribe messages. As tightly as human ingenuity could devise, the security lid was bolted.

It was Pavlov's move. Among the things he did not know was how much his opponents knew. Sir William was waiting to play against his moves, not for anything so pedestrian as arrest, but to go "up the ladder," that is, have him reveal more in his efforts to conceal his loss. The stakes were heavy: Sir William was playing to get more than espionage information. This was counterespionage action, which compares to espionage as chess to checkers, because somewhere in the Canadian, American, and British Governments, Pavlov had his own men. Pavlov, aside from his professional duties, was playing for heavy stakes also: A man who had reported a fender dent had subsequently to report that vital documents and a key cipher clerk had departed, news which Moscow usually greeted with an automatic with silencer.

In any event, the deadly game was on. Its stakes were to increase.

On September 8, Pavlov made the conventional opening, preparing a routine document and the routine intelligence lies that go with it, treating the disappearance of Gouzenko as a routine embezzlement. The document gravely stated that a member of the Embassy having failed to report for work, Consul Pavlov and two other colleagues visited his apartment at 11:30 September 6, opening it with his duplicate key. (The thirty-six-inch long duplicate.) Pavlov continued that it was later established that the employee had stolen some money and disappeared. Accordingly, would the Department of External Affairs seek and arrest him, and hand him over for deportation as a capital criminal?

Ordinarily, official procedures being what they are, it would mean a stabilized field for at least twenty-four hours, during which the Canadian Government would presumably answer. But Pavlov could not wait. He called the Under Secretary's office that evening and (if he had only known!) interrupted a meeting caused by the information given that day by his quarry. More particularly, the RCMP had brought in detailed information on Canadian personnel in the Soviet spywork. The meeting had been convened at once in the Under Secretary's office to determine what immediate steps should be taken to neutralize the activities of the known agents.

In the middle of the meeting, Pavlov called the Under Secretary asking if a note from the Russian Embassy concerning the disappearance of an employee had been received. Pavlov was informed that such a note had in fact been received, translated, and transmitted to the RCMP, who would undoubtedly take immediate steps. In fact, the RCMP did. As a cover, numbers of constables throughout Canada were sent out to look for Gouzenko. A conference continued into the late hours, sustained by a bottle of Corby's Canadian Rye Whiskey. After the meeting it was necessary to give Gouzenko a code name; the Under Secretary simply pointed to the label on the bottle, and Mr. Gouzenko became Mr. Corby. Stephenson nodded and wired London "Subject will be referred to as Corby, repeat Corby." It was still Pavlov's move, and all hands adjourned.

Pearson uncovers Great Spy Case and interviews masked Russian diplomat.

What Corby had to say the next day was an eye-opener. While Zabotin had instructions as Task Number One to get all information on atomic fission, his general orders would only have been issued if Russia were preparing for hostilities against the United States, Britain, and Canada. American troop movements, personnel changes in American divisions, location of paratroopers, size, quality, and quantity of ammunition in field units, were marked as urgent. Information on electronic shells used by the American Navy, depth bombs, and double-charge shells for cannon were marked for highest priority. Very apparently, Russia was preparing to go on a daring diplomatic offensive, which did not in the least discount war against the Western Allies.

Corby's revelation the next day made it imperative that Stephenson take immediate action. The disclosure was supported by a telegram from Zabotin under the cover name of "Grant," indicating that Zabotin had gotten not only the atomic bomb secret, but samples of the bomb explosive. The telegram read, "Alek delivered us platinum with 160 micrograms of Uranium 233 in form of acid, contained in a thin lamina." "Alek" was Britain's top flight physicist, Dr. May, working right in the center of the National Research Council at Montreal, the combined research center of British and Canadian science on atomic fission.

In greatest secrecy it was ascertained that May had knowledge of the construction of the U.S. graphite pile; knowledge of the methods of separating Plutonium of U-233, access to small samples of U-233, and possible access to uranium metal irradiated in the X pile and containing plutonium. May, from an Intelligence standpoint, was as loaded as the atomic bomb itself.

The precipitating factor was that May was due to return to London. Both London and Washington warned that it would be an international catastrophe if there were further disclosures of intelligence moves or capture of Red spies. An Order-in-Council was even prepared for May's arrest, but Stephenson overruled both governments. May went to London, but was covered every foot of the way, and MI 5, British Intelligence, was waiting for him at Prestwick Airport. There was an odd thing about the shadowing of May. As might be imagined, there was scarcely a move he made that was not completely covered. It takes a large number of men to do this. Coverage was thought to be complete, but an unexpected problem arose: May appeared to be talking to someone in his room, and MI 5 could see no one going either in or out. Yet voices came over the "bug." As finally resolved, it was found that May talked aloud to himself, asking and answering his own questions as if he were two different people, even to the sound of two different voices. It was an imaginative but vain effort to confuse his pursuers.

In what is undoubtedly one of the highest-stake games in the annals of Intelligence, Stephenson had elected to attempt to locate the whole Soviet atomic network, and in order to do that he had to gamble the atomic bomb itself. Not even D-Day on the Normandy beaches was such a wager, and in this instance it was gambled by one man. But if it was his play, he also had an ace. Stephenson knew that Soviet Intelligence had a rendezvous with May in London. He had the details down to the recognition signals. The alternative dates were October 7, 17, or 27; the place was in front of the British Museum in London, on Great Russell Street, at the opposite side of the street. May was to have under his left arm a copy of the *Times*. The Soviet contact man was to have in his left hand the magazine *Picture Post*. Upon this exchange of signals, May was to open with "Best regards from Mikel."

Of course, if Soviet Intelligence had made the contact, the game would have been over then and there. May would have had to be arrested. Fifteen teams of RCMP's were poised to make simultaneous arrests in Canada. No one knows how many interested parties watched that rendezvous point that night. It is certain that Soviet Intelligence and Soviet Counterintelligence spying on Soviet Intelligence were there. The non-appearance of the Soviet contact man meant that Pavlov had reported Gouzenko's disappearance, thus routinely activating top security measures. But it also meant that the Soviets did not know how much Stephenson knew, or there would have been an attempt to capture or kill May.

An insight as to what was going on inside the NKVD was furnished by the FBI. Soviet Intelligence had secured a Canadian passport abroad and substituted for its rightful owner a Soviet agent. Ignacy Witczak was the correct name on the passport, and Ignacy

Witczak became the name of the Soviet agent. Under this name, he and his wife landed in New York on September 13, 1938, and proceeded to California where he settled down ostensibly as an inconspicuous student at the University of Los Angeles. But Witczak's phony Canadian passport was expiring in late 1945, and hence had to be forged all over again. That Witczak was of considerable importance was obvious: the Director of Military Intelligence himself was sending personal wires on the subject to Ottawa. He was informed that V—— (Witczak's code name) would get his passport, but that the Executor could act for nothing less than three. This simply meant that a Canadian in the Passport office had been bribed for $3,000 to pass the spurious documents, according to Gouzenko. Thus, a second dilemma was presented to Soviet Intelligence: Should they apply or should they not? Did or did not the Canadian Government know? Witczak was ordered to make contact with Soviet Intelligence in New York.

One thing was now certain to Witczak: He knew he was the object of scrutiny by anti-Soviet Intelligence services, and by his own. From one of the most valued agents he now became one of the most dangerous to his own service, a service not famous for respecting human beings or sympathizing with their ill fortune. Witczak started to crack up. He wrote to his wife, Bunia, in open code, which is an open book to experts. For example: "Today I was worried all day because my uncle called me, saying he wanted to see me at two—so up to two there were worries. Anyhow, everything is OK, and he just wants me to go with him to Washington for a visit." This simply means he was ordered to Washington.

Referring to himself as Harry, Witczak next wrote: "When one Harry arrived in D.C. at the station he was met by two doctor specialists and for three hours they did not take their eyes off Harry. Now if everything was OK why such a fuss? It is quite possible that doctors in the U.S. were informed from Canada about Harry's illness. Harry did not sleep for a whole week. He was very attentive to every little noise outside his room. Harry was told in case of bad attack he should go to New York hospital immediately and stay there."

It was now clear that Zabotin and Pavlov had spread the alarm, although this of course involved mortal admission of negligence on their part. Witczak's "doctors" were NKVD counterespionage people, intent on saving as much of the network as possible. The N. Y. hospital was the Soviet Consulate General.

Witczak's subsequent conduct could perhaps be a case history of an individual in the twentieth century, sort of a Victor Hugo horror tale. Far more afraid of his own organization than its opponents, he had no place to go, no place to hide, and no one to trust. Yet he knew many eyes were upon him. Overcome by this terror, he stampeded mentally. He would register in a hotel under a false name, then immediately vacate the room. He spent several nights sleeping in the waiting room of Pennsylvania Station and Grand Central, changing in the middle of the night. Sometimes he went to a Turkish bath, not to bathe but to toss in frenetic slumber for a few hours. He neither bathed, shaved, nor changed his clothes, which caused him to be noticed by passers-by. If one of these cast a second glance, Witczak would run for several blocks. He wrote his wife that he did not dare stay in one place long enough to make a long distance call because "it gives an opportunity for attacking liver to appear again." It is a normal defensive measure for a man who believes he is being followed to pass through a revolving door and move quickly to one side to observe who follows him through. The poor crazed mind of Witczak apparently believed that revolving doors could scrub his pursuers away. He entered one, refused to leave, and went round and round until forcibly ejected by the hotel clerks. Witczak's terror reached its climax when he rushed for the subway. There he took trains back and forth in an effort to shake off pursuers. This also is standard operational technique, being reasonably effective in elevators or subways unless the subject is under fullest surveillance. Apparently, though, Witczak had an end objective. It turned out to be, in late afternoon, a bus ride to the empty football stadium on Randall's Island. Walking through the seats, and looking around carefully at every step, he picked his way down to the field itself. As soon as his feet touched the field, he burst into a mad run down the sideline and disappeared on the far side. He finally reeled aboard the train for California and returned to his wife, to await the call he knew must come from his Big Brothers in Moscow.

The stakes were too high for the slightest humanity to enter into the decision. To have picked up Witczak would be to inform NKVD that not only did RCMP and FBI know, but under the circumstances, to inform NKVD that RCMP and FBI *knew* that NKVD knew. Poor little Mr. Witczak's role was to inform the West that the general alarm had been sent throughout the Soviet Intelligence system—and that the NKVD were putting unholy pressure upon Soviet Intelligence to find out how deeply it had been penetrated. As of now, NKVD's position was that the network was compromised enough not to be used, but too valuable to be given up. It is a military axiom that the worst possible estimate must be made of an unknown situation. Accordingly, it was obvious that Zabotin et al. had to produce Gouzenko and produce him in a hurry, or stand the consequences of trial in Moscow. But Corby-Gouzenko's whereabouts were known only to a very few men. So carefully did Stephenson guard his hiding place, that when Mrs. Gouzenko's second child came, purchase of a blue-and-pink layette was made at Best's through a dupe in New York. The young matron in New York, who made the purchases, had no notion then nor now that she was blocking any possible NKVD knowledge of the blessed event. Purchase of a layette in Canada was deemed an unnecessary risk.

The lines were drawn now. Involved were RCMP, MI 5, and FBI versus Soviet Military Intelligence and NKVD, with NKVD against all, including Soviet Military Intelligence. And assuredly if Soviet Military Intelligence could not deliver Gouzenko, NKVD was going to deliver Soviet Military Intelligence for severest discipline.

That is what happened. Colonel Zabotin left for Washington ostensibly to visit his colleagues in the Soviet Embassy. But under the very alert eyes of the FBI he slipped to a darkened pier in Jersey City and quietly boarded a Russian freighter bound for Murmansk. The Canadian Government was not even officially informed of his departure. Lieutenant Colonel Sokolov, his assistant, made a trip to Washington and left from Philadelphia aboard another Russian freighter bound for Odessa. He disappeared into the broad Atlantic and the maze of NKVD's internal police system. That phase of the game had ended: The Reds assumed that Stephenson had Gouzenko.

That they intended to cautiously but daringly rehabilitate as much of the Zabotin system as they could was evidenced by a fortuitous circumstance. In this instance, Stephenson once again demonstrated that the mortal terror by which NKVD ruled was its own greatest vulnerability. On February 2, the Toronto Police picked up a man from the streets in a state of advanced intoxication. A card in his wallet showed him to be Roler, the newly arrived Soviet Assistant Military attaché. Also in his wallet was a receipt for "medical expenses" signed by the cover name of one of Grant's agents, dated only a few days previously. Roler, like Witczak, had broken under the strain. Nothing was said to him when he sobered up next day; he was certainly not going to put himself on report to the very organization he feared. But his lapse of security had provided the only information necessary to call the hand of NKVD.

Scotland Yard closed in on Dr. May. On the second questioning he too broke and completely confessed.

With Orders-in-Council already prepared, Canada acted; both the British Prime Minister and the President of the United States had been kept fully advised of the coming action. Prime Minister Mackenzie King had ruled from the beginning that any intelligence or police action must be considered subordinate to diplomatic consideration.

On February 15, 1946, at dawn, the RCMP closed in. The arrests were made, the Prime Minister went before the House, and the Royal Commission began its work at once. The Grant network was exposed to the world, including the atomic bomb spying, with historical diplomatic repercussions.

Three days later, Pearson's column carried the first public inkling of the momentous events. For Pearson, this was a terrifying story to uncover because it demonstrated the Russian technique, of which both the British and Canadian governments were acutely aware. Of course there were Russian spyworks operating in practically every sensitive department of the U.S.; they were in deeper and in greater numbers than the penetration of the British and the Canadians. But there was this difference: Stephenson had experienced governments to deal with. J. Edgar Hoover did not. Like Cassandra, he told and re-told the details of Soviet activity, but his warnings fell upon the ears of those who were, at best, utter amateurs. Throughout the war, intelligence warnings were often countered by statements such as, "Why, I've known the man for years," as if that closed the matter. (President Roosevelt said that of Harry White.) The truth is, then and now, that if Canada and Britain were leaking, the U.S. is and was a sieve. As one American official privately conceded: "Are they in our department? Four deep, as Knute Rockne used to say, in every sensitive area."

Gouzenko's documents disclosed the incredible dimensions of Soviet espionage in the Western Hemisphere. The Russian Embassy in Ottawa radiated into the eastern United States. Agents in the western part of the United States relayed information by courier in Southern California, and then to Mexico City, headquarters for Soviet Latin-American espionage. The Mexican spy apparatus had been established by former Washington Ambassador Oumansky. The Russian diplomat had been most unpopular in Washington. He was a nasty, testy, perpetually sneering person. He occasionally joined the dinners Pearson frequently gives for foreign diplomats, and one time a guest asked Oumansky: "What do you think is the most unusual characteristic of the American people?" He growled: "Panic. I've sent home everything I can find on the panic created by the Orson Welles broadcast. It shows the American people have no emotional stability. They are afraid."

At any rate, Oumansky headed a chain of two thousand agents south of the border. He was later killed in a plane "accident." His plane crashed during a Mexico City take-off. Later, U.S. Intelligence agents learned that Oumansky was murdered by Russian assassins.

Originally, the American press reaction to Pearson's monumental scoop was a blend of skepticism and caution, since there was no official confirmation for several days. It would be thought that the columnist's achievement would be publicly welcomed with brass bands and a showering of rose petals. However, this incident offered a staggering illustration of the occasional perversity of human nature. Pearson was deluged with mail denouncing him as a warmonger, a disrupter of American-Russian relations, a threat to world peace and a liar.

The deluge ceased after Canada's Prime Minister Mackenzie King issued an official statement confirming the spy ring. The official confirmation inspired American editorialists to express alarm and dismay. Nevertheless, only a few newspapers gave Pearson credit for breaking the story. As Pearson said: "You should know newspapers never give anyone credit for anything. They're very jealous."

Part two of the spy story took place about six years later. In January 1954, Pearson spent the greater part of two days in an exclusive interview with Igor Gouzenko "somewhere in Canada." His first talk with Gouzenko was in a private home "whose owner I did not entirely know and whose identity I could not reveal even if I wanted to." Then they dined at a private club "which I couldn't possibly find again," says Pearson. They huddled in a kitchen of a small farmhouse cluttered with television cameras, lights, electricians, and cables. Gouzenko gave Pearson his first television interview. He wore a mask while he was in front of the cameras.

The interview collected headlines around the world. During the interview, excitement ran high. Gouzenko was constantly roving, constantly on the alert, on the prowl for the slightest indication of danger. He glanced nervously over his shoulder as he spoke. He leaped up and peered out the window at the first throb of a passing car. He kept his eye on a passerby strolling down the street. Emotionally, Gouzenko seemed to be a hive of activity, forever buzzing. Of course, there was good reason for his extreme wariness. He knew he was one of the Kremlin's most wanted men. He was aware Soviet agents had reached into Mexico to murder Trotsky; he knew that Red chiefs would relish making him an example in order to discourage other possible defectors. So he lived as one who was being hunted, as indeed he was, under the twenty-four-hour house protection of the Canadian Royal Mounted Police.

Gouzenko's interview was highlighted by certain revelations: Colonel Zabotin, the top Russian spy in Canada, often toasted, "Today Our Allies, Tomorrow Our Enemies!" He heard from one of his colleagues returning from Moscow that the Kremlin was cooperating with an assistant to Secretary of State Stettinius during the San Francisco conference which created the United Nations. At the time, Stettinius' chief assistant was Alger Hiss.

Gouzenko told Pearson: "In front of every potential escapee there is a problem. He has to think, will he be accepted as a member of society in the free world? So you must give him assurances in advance. He must be sure of a job, of police protection, and material help. There is also the matter of dignity involved. Sometimes a high Russian military attaché or General would like to come over to the West, but he continues on with the Soviets simply because he is afraid he will be humiliated there, and perhaps be put to work as a janitor or a doorman in front of a New York nightclub."

Pearson recalled his experience in Germany where he found various high Russian escapees had been shunted back and forth between Frankfurt and Washington by the U.S. military, milked dry of their information, then allowed to sit and rot in concentration camps outside Frankfurt. As a matter of fact, Pearson persuaded fourteen Senators to introduce a bill to study the entire problem of Russian escapees, but the legislation was lost in the shuffle.

Pearson's television interview with Gouzenko was an exciting epilogue for a drama that was played in February 1946. The breaking of the spy case had an incalculable effect on the world's military and diplomatic structure, especially in those powerful circles dominated by suspicion and the mad clangor of arms. In terms of history, it was a significant chapter. In terms of journalism, it was high drama, a first-rate spectacular.

...kages containing foodstuffs for the needy of Europe being placed in cars at Hollywood for cross-country trip

Associated Press Wirephoto

...Germans' Art Loot From Italy Traced by List Found in Rome

Papers Found Saturday, Showing Hitler's Interest in Booty, Given to Government by U. S. Envoy at Exhibition

By CAMILLE M. CIANFARRA

Special to The New York Times.

ROME, Nov. 9—Methods used [by] German armies to plunder Ital[ian a]rt treasures were disclosed to[day] by documents that United [State]s Ambassador James C. Dunn [hand]ed to the Italian Govern[ment].

...more effectively since the Italian Government will be fully informed of the German policy and organization in these matters."

The first news of the discovery was received by Paul H. Bonner, economic adviser to Ambassador Dunn, yesterday afternoon. The case containing the documents had been lying in the American Military Government building in Rome for nearly two years. When the military government evacuated the building yesterday in accordance with the peace treaty it asked the United States Embassy whether it could hand over a number of cases to the Commission for the Liquidation of German Assets. An inventory revealed the documents.

The documents gave the disposition of sixty paintings looted from the Pitti and Uffizi galleries and the National Museum in Florence, which included oils by Raphael, Michelangelo, Georgione, Rubens, Caravaggio, Titian, Tiepolo and others. The Germans transported these paintings to Germany on the pretext that they would be better protected.

The files disclosed a German suggestion to Italy that the Vatican be asked to appeal to the Allies to spare the Carthusian monastery of Pavia. Benito Mussolino's body was concealed there after it was secretly exhumed from Milan's cemetery by Fascists last year. The monks were accused of complicity...

FRIENDSHIP T[RAIN] GROWS TO 29 [CARS]

Reaches Reno and Add[s to] Accumulation of Food for People of Europ[e]

RENO, Nev., Nov. 9 (UP)—[The] Friendship Train moved i[nto] its second state tonight, ... here to take on two more ca[rs] of food for hungry Europe b[efore] proceeding on its cross-co[untry] trip.

Adding sections at every ... the train now has twenty-nine cars packed with food—more ... triple the number with whic[h it] started from Los Angeles Fr[iday] night.

Nevada's two carload gift, d[ou]ble the state's quota, was coup[led] to the train at ceremonies attend[ed] by Gov. Vail Pittman, Ren[o] Mayor, Francis W. Smith, and a[n] Indian band in full tribal regalia.

Earlier today the train stoppe[d] in Sacramento, Calif., where tw[o] cars of food from the Sacramento Valley were attached. California's Gov. Earl Warren officially turned the train over to Governor Pittman, who rode with it to Reno.

At Oakland, Calif., seven cars of flour, evaporated milk, baby food, dried peas and beans, spaghetti, macaroni and canned goods had been added. San Francisco and neighboring cities made a $10,000 cash donation.

Two carloads of sugar, personally presented by Gov. Ingram Stainback on behalf of the people of Hawaii, arrived at Oakland in time to be waiting for the train.

The train is scheduled to arrive at New York in two sections Nov. 18 with at least 200 carloads of food to be shipped to Europe for Christmas.

Northwest Sending Food Ship

SALEM, Ore., Nov. 9 (UP)—Plans for a "Christmas ship" loaded with Northwest grain and food for the hungry of Europe and Asia are being made by the Washington State and Oregon Councils of Churches, Dr. Chester Hamblin of Salem, president of the Oregon Council of Churches, announced here tonight.

Dr. Hamblin said the ship would carry the contributions of many persons of the Northwest who were unable to get their gifts aboard the Friendship Train.

OUTPUT CLIMBING

...7 (UP)—Russia's ... pushed up the ... Soviet food in... rising rate. A ... Moscow News ...

Hollywood Fanfare Sends Friendship Train East to Collect Contributions for Europe

Special to The New York Times.

LOS ANGELES, Nov. 7—A klieg-lighted Hollywood gala party, replete with bands and movie stars, tonight sped the Friendship Food Train on its ten-day cross-country tour to gather contributions for Europe.

In typical Hollywood fashion the actual train itself was ignored while an eight-car "dummy" was contrived as the cynosure of festivities.

... ceiving a succession of messages from points en route reporting food carloads waiting.

The train will travel over Southern Pacific tracks to Ogden, Utah, and thence over the Union Pacific to Chicago where it is scheduled to arrive Nov. 14.

There it will be split into two sections, one taking the New York Central Railroad's northern route and the other the Pennsylvania Railroad's midland route, arriving in New York Nov. 18.

... conceived by Drew ...

FLANDERS FOR RATION TO CURB MEAT PRICES

SPRINGFIELD, Vt., Nov. 7 (UP)—Meat rationing without price controls was proposed today by Senator Ralph E. Flanders, Republican, of Vermont, as the only way he knew to check spiraling prices.

Mr. Flanders, who headed a Congressional inquiry into high living costs in the East, said that meat was the "key" to the whole situation.

"Food should take up about one-third of the total income in the family budget, but now is eating up as much as 40 to 60 per cent of the low and middle class family incomes," he said.

Clinton P. Anderson, Secretary of Agriculture, said recently that meat rationing would take too ...

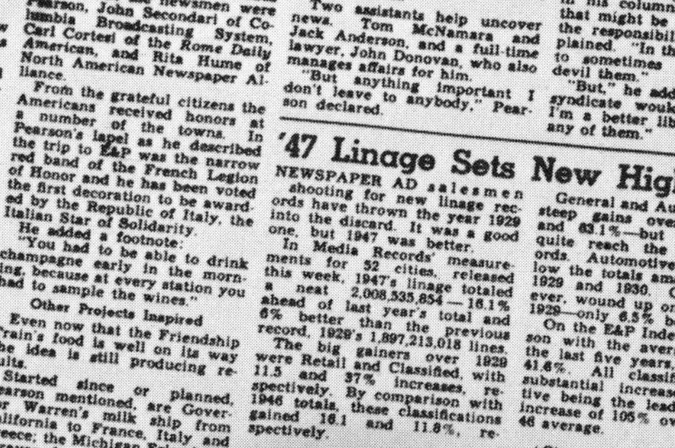

...son Wins Friends [for] Friendship Train

...M. Staunton

...train. Pearson was on the first train with Geoffrey Parsons of the European Edition of the *New York Herald Tribune*. On other French trains were Lansing Warren of the *New York Times*, Paul Ghali of the *Chicago Daily News* and Bob Parker of International News Service.

"We did feel that we were obligated to go and tell the people what the Friendship Train was," explained Pearson.

In Italy the same flatcar speeches by newsmen accompanied the dropping of carloads of food, but the newsmen were Pearson, John Secondari of Columbia Broadcasting System, Carl Cortesi of the *Rome Daily American*, and Rita Hume of North American Newspaper Alliance.

From the grateful citizens the Americans received honors at a number of the towns. In Pearson's lapel as he described the trip to E&P was the narrow red band of the French Legion of Honor and he has been voted the first decoration to be awarded by the Republic of Italy, the Italian Star of Solidarity.

He added a footnote: "You had to be able to drink champagne early in the morning, because at every station you had to sample the wines."

Other Projects Inspired

Even now that the Friendship Train's food is well on its way the idea is still producing results.

Started since or planned, Pearson mentioned, are Governor Warren's milk ship from California to France, Italy and Greece; the Michigan Friendship Caravan from 70 Junior Chambers of Commerce to France; two Abraham Lincoln Friendship trains leaving Lincoln, Neb., and Springfield, Ill., Feb. 12 for Germany and Austria; the Northwest Friend Ship to Austria and either Germany or Czechoslovakia; the New England Friend Ship to Greece; the North Carolina Friendship clothing drive, and the campaign by New Orleans to adopt Orleans in France.

He estimated the new drives would produce another 20,000 tons of food and clothing.

Pearson disliked the organization detail work, but he admitted: "I got a tremendous amount of satisfaction because it accomplished something and a hell of a satisfaction to see the response in this country and even more abroad."

The comment was typical of the columnist who has been one of the most controversial personalities of the press since he collaborated with Robert S. Allen on the first "Washington Merry-Go-Round" book.

"I think I'm still in bad with an awful lot of people," he remarked with a twinkle. "I have a lot of enemies and a few good friends. Right now some people are saying some nice things about me, but it probably won't last long."

Early Bird Columnist

Describing how he works on his column, Pearson related: "I get up at 6 or 6:30 and finish writing the column before breakfast. I write one column a day except on Wednesday when I write two, and on Saturday I write none. In summertime I get up at 4 a.m. As I get up early, I know my farm hands get up early too. I get them started and then work on the column."

He reserved his greatest enthusiasm for that sizable farm of his and sunrise on the front porch, climaxing with the fact that "You can spit right into the Potomac, if you spit 150 feet, straight down."

Two assistants help uncover news, Tom McNamara and Jack Anderson, and a full-time lawyer, John Donovan, who also manages affairs for him.

"But anything important I don't leave to anybody," Pearson declared.

On his own schedule the day of the interview was a talk with a cabinet member and a long-distance call that might uncover another story. He was, he revealed, on the trail of the "real reason" for Eisenhower's withdrawal from the presidential race.

No New Libel Suits

Pearson mentioned that since he has been writing for Bell instead of United Feature Syndicate he has had no new libel suits filed against him.

"I do the filing now," he twinkled, referring to his withdrawn suit against Westbrook Pegler and another against a rival publisher who called him a communist.

Bell never questions anything in his columns except a point that might be libelous. "I take the responsibility now," he explained. "In the old days I used to sometimes put stuff in to devil them."

"But," he added, "I think the syndicate would tell you that I'm a better libel lawyer than any of them."

Pearson

'47 Linage Sets New High Mark

NEWSPAPER AD salesmen shooting for new linage records have thrown the year 1929 into the discard. It was a good one, but 1947 was better.

In Media Records' measurements for 52 cities, released this week, 1947's linage totaled a neat 2,008,535,854—16.1% ahead of last year's total and 6% better than the previous record, 1929's 1,897,213,018 lines.

The big gainers over 1929 were Retail and Classified, with 11.5 and 37% increases, respectively. By comparison with 1946 totals, these classifications gained 16.1 and 11.8%, respectively.

General and Automotive made steep gains over 1946—18.1% and 63.1%—but they couldn't quite reach the previous records. Automotive was far below the totals amassed in 1928, 1929 and 1930. General, however, wound up on the heels of 1929—only 6.5% behind.

On the E&P Index, a comparison with the average total for the last five years, 1947 gained 41.6%. All classifications had substantial increases, Automotive being the leader, with an increase of 105% over the 1942-46 average.

(City report on pages 56-58)

NEWSPAPER LINAGE—52 CITIES

(compiled by EDITOR & PUBLISHER from Media Records measurements)

	1947 Linage	1946 Linage	% of 1946	E&P Index
Total Advertising				
12 months	2,008,535,854	1,729,713,225	116.1	141.6
December	186,913,274	163,257,097	114.5	140.8
November	198,906,481	164,120,122	118.7	143.2
Display				
12 months	1,534,985,617	1,306,051,096	117.5	140.1
December	149,383,134	128,853,119	115.9	140.5
November	153,361,247	127,347,828	120.4	142.1
Classified				
12 months	473,600,237	423,662,129	111.8	143.9
December	37,530,140	34,403,978	109.1	179.2
November	41,447,234	36,772,294	112.7	147.6
Retail				
12 months	1,127,242,002	971,283,756	116.1	140.9
December	117,247,075	101,155,323	115.9	145.1
November	113,367,458	94,052,153	120.5	146.3
Department Store				
12 months	427,512,988	380,247,319	112.4	130.3
December	43,048,470	37,797,560	113.9	134.8
November	42,989,466	36,767,896	116.9	133.4
General				
12 months	314,605,173	266,285,155	118.1	125.1
December	24,935,208	22,388,220	111.4	119.2
November	32,003,957	26,595,729	120.3	129.0
Automotive				
12 months	68,671,744	42,106,120	163.1	205.0
December	5,214,631	3,415,405	152.7	132.6
November	5,956,985	4,674,652	127.4	149.1
Financial				
12 months	24,416,698	26,376,065	92.6	119.4
December	1,986,220	1,894,171	104.9	104.8
November	2,032,847	2,025,295	100.4	121.7

...A LIMIT ...ON CURBS

City Hails Friendship Trai[n]; Food Total Is Put at 270 C[ars]

By CHARLES GRUTZNER

[F]RENCH HEADS ... A GENERAL S...

Communists Step U[p] ... of Walkouts—Nati[on] ... in State of De...

By HAROLD CA...

...Summarized

NOVEMBER 19, 1947

Continued on Page 5, Column 3

2 U. S. Crews Back Fr... Bar Troops From Unl...

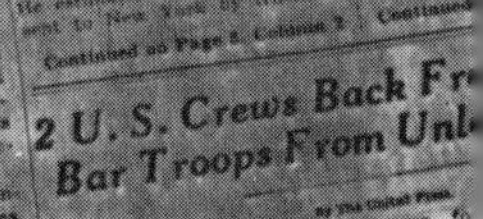

6

THE FRIENDSHIP STORY

In October 1947, sitting in his 200-year-old Georgetown home, Pearson came across a news item buried on an inside page: In Marseilles harbor a cargo of Soviet wheat entered with flags flying and bands playing. There were street parades, a municipal holiday was declared, and praise was heaped on the benefactors of the French people—Soviet Russia. Actually the Russian cargo was a mere driblet compared to the millions of tons of food the United States was shipping to France without fanfare. After pondering the item for several moments, Pearson went to his typewriter and began pounding out a column in the form of an open letter to Charles Luckman, Chairman of the Citizens Food Committee. He wrote: "Why not dramatize the story of America's sacrifice by running a 'Friendship Train' straight across the United States, through the heart of America, collecting food as it goes, inspiring housewives and farmers of the nation to spare a bag of flour or a bushel of wheat and bring it down to the 'Friendship Train' as their contribution toward friendship with the people of Europe."

Pearson argued that a government-to-government barter system rarely conveys a sense of human warmth. Governmental institutions, despite the purity of their intentions, represent intricate mechanical processes that defy translation in human terms. Additionally, cynical diplomatic expediency is closely interwoven with the entire fabric of a government's moral conceptions. In other words, it is easy to recognize the importance of government as an agency in the program of international economic recovery, but at the same time the limitations of its effectiveness as an instrument of human concern must be acknowledged.

Pearson concluded: "How much more important, if the recipients of this food interpret it not as a cold and calculated move, but rather what it really is—a movement by the American people to stint on their own dinner tables to help neighbors in distress who in turn are helped to make democracy live. Perhaps I'm cockeyed on this, or perhaps you have a better way of getting this idea across. In any event, this is merely a suggestion from one citizen vitally interested in the success of your Citizens' Food Committee."

Drew originally intended to start with one boxcar in Los Angeles and load food along the way. He contributed $10,000 to launch the project. Privately, he was worried sick that he would be unable to fill a single boxcar. Of course, Pearson's project was in the grand journalistic tradition. Over the years, numerous newspapers have engaged in charitable affairs, which are generally confined to local communities. Newspapers have raised funds for children's playgrounds and for the sick and needy. Now and again, they promote financial support for the victim of a rare disease. One branch of journalism is confined to what is commonly known as sob-sisterism. Recorded tales of woe, often dripping with syrupy sentiment, they elicit donations from readers.

However, the Friendship Train, in terms of journalistic charity, is unmatched in scope and international impact. The project mushroomed beyond Pearson's brightest visions. It caught fire and spread welcoming bonfires throughout the United States and Western Europe.

Pearson organized a committee headed by movie mogul Harry Warner and including representatives of farmers, labor unions, businessmen, and service clubs. The Friendship Train became a reality as soon as the railroads offered to haul the train free of charge. It began its journey in Los Angeles on November 5, 1947. The inaugural was a kleig-lighted Hollywood gala, with bands, movie stars, and assorted luminaries. The crowd ignored the actual train, while an eight-car "dummy" attracted attention. It was a typical Hollywood show, and the notables were headed by Pearson,

Governor Earl Warren, and Charles Luckman, the Citizens Food Committee chief. Incidentally, Earl Warren and his wife were generous with their assistance. They rode the Friendship Train for two days, until it left California.

The Friendship Train moved through Los Angeles on street railway tracks as the crowds cheered. Meanwhile, from freight docks scattered throughout the city, the Southern Pacific Railroad assembled the components of the actual train for its midnight departure. Before the train left Los Angeles, it collected twelve carloads of foodstuffs. The train, with two engines, also included seven auxiliary cars—a diner, two Pullmans, a tourist car, an officer car, a coach caboose, and a flatcar as a platform for en route celebrations.

Before the train left for Los Angeles, Pearson received messages from points throughout the country reporting food carloads waiting. In addition to actual gifts of food from the public collected at Los Angeles schools and other public agencies, the Friendship Train received about $10,000 in cash contributions as a nucleus for a national fund.

The train had grown to twenty-nine cars by the time it reached Reno, Nevada, forty-eight hours after leaving Los Angeles. Along the way it picked up seven cars of flour, evaporated milk, baby food, dried peas and beans, spaghetti, macaroni, and canned goods. San Francisco and neighboring cities made a $10,000 cash contribution. Two carloads of sugar, presented on behalf of the people of Hawaii, arrived at Oakland in time to be waiting for the train. On November 9 the Associated Press carried a story datelined Salem, Oregon: "Plans for a 'Christmas Ship' loaded with Northwest grain and food for the hungry of Europe and Asia are being made by the Washington State and Oregon Councils of Churches. The ship will carry the contributions of many persons in the Northwest who are unable to get their gifts aboard the Friendship Train."

On November 14 an airborne addition to the Friendship Train went into operation on a coast-to-coast basis. Foodstuffs contributed too late to catch the train en route were flown from western cities to Newark (New Jersey) Airport each evening.

The Friendship Train gave Pearson an education in food shipping. Anything packed in glass cannot be shipped. Also, most canned goods contain so much water that accepting them for overseas shipment is uneconomical. But these were minor problems. The fact was that just a few weeks after Pearson sent the Friendship Train concept soaring—and privately hoped he could fill a single boxcar—the people had hooked onto the train almost two hundred boxcars. The immense outpouring of generosity was warmed with numerous incidents: At Spencer, Iowa, a freight train on the Milwaukee Road stopped opposite radio station KICD while the train crew trudged through the snow to the radio station to contribute to the Friendship Train. And in Los Angeles the musicians' union contributed, gratis, eight 40-piece bands for the parade. Teamster union locals in many cities furnished volunteers to load and pack boxcars. The Hershey Chocolate Company sent a boxcar of sugar by boat from Cuba on the same day the Friendship Train left Los Angeles; it met the train in New York. Sidney, Nebraska, population 4,000, rolled up two full boxcars of wheat.

Pearson rode the Friendship Train. He remembers it as "the most exciting and exhilarating experience of my life. I got a lot more kick out of writing about the Friendship Train than I ever did peeking through keyholes in Washington."

Even President Truman, who was bitterly at odds with Pearson, made a contribution. The Friendship Train required several thousand French and Italian posters to be sealed on the boxcars for Europe, so that Europeans would be aware of the food gift from Americans. One of the columnist's friends in the State Department arranged to pay for the printing of the posters out of President Truman's confidential-expense fund. Truman was unaware of his donation until Pearson told him about it years later.

Numerous American communities not on the main line of the Friendship Train rushed voluntary contributions to the ship. The city of Nashville, Tennessee, entirely unsolicited, loaded up one hundred pounds of flour and trucked it all the way to Philadelphia. Chattanooga did likewise with two huge truckloads of evaporated milk. The students of Virginia's Intermount College voted to forego their Thanksgiving banquet and contributed the money to the Friendship Train. Radio stations and newspapers in towns and cities far from the main line of the Friendship Train loaded cars and sent them toward the terminus. As a matter of fact, the State of Virginia concocted a special Friendship Train of its own.

Meanwhile, back in Hollywood, Charles Skouras called in his theatre managers and urged them to publicize the Friendship Train. One manager argued: "But we're just opening *Forever Amber*. We can't plug both." Skouras shot back: "What is more important, your country or *Forever Amber*?"

One day prior to the train's arrival, the November 18, 1947, *New York Times* editorial page extended a welcome:

> It started from Los Angeles as a single train of twelve cars, easily pulled by one locomotive. At Oakland it picked up seven more cars. It left Reno on Sunday with twenty-nine, Ogden on Monday with thirty-one, Kearney, Neb., on Wednesday with fifty, Council Bluffs on Friday with sixty-two. It got too big and had to visit too many cities to remain one train, and cars were being added so rapidly yesterday that counting was difficult. But the twelve cars had grown to more than two hundred, approaching this city on both banks of the Hudson. It is now New York's turn to add to these gifts of the American people for hungry Europe's Christmas. In this port the Friendship Train ends its dramatic food journey.
>
> This is a small part of the harvest of our broad land; fruits of California, the grain of the Middle West, milk of Wisconsin, dried peas and beans, some, perhaps, directly or indirectly, from all the states. We in this city can do our own part by gifts of food or money, which may be sent or taken to any school or police station or firehouse. Today's parade and ceremonies at City Hall will warm the heart like a rehearsal for Christmas. Friendship Train carries no burden of politics. It is a message from people with something to spare to people with less than enough.
>
> Friendship Train is an expression of America, just as is the Freedom Train; the one is a reaffirmation of our basic faith, the other is that faith in simple, human action. These are stern days, which we will need strength and courage to get safely through. But the pioneer who could labor and endure also gave freely of his substance when his neighbor was in trouble; that was, and is, America, too.

Friendship Train starts in Los Angeles.

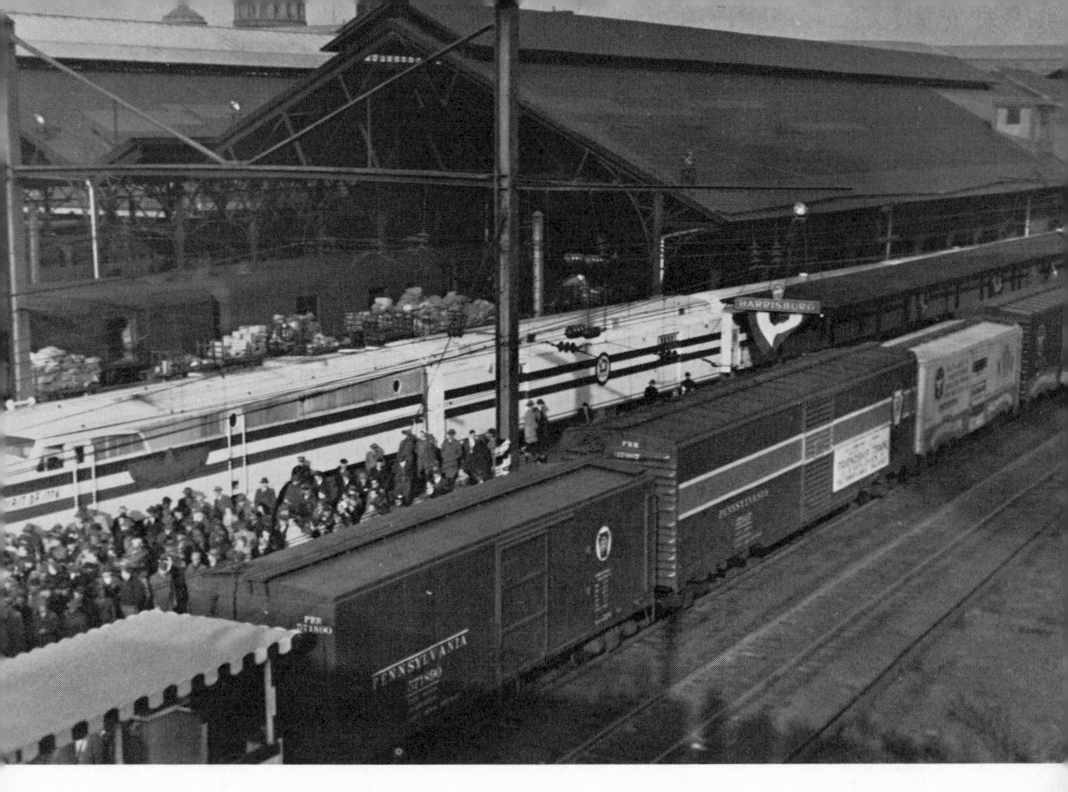

Friendship Train welcomed in Harrisburg.

Friendship Train cheered by Italian children.

The foregoing tribute was representative of the American press in general. Newspapers encouraged and promoted the Friendship Train. Many of them saluted Pearson, albeit his column appeared in opposition papers. This was one of the minor miracles performed by the Friendship Train. For once, it suspended journalistic hostilities and jealousies in a truly notable illustration of the Christmas spirit.

The spirit expressed in *The New York Times* editorial spread across the city. A rousing salute in the bay for the Friendship Train was followed by a parade up Broadway to City Hall. Eight trucks laden with fruit rolled behind brass bands, while crowds lining the sidewalks cheered. The cargo was a token of the donations. This event was preceded by a string of boxcars on railroad floats in a marine procession, with fireboats and police launches, sailing past the Statue of Liberty.

At City Hall, Mayor O'Dwyer said the Friendship Train "was a material symbol of the desire of our people to relieve the hunger and suffering of our fellow humans in Italy and France."

The New York papers described Pearson as "the father of the Friendship Train" and quoted his forecast that "New York's contributions being made at schools, police stations, and firehouses, would amount to thirty or forty carloads. In addition, the food sent to New York by trucks and planes would bring total collections to 275 cars." Drew noted also that arrangements had been made by the French and Italian governments for assembling two Friendship Trains in Europe to take the food to communities in France, Italy, and Greece. The food would be carried to Europe without charge by shipping companies.

The railroad floats in New York harbor carried fifteen cars, including the original Los Angeles boxcars. They were painted blue, white, and yellow and bore such slogans as "Vive la France," "Viva L'Italia," and "From the Heart of the American People." Some boxcars had French and Italian flags painted on their sides. The floats flew the flags of the United States, France, and Italy.*

* One news story noted a minor problem: Railroad officials ran into temporary difficulty getting Italian flags. The flag dealer who usually supplied them said there had been no call for Italian flags since before the war, and

Police estimated that the Friendship Train parade up Broadway was witnessed by more than one hundred thousand people, and over twenty-five thousand turned out to observe the ceremonies at City Hall, where the marchers were welcomed by Police, Fire, and Sanitation department bands. They were joined by Boy and Girl Scouts and persons of French and Italian extraction in national costume. Several thousand children had been excused from school, and they formed a cheering section on Broadway; other students had seats at the City Hall exercises. Many of the children presented gifts from their schools, and they made the presentations in French and Italian. In a shortwave broadcast from France, the crowd at City Hall heard a French child express thanks for America's food gifts.

The French Consul General in New York, Ludovic Chancel, told the crowd, "France shall never forget the generous nation who came to her aid in the hours of grief." The Italian Consul General, Luigi Nardi, echoed the sentiments of his diplomatic colleague. The Italian Ambassador's wife, Signora Alberto Tarchiano, rode the Friendship Train from Chicago to New York.

Warren R. Austin, United States permanent delegate to the United Nations, concluded the ceremonies at City Hall by stating in part: "The hundreds of thousands of carloads of food which have gone through this port since the war were no less characterized by the spirit of friendship. But the cars of the Friendship Train have brought the personal touch and the individual sense of responsibility to bear on the process of helping people to help themselves."

Twenty-four hours after the Friendship Train came to New York, gifts of food and money continued. For example, mail addressed to Postmaster General Albert Goldman yielded over $11,000. Some of the money represented collections in shops, offices, and neighborhoods. Residents of New England, a section not covered by the Friendship Train, sent food by truck. A group of 500 students from fifty-six countries donated $2,500. Several hundred New Yorkers sent in one-day salary checks. Incidentally, the total food supply

---

those in stock had the crown and shield of Savoy. This royal insignia was deleted to make the flags representative of the new republic of Italy.

collected by the Friendship Train was valued at more than $40 million.

New York's generosity was typical of every city and town touched by the Friendship Train. Several weeks later, Europeans radiated similar heartwarming sentiments.

On Christmas Eve, Drew Pearson was in Marseilles. He headed a parade down the city's main boulevard. Only a few months before, the French street had been the scene for waving hammer-and-sickles. Now Pearson beheld a different spectacle. The Stars and Stripes whipped in the breeze. Sidewalks were lined with cheering Frenchmen. Mademoiselles tossed flowers and blew kisses. Bands cracked the air with rousing sounds. Pearson was hugged and smooched and applauded.

The next day was Christmas and it was cold and clammy. The weary Pearsons were in an unheated hotel. The euphoria of the previous day's parade was replaced by aching muscles and chills. Drew and Luvie Pearson shivered as they waited for their laundry, hung in the room, to dry. The dampness persisted. Eventually the Pearsons were compelled to pull on their moist clothes and listen to their teeth chatter. The real warmth was provided by the reception of the people.

Pearson set up a committee so that there would be one newspaperman on each train. He was on the first train with Geoffrey Parsons of the *Herald Tribune*. On the other French trains were Lansing Warren of *The New York Times,* Paul Ghali of the Chicago *Daily News*, and Bob Parker of International News Service.

As Pearson explains: "We were obligated to go and tell the people about the Friendship Train. If we had just arrived in France with a ship that was loaded by the American Government, we would have gotten nowhere. Newsreels taken in the United States were shown in French theatres before we arrived. I didn't leave anything to chance. The French people knew it was a bona fide gift from the American people."

In Italy the same flatcar speeches by newsmen accompanied the delivery of carloads of food. John Secondari of the Columbia Broadcasting System, Carl Cortesi of the Rome *Daily American*, and Rita

Hume of North American Newspaper Alliance were active participants.

The newsmen were showered with honors as they moved from town to town. Pearson's major problem consisted of indulging in the traditional toasting as he traveled from place to place. The columnist sighs, "You had to be able to drink champagne early in the morning, because at every station you had to sample the wines."

Three weeks after the first Friendship Train arrived at Le Havre, the French newspapers were still headlining stories about subsequent trains. *France Soir*, for example, announced that the Ministry of Education had officially accepted a plan for a Friendship Contest in the schools. Prizes were to be awarded for the twenty best letters on the Friendship Train. These letters were later compiled and exhibited by two French children on a tour of the United States.

Various proposals were made in Italy to thank the American people for the Friendship Train. *Momento Sera*, a Rome newspaper, suggested that some ancient and highly prized work of art be dispatched to Washington for exhibition in the Smithsonian or National Museum. In Florence a group of artists proposed sending several art gifts to the American people, while an Italian film company produced a movie titled *Thanks, America*, showing the Italian reception of the Friendship Train. Premier Alcide de Gasperi and Foreign Minister Carlo Sforza (and their assistants) contributed twenty thousand lire out of their own pockets to pay for the film's production.

As expected, the one sour note was provided by the Communists. The French Communist newspaper *Humanité* blasted the columnist editorially as a "blackguard and one with ill breeding. . . . To Drew Pearson and his accomplices, our contempt. . . . It is scandalous that in cities of the East ravaged by floods, trucks display streamers showing the Friendship Train when the products being distributed do not come at all from across the Atlantic. It's a swindle."

Le Figaro responded editorially to the Red attack: "It would have been better, no doubt, if some clever sabotage had derailed the Friendship Train. But since it has unfortunately come safely into port, the attack must be made on this terrible Drew Pearson.

For this wicked aggressor, Drew Pearson, is none other than a journalist who launched the idea of the Friendship Train. He might well have expected that the Communists would not let such insolence pass without comment."

Later there was another unhappy incident. One Italian mayor spurned the Friendship Train. His hostility was the consequence of a Pearson exposé. Early in 1947, Drew published a confidential report of Communist plans to seize control of Italy. Included in the exposé were the locations of secret Communist ammunition dumps and the names of Communist leaders, among them Guiseppe Dozza, Mayor of Bologna. Four months later, when the Friendship Train reached Bologna, Mayor Dozza furiously waved the clipping to American newsmen and denounced Pearson as well as the Friendship Train. He was the only mayor in Italy who refused to welcome the train.

Communist furies heightened the Friendship Train drama, marred only, as far as Pearson was concerned, by a pair of minor irritations. One was the onerous organizational details and the other involved celebrity ceremonials. The Friendship Train made Pearson an international celebrity. And it enhanced his box-office appeal.

Whether they like it or not, columnists are engaged in the box-office sweepstakes. Their products are merchandised on national and international markets. It naturally follows that the more interest they generate in their products—and in themselves—the greater will be their attraction.

Over the years, some of the most colorful chapters in the annals of newspaperdom have been compiled by the flamboyant. They not only observed the news, they participated in it. Horace Greeley, Joseph Pulitzer, William Randolph Hearst, James Gordon Bennett published and created news. An outstanding radio-television example was Edward R. Murrow. During the past three decades, columnists have led journalism's showmanship parade. The prime illustrations are Drew Pearson and Walter Winchell. The latter's gifts for showmanship can be attributed to his apprenticeship in vaudeville.

At any rate, while Pearson decried some of the hoopla that went with the Friendship Train, he confessed that "it was necessary." And when his mission ended, he accepted the applause. The *Christian Science Monitor's* Roscoe Drummond hailed the Friendship Train as "one of the greatest projects ever born of American journalism." *Time* magazine quoted the comment with approval. *Editor and Publisher*, the publisher's trade journal, reported: "In recent years no non-government gesture has created such international good-will as the Friendship Train, and few have received such spontaneous backing all over the country. The man with the idea for the train—and the man who got handed the job of organizing it—was Drew Pearson. The success of the Friendship Train is largely a tribute to the whole-hearted cooperation of newspapers along the routes. Whether or not they were among the dailies and weeklies using Pearson's column, they joined almost unanimously in sparking the food drives in their own communities."

Pearson agreed: "To a large extent it was a newspaper show over here and over there." Actually, the French newspapers in particular helped produce the successful show. France was swept by strikes and unrest when the Friendship Train arrived. However, French newspapers gave much of their precious space to welcoming and explaining the project. Pearson feared the strikes might prevent the food from being distributed, but the newspapers and newsreels communicated the generosity of the American people.

Incidentally, one newspaper stunt was particularly effective. Amon G. Carter, publisher of the Fort Worth, Texas, *Star-Telegram*, held up sixteen carloads of flour from there while he had the bag stamped with messages of friendship from Fort Worth. In Italy the bags were transformed into clothes and towels.

In addition to the journalistic accolades, Pearson received the French Legion of Honor, and he was voted the first decoration to be awarded by the Republic of Italy, the Italian Star of Solidarity. Moreover, the Friendship Train concept spawned other humanitarian endeavors. Governor Earl Warren's milk ship from California to France, Italy, and Greece; the Michigan Friendship Caravan from seventy Junior Chambers of Commerce to France; two Abraham Lincoln Friendship Trains leaving Lincoln, Nebraska, and Springfield, Illinois, for Germany and Austria; the Northwest Friend Ship to Scotland; the North Carolina Friendship clothing drive, and the campaign by New Orleans to adopt Orléans in France.

Pearson treasures a letter he received from a French child: "Dear Friend of America: For us, the children of Dijou, the arrival of the train of Friendship in the capitol is a great event. It shows that, over thousands of kilometers of ocean, a great democratic nation, our ally in wartime, is aware of the difficult situation of our country and takes a generous part to the suffering of the less favored part of the French population."

As he sat on the porch of his farm ("you can spit right into the Potomac," he remarked suddenly, "if you spit one hundred and fifty feet straight down") he squinted at the twilight balancing night and day on the horizon, and said: "I got a tremendous satisfaction out of the Friendship Train because it accomplished something. It was a hell of a satisfaction to see the response in this country and even more abroad." One satisfying response was offered by the French people. As a gesture of gratitude, French citizens launched a "Merci America" train of forty French boxcars that was shipped across the Atlantic, loaded with such gifts as Sèvres vases from the President of France and bronze school bells from Caen. Pearson spent four weeks with the French Gratitude Train, covered most of the country, and helped Frenchmen meet state governors, address state legislatures, and distribute souvenirs.

The Friendship Train expanded Pearson's dimensions. He functioned not only as a reporter and humanitarian, but also as a newsmaker and propagandist. In this case, Drew was a man of ideas and a man of action, who succeeded in putting his ideas into practice. The practical success of his idea resulted in a significant propaganda victory for the United States. One measure of this triumph is the fury directed at Pearson by Communists and their newspapers.

Pearson, nevertheless, was aware that the good grace bestowed on him by the Friendship Train was, unfortunately, to be ephemeral. Shortly after he completed his humanitarian effort in Europe and returned to the United States, he ruefully observed: "I think I'm still in bad with a lot of people. I have a lot of enemies and a few good friends. Right now some people are saying some nice things about me, but it probably won't last long." *

Pearson believes the major accomplishments of the Friendship Train were, first, making Western Europe aware that the United States cared; second, making President Truman realize that the American people were willing to sacrifice. Prior to the train, Truman was hesitant about aid to Europe. However, when Senator Vandenberg arose on the Senate floor to point to the fact that a train crossing the continent clearly demonstrated that the American people were ahead of their government, Truman moved to launch the Marshall Plan with massive aid for the reconstruction of Europe.

* He was right. His foes remained implacable. For example: On the memorial bridge facing the Lincoln Memorial stand a pair of golden horses, contributed by the people of Italy to the people of the United States. The plaque fails to note this gift represented an expression of gratitude for Pearson's Friendship Train. When the horses were presented, Truman was in the White House. Although the Italian Ambassador made it clear the gifts were in recognition of Drew Pearson's efforts, Truman aides went to great pains to withhold this from the public. Pearson was not invited to attend the dedication ceremony.

Y, MARCH 12, 1954.

ARMY CHARGES M'CARTHY AND COHN THREATENED IT IN TRYING TO OBTAIN PREFERRED TREATMENT FOR SCHINE

SENATOR ATTACKS

Hits Back at Stevenson, Murrow and Flanders in Radio Broadcast

Cohn Scored When Woman Denies McCarthy's Charges

Mrs. Moss Counters Accusation as Red While Senators Decry 'Innuendo'—Crowd Applauds Hearing Scene

STEVENS A TARGET

Report Quotes Counsel As Saying Secretary Would Be 'Through'

The text of the Army's report is printed on Page 9A.

By W. H. LAWRENCE

WASHINGTON, March 11—The Army reported today it had been subjected to direct threats by Senator Joseph R. McCarthy and his chief counsel, Roy Cohn.

Continued on Page 10, Column 3

As Pegler Sees It

Reiterates His Charges About Columnist Pearson

By WESTBROOK PEGLER

DREW PEARSON HAS ANNOUNCED in a manner calculated to give his charge the maximum publicity that he is suing me and King Features Syndicate, which distributes my compositions, for libel. He alleges that I libeled him in certain statements published under my name soon after the tragic death of James Forrestal.

Pearson had broadcast the false and defamatory charge that Forrestal, a brave man with a proven record for courage in mortal danger, had run "out of the back door of his house into the alley, leaving his wife to cope with a jewel robbery alone."

As on a past occasion, Pearson put himself in the position of an injured innocent in the preliminary publicity and immediately began private overtures looking toward a settlement which would permit him to dodge the question whether he is or is not a lying blackguard. He is willing to withdraw his present suit if I would apologize and say publicly that he is neither a liar nor a blackguard.

I reiterate that he is both. He complains further that he was injured in his reputation, such as it is, by my revival of a statement published years ago by his ex-mother-in-law, the late Cissie Patterson, of Washington. Her paper alleged that ..., as a Quaker, had "thee'd and thou'd" his way out ... First World War.

... not know whether he did "thee and thou" his way ... that war. Pearson did spend a brief time legally ... rms as a member of the Student Army Training ... For all I know to the contrary he satisfied the re... ts. I affirm that Mrs. Patterson did publish the ... t I repeated and that Pearson let it pass without ... in court.

... IS THE SECOND TIME Pearson has sued me. In ... cases it is the usual practice of defense counsel to ... e defendant to drop the subject until the suit is dis... lest the plaintiff be given ground to charge that ... er publications prove malice. In the present case, ... neys agree with my belief that Pearson brought ... to muzzle me. Therefore, I am disregarding the ... rse.

... e first case, Pearson soon came crawling and the ... was withdrawn by Pearson and his co-plaintiff,

WESTBROOK PEGLER

RIL 23, 1954. FIVE CENTS

EVENS SWEARS M'CARTHY FALSIFIED, YS 'PERVERSION OF POWER' TO HIM; NATOR IMPUGNS GENERAL'S MOTIVES

HEARING IS STORMY

Gen. Reber Asserts Cohn ...

ncipal Witnesses at the McCarthy-Army Inquiry

Secretary Robert T. Stevens

Maj. Gen. Miles ...

URE E. D. C. TIE ... TED AT BY TITO

273 Housing Units ... By U. S. Because of ...

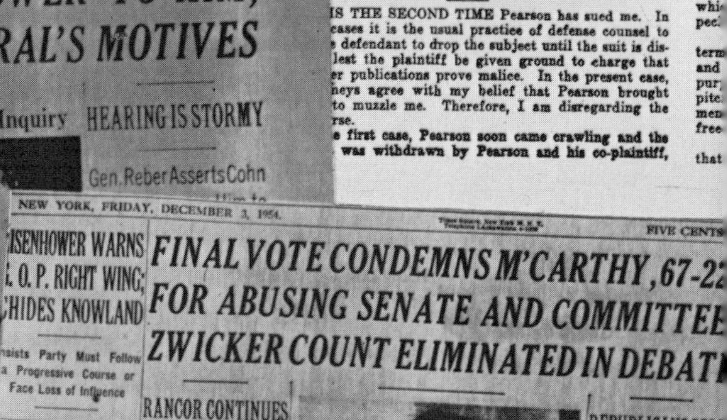

NEW YORK, FRIDAY, DECEMBER 3, 1954. FIVE CENTS

FINAL VOTE CONDEMNS M'CARTHY, 67-22, FOR ABUSING SENATE AND COMMITTEE; ZWICKER COUNT ELIMINATED IN DEBATE

EISENHOWER WARNS G. O. P. RIGHT WING; CHIDES KNOWLAND

Insists Party Must Follow a Progressive Course or Face Loss of Influence

Transcript and summary of the news conference, Page 18.

By WILLIAM S. WHITE

RANCOR CONTINUES

Welker Refuses to Let Flanders Apology Go Into the Record

By JAMES RESTON

REPUBLICANS SPLIT

Democrats Act Solidly in Support of Motion Against Senator

By ANTHONY LEVIERO

CONDEMNED ON TWO COUNTS: Senator McCarthy as he left the Senate floor last night after members adopted a resolution condemning his conduct. The vote was 67-22.

PRESIDENT ALERTS MAYORS ON ATTACK

Cities Are Front-Line Targets, He Warns—Asks Teamwork

SENATORS CLEARED ON M'CARTHY MAIL

Inquiry Indicates Request for Check Was Handled by ...

7

BETWEEN DARKNESS AND LIGHT

Joe McCarthy personified the classic case of a man in a hurry. The end justified the means, and there was never a pause at the crossroads. After graduating from Marquette University, he bulled his way to a Wisconsin Circuit Judgeship and became known for his instant divorces, turning them out in five minutes or less. It gave him a reputation for eccentricity, but also offered him the attention he desperately desired. McCarthy was a World War II Marine and later described himself dramatically as "tail-gunner Joe." Actually, he had been a desk pilot. After being elected to the Senate in 1946, his craving for adulation amounted to addiction. On one occasion he generated a certain amount of negative interest by defending the Nazis on trial for the murders of Malmédy.

During his early years in the Senate—and numerous Washington bars—McCarthy made no secret of his opportunism. He was constantly buttonholing friends and asking for publicity-inciting gimmicks. Naturally, he sought to cultivate newspapermen. One of his friends was Jack Anderson, Drew Pearson's associate. Now and again, McCarthy and Anderson double-dated. His friendship with reporters gave him a valuable working knowledge of the journalistic profession. He often confided to newspapermen his desire to electrify the nation in some manner. Journalists reacted to McCarthy's ambitions with a shrug or a chuckle. They generally considered him as an amiable mediocrity who would pass from the Washington scene without creating more than a ripple.

In the beginning, McCarthyism was nothing more than the usual political opportunism. One year before Senator McCarthy discovered Communism, he confessed to reporters that the future for him appeared dark. He was uncertain about his chances for re-election. And even more meaningful for McCarthy, he was relatively unknown. Time and again he urged friends for suggestions to create a vote-catching image. One friend advised him to support the St. Lawrence Seaway project, which would enhance the Great Lakes and invite new business to his home state of Wisconsin. It was also suggested that he concentrate on closer industrial cooperation between neighboring Canada and the Great Lakes states. Eventually, the anti-Communist crusade was suggested.

Pearson later reported: "The man who urged the anti-Communist campaign was Father Edmund A. Walsh of Georgetown University. Father Walsh is not happy at the outcome, while Republican leaders are getting unhappier by the minute at the antics of the junior Senator from Wisconsin."

The foregoing appeared in the March 14, 1950, Pearson column. Although the columnist was in the forefront of the McCarthy debunkers, in disclosing the origins of the witch-hunt, Pearson described him as "the likeable young Senator McCarthy of Wisconsin." At that point in the McCarthy career, it would have taken 20-20 foresight to predict his emergence as a major menace. The Washington press considered him a minor nuisance—at first.

The sting of the McCarthy saga is that so many Americans—and so many politicians and newspapermen—entered into a conspiracy to conceal a melancholy truth: They were motivated by fear and they were in servitude to a demagogue as dogs are to men. From the President of the United States to the file clerk in the Bureau of Census, all made obeisance to the terror. Only a few originally found the courage to oppose it. One was Drew Pearson. His allies were pitifully few in number. Among Washington journalists, the pioneer battlers against McCarthy, in addition to Pearson, were Columnist Joe Alsop, the Washington *Post* and its gifted cartoonist Herblock (who coined the word "McCarthyism"), plus Washington correspondent Richard H. Rovere, who was quick to note that McCarthy "was in many ways the most gifted demagogue ever bred on these shores. No bolder seditionist ever moved among us—nor any politician with a surer, swifter access to the dark places of the American mind."

The editorial pages of *The New York Times,* the New York *Herald Tribune,* and several other papers joined the small band of anti-McCarthy Washington journalists. They represented a small but gallant brigade. At a time when Senator McCarthy was pitting one American against another and spreading fright in almost every field of endeavor from politics to show business, this journalistic group stood up and fought. If they had done nothing else, their defiance of McCarthyism would have entitled them to a place of honor in journalistic annals.

Ironically, McCarthyism took shape in the most serene atmosphere. In February 1950, McCarthy was scheduled to appear before the Ohio County Women's Republican Club of Wheeling, West Virginia. His topic was announced in advance: "Communists in Government." The ladies undoubtedly expected the customary anti-Democratic breast-beating oratory that comes upon Republicans near Lincoln's Birthday.

But what McCarthy told the unsuspecting ladies forever jolted him from relative obscurity. At the Hotel McLure in Wheeling, the ladies listened to Senator McCarthy voicing political sounds, words that never get beyond the ears, like radio or television commercials. But midway in his speech, McCarthy suddenly startled them with a gesture that was to become part of his act. He held up a sheet of paper and paused for dramatic emphasis, "I have here in my hand," he announced, "a list of two hundred and five, a list of names that were made known to the Secretary of State as being members of the Communist Party and who nevertheless are still working and shaping policy in the State Department." His announcement inspired twittering among the assembled ladies. The following evening during a radio interview, McCarthy's number had dropped to "fifty-seven card-carrying Communists."

Although McCarthy's Wheeling diatribe had caused little stir in the nation's press, Washington's officialdom was stunned and fearful. Secretary of State Dean Acheson conferred with the Democratic majority in the Senate. The result was a demand that McCarthy document his charges. The spotlight was intensified. The junior Senator from Wisconsin moved to center stage.

Thus on February 20 he gave his performance. He leaped out of his Senate seat and proceeded to thunder for six hours.

In a half-dozen hours he began to chip away 174 years of freedom. He started by proclaiming he had shattered "Truman's iron curtain of secrecy," and then launched into a lengthy discussion of eighty-one security risk cases which, he conceded, had been investigated by the State Department Security Office.

He then added: "I must say that I know that some of these individuals whose cases I am giving the Senate are no longer in the State Department. A sizable number of them are not. But there is sufficient information in the files to show that there is something radically wrong. Since neither Truman nor Acheson was prepared to do anything about it, I thought the only thing to do was what I have done, namely to let the people of the country know what is going on, and then hope that the pressure of public opinion would be great enough to force the President to clean house."

Thus the era of McCarthyism began. It was followed by a Pearson column that was destined to become an almost reflex action. When McCarthy attacked, Pearson debunked. On February 28, 1950, he reported: "You have to have a card-index system these days to keep up with the accusations of certain Congressmen regarding Communists in the Federal Government. Unfortunately the average citizen doesn't have time to keep a card index, so he gets confused over harum-scarum Senator Joe McCarthy's recent accusation that there were 57 card-carrying Communists in the State Department. When the Senator from Wisconsin finally was pinned down, he could produce not 57, but only three names of State Department officials whom he claimed were Communists."

The three names were Dr. Harlow Shapley, Gustave Duran, and Mrs. Mary Keeney. Pearson checked McCarthy's accusations and discovered that Dr. Shapley had never worked for the State Department. As for Gustave Duran and Mrs. Mary Keeney, they had resigned from the State Department four years before McCarthy made his charges. Further digging by Pearson disclosed that McCarthy's charges were old hat. Three years before McCarthy leveled his blast, Congressman Bartel Jonkman of Michigan made similar charges against Keeney and Duran.

In countering McCarthyism, Drew Pearson made the point that "McCarthy's witch-hunt for Communists inside the State Department has disrupted our entire foreign service at a time when our foreign relations are more delicately balanced than ever." Columnist Joe Alsop later buttressed Pearson's comment when he wrote: "It was McCarthy's great service to the Kremlin, of course, that he was able to direct so great a share of the nation's attention and emotional drive away from the danger to national survival inherent in the Kremlin's growing power."

Meanwhile, Pearson continued to expose McCarthy while McCarthy was allegedly exposing Reds. In 1943 when Wisconsin claimed he failed to disclose an income of $42,000, McCarthy explained he made money speculating in stocks while he was overseas and not a citizen of Wisconsin; hence he refused to pay the State income tax. Pearson went on to report that McCarthy still held office as a State Judge at the time he claimed he was not a citizen of Wisconsin. In the end, tax authorities accepted a compromise payment. In 1944, McCarthy was defeated by Senator Alexander Wiley in the primaries and received total campaign contributions from his father, brother, and brother-in-law of $18,000. When the campaign was over, it was discovered that McCarthy's father lacked enough income to file a tax return, while neither the brother nor brother-in-law reported an income of more than $2,000. The source of the $18,000 campaign contribution was never explained. Moreover, during his 1946 campaign against Senator Bob La Follette, McCarthy not only failed to resign from the bench, but swapped circuits with other judges in various parts of Wisconsin, with the result that the Board of Bar Commissioners recommended to the Wisconsin Supreme Court that he be disbarred. The Wisconsin Supreme Court stated that the Senator had violated the State constitution and the Code of Ethics of the American Bar Associations, yet failed to disbar him.

Because of Pearson's reporting, a special subcommittee under the chairmanship of Senator Tydings launched a comprehensive probe of the charges. The committee sat for four months, amassed

2,500 pages of testimony and documentation, gave witness McCarthy all the time he desired. In the end, the Democratic majority on the Tydings Committee cleared both the State Department and the individuals involved. The report stated in part: "Starting with nothing, Senator McCarthy plunged headlong forward, desperately seeking to develop some information which, colored with distortion and fanned by the blaze of bias would forestall the day of reckoning. . . . There is not one member of the Communist party or of a "spy ring" employed in the State Department known to the Secretary of State or other responsible officials of that department."

The Democratic majority concluded that the charges were "a fraud and a hoax perpetrated on the Senate of the United States and the American people. They represent perhaps the most nefarious campaign of half-truths and untruth in the history of the Republic."

The slapdown by a Senate committee failed to discourage McCarthy. On the contrary, it was like a red flag to the bull in him. His rampage was intensified. He ranted that the Tydings Report was "a green light for the Reds." Concurrently, the onset of the Korean War heightened passions and made Americans increasingly sensitive to problems of internal security. Seizing the bullwhip, the junior Senator from Wisconsin stampeded Washington. Joe McCarthy went on a headline binge.

His successful headline hunting was immeasurably aided by his Republican allies. Senator Jenner, for example, denounced Tydings for conducting the "most scandalous and brazen whitewash of treasonable conspiracy in our history. . . . The crowd of master conspirators in the State Department had not only sold out China, but now they were undermining Korea. The sad thing about it is that those who are being pushed now in Korea are the sons and mothers of America."

Senator Jenner's vituperative attacks dominated the headlines in the Hearst press, the Chicago *Tribune,* the Washington *Times-Herald,* and, sad to relate, most of the American press. Further, McCarthy received a major assist from the most respected Republican leader of the era, Senator Robert A. Taft. Several Washington correspondents quoted Taft as saying: "McCarthy should keep on talking, and if one case doesn't work out he should proceed to another." Taft contended he had been misquoted and explained: "Truman had the bad judgment to assume the innocence of the persons mentioned in the State Department. Whether Senator McCarthy has legal evidence, whether he has overstated or understated his case, is of lesser importance. The question is whether influence in the State Department still exists."

One Washington correspondent described the mood of the Senate: "It is something to remember. No one who sees this show will ever underestimate young Mr. McCarthy again. He is the most formidable figure to hit the Senate, we think, since Huey Long. He has the galleries with him. The Republicans around him beam. Taft and Bridges exchange enthusiastic smiles as he sidesteps hostile questions again and again. . . . It would seem easy to pin down the preposterous utterances, but no; McCarthy is as hard to catch as a mist—a mist that carries lethal contagion."

The *Times* of London described the McCarthy hysteria as "a revolt of the primitives against the intelligent in the complexities of foreign affairs."

The Washington *Post* published sixty-two editorials on the subject of McCarthyism before, during, and after the Tydings investigation. They were unanimously critical of Senator McCarthy's motives, methods, and objectives. The *Post,* noting the changing numbers in McCarthy's list of Reds, editorially stated that "rarely has a man in public life crawled and squirmed so abjectly." The paper maintained McCarthy's animus was focused on "those persons who had intelligence and understanding in reporting on the China situation. Their sin, in his view, it would seem, was that they were prematurely right about a foregone conclusion." The *Post* prodded the Tydings Committee to "expose Senator McCarthy without exposing innocent persons whom he has tried to victimize." Later, the editorialist warned: "The State Department has answered McCarthy's charges. It's about time. For the McCarthy attempts to make the department a pariah could easily result both in the paralysis of foreign policy and an establishment manned by timid second raters." The *Post* approved the report issued by Tydings and the Democratic majority. The paper contended the witnesses called at McCarthy's behest failed to reveal "the presence in the State Department of a single employee who could reasonably be called a Communist, or an agent of the Soviet Union, or even a security risk."

The other side of the journalistic coin was the Washington *Times-Herald*. Before McCarthyism appeared, the paper was first with the most exposés of alleged Communists in the government. After the Tydings Committee was formed, the paper editorially commented that "everybody knows good and well that Communists have done this country terrible damage and that they have got in some of their most tremendous blows in the State Department." Later the editorial page contended that "the known failures of high officials of the State Department in dealing with subversion, pinkers, and Communist agents have destroyed public confidence in this important branch of government. . . . The Communists who are and have been wrecking American foreign policy from within the State Department. Communists are still where they always were, and the disaster to the United States is obvious to every man, woman, and child."

The Washington *Post* anti-McCarthy editorials and the Washington *Times-Herald* pro-McCarthy editorials were closely matched numerically. After the Tydings Committee completed its probe and issued its report, the *Times-Herald* devoted a full-page editorial to an ugly attack against the New Deal, the Truman Administration, and the Democratic Senators on the committee. "The report," it editorially remonstrated, "was a whitewash that nobody believes." Several days later, it stated that "the committee did not do its job, which was "to find out who is or has been doing Stalin's work in the State Department."

This was the journalistic pattern that remained rigid in Washington during the McCarthy Era. Outside of the capital, three papers maintained a continual barrage against McCarthyism. They were the New York *Post,* the Milwaukee *Journal,* and the St. Louis *Post-Dispatch*. As was to be expected, McCarthy frequently accused these papers of distorting news about his activities.

McCarthy's handful of journalistic critics, at first, were no match for the incessant page-one uproar he provoked. It must be conceded he had an evil genius for manipulating the press. As Cabell Phillips, *The New York Times* Washington correspondent, accurately reported: "McCarthy used the press as assiduously as he used the Senate in his campaign. He was always available to reporters; when they didn't seek him out, he would seek them out, often summoning them out of the press gallery with a meaningful wink and a nod of the head. He knew about deadline and edition times, and how to blanket an unfavorable story with one that served his purpose. He would throw a heavy arm about a favorite reporter's shoulder while walking down a Senate corridor, or would take him to his office for a drink and give him a tip on the next 'exposé.' What many reporters suspected then was later proved to be true—namely, that McCarthy had laid pipelines into State and other government departments."

The author had first-hand knowledge of strategically placed malcontents in the bureaucracy who were acting as spies for McCarthy, feeding him material from security files and confidential documents. In turn, McCarthy fed the "scoops" to favored reporters and columnists. One national columnist was phoned several times a day by McCarthy or by one of his associates and given "inside" news. In effect, he had his own news service, and it helped him create a wide network of journalistic allies.

McCarthy's successful news management goaded Secretary of State Acheson into a scathing comment before a meeting of the American Society of Newspaper Editors: "Senator McCarthy has continued to assault the State Department. Now I don't ask for your sympathy. I don't ask you for your help. You are in a worse situation than I am. I and my associates are only the intended victim of this mad and vicious aberration. But you, unhappily—you by reason of your calling—are participants. You are unwilling participants, but nevertheless participants. And your position is far more serious than mine."

Secretary Acheson's finger-pointing was a disturbing reminder for Washington correspondents and editors. He was pointing in the right direction. The overwhelming majority of reporters and editors were aware of McCarthy's lies, but they published the falsehoods in the name of journalistic "objectivity" and in the contention that lies or not, McCarthy's charges were "news." During the height of

McCarthy's attacks, Glenn Neville, managing editor of the New York *Daily Mirror*, was asked why his paper published McCarthy's lies. He replied: "Sometimes lies and half-lies will smoke out the truth. McCarthy isn't all wrong. There are lots of damn Reds in the government. Communists are gangsters. You can't fight them according to the rules. You try to hurt them even if it means hitting below the belt. Besides, McCarthy helps sell newspapers. Every editor knows that. It's part of the game."

On the other hand, columnist William S. White observed: "Objectivity is sometimes taken to mean only a careful—indeed, a meticulous—measuring out of absolutely even-handed credit and blame to this man against that, or this movement against another. The theory seems to be that all's fair—and nobody has been impermissibly subjective—so long as everybody and everything comes out even in the end. This has sometimes put a curious veil over great and harsh issues."

Later, the theme was analyzed by correspondent James Reston of *The New York Times*: "The news agency is especially vulnerable to the cult of objectivity, which has done so much in the last generation to confuse 'news' with truth. Since it serves newspapers of varying political opinions, the agency is not so vulnerable to the old sin of slanting the news. A Republican or a Democratic paper can print all the news that fits its political bias and ignore or cut and hide all the news that doesn't, but not a news agency filing to both Republican and Democratic, isolationist or internationalist papers. The news agency led the way in what was called 'objective reporting,' which for a long time has come to mean that 'news' was anything any big shot said. If Senator McCarthy said that there were over one hundred card-carrying Communists in the State Department, out it would go on the wires regardless of whether or not what the Senator said was true. And the newspapers not only published and repeated endlessly rubbish of this kind, but fell into the same habit of following the technique themselves, all in the name of 'objectivity.' "

Week after week the "objective" journalists and McCarthy's newspaper allies amplified the Senator's power. As his influence expanded, McCarthy became more viciously arrogant and punitive. One of his first victims was Senator Tydings. With the aid of a composite photograph that gave the impression that Tydings and Earl Browder, the former chief of the Communist Party in America, were working partners, the Maryland electorate defeated Tydings. "I have been vindicated," McCarthy gleefully informed reporters after Tydings' defeat.

Shortly thereafter, McCarthy damned General George C. Marshall as "an instrument of the Soviet conspiracy" and charged Adlai Stevenson "would continue the suicidal Kremlin-shaped policies of the nation." But his primary journalistic target was Drew Pearson, and for good reason. The Pearson column kept hammering away at McCarthy.

McCarthy soon retaliated. On December 15, 1950, he excoriated Pearson for more than an hour on the floor of the Senate. In part, he rasped: "Only a man as diabolically clever as Pearson could continue to maintain his huge reading and listening audience after being so completely and thoroughly labeled an unprincipled liar and fake. . . . The head of any of our intelligence agencies would testify that one of the principal aims of the Communist Party is to gain control of our lines of communication; that is, newspapers, television, motion pictures, and so forth. It, of course, would be a miracle if they had not recognized in Pearson the ideal for them . . . an unprincipled, degenerate liar—but with a tremendous audience both in the newspapers and on the airwaves—a man who has been able to sugarcoat his wares so well that he has been able to fool vast numbers of people with his fake piety and false loyalty."

Ironically, only a few months before McCarthy sought to smear Pearson, a Russian magazine published a lengthy attack against the columnist. Among other things, the Communist periodical called Pearson "the chained dog of monopolists of Wall Street." Actually, the same week McCarthy roughed up Pearson, the Communist *Daily Worker* in New York carried several anti-Pearson editorials. The Soviet's official wind machine, *Pravda*, had charged "the Pearson news cocktail is a mixture of one or two facts with a dose of anti-Soviet lying."

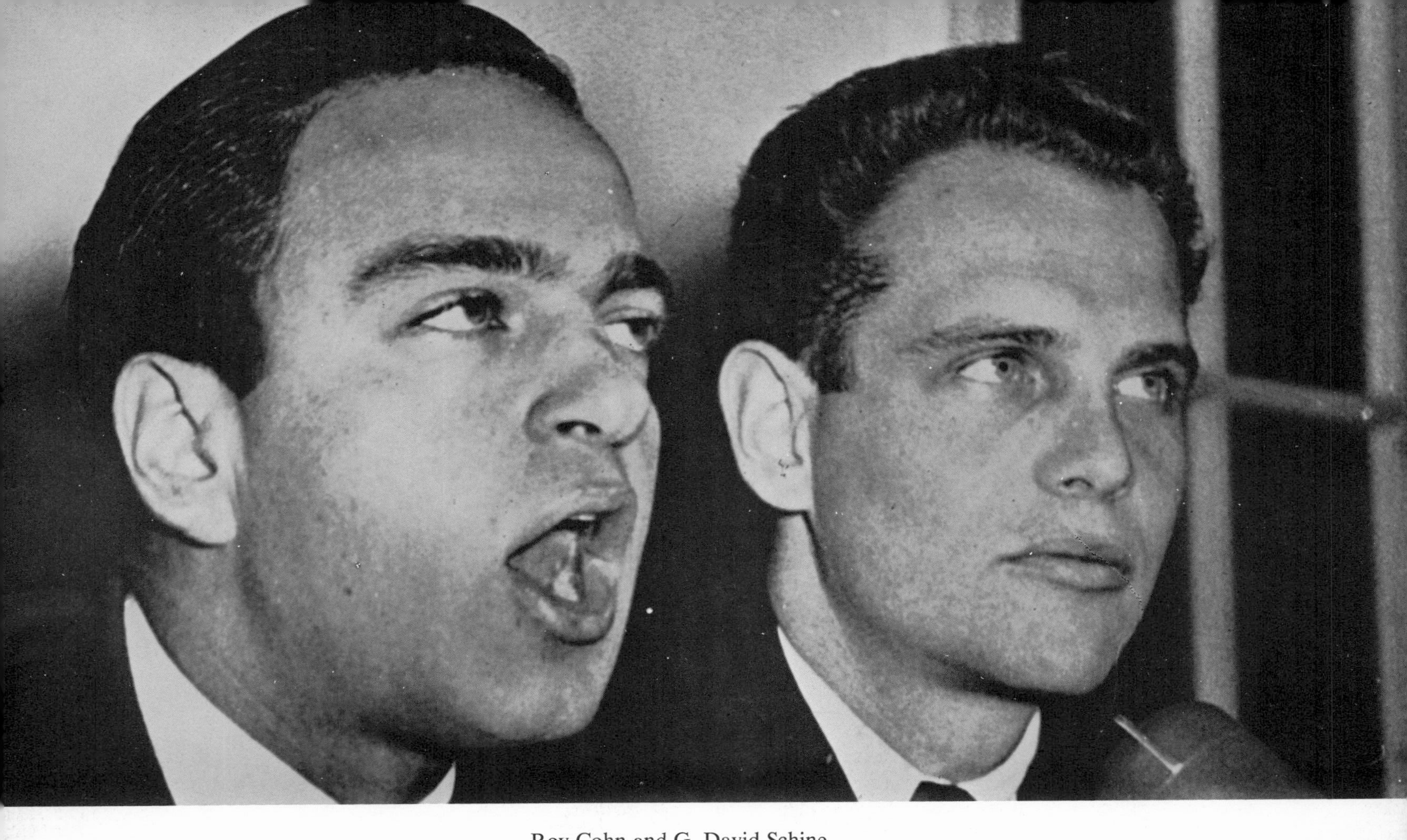

Roy Cohn and G. David Schine.

Senator Joe McCarthy reaches for a headline.

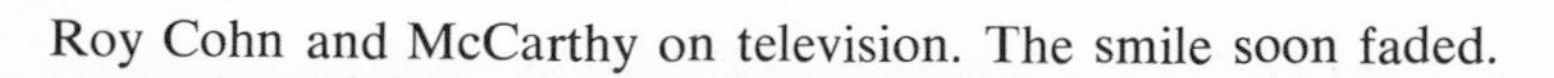

Roy Cohn and McCarthy on television. The smile soon faded.

While McCarthy told the Senate that "Pearson's job was to lead the character assassination of any man who was a threat to international Communism," *Universul*, the Communist Party organ in Bucharest, wrote in June 1950: "The international organization of journalists has expelled all journalists who have compromised themselves by carrying on racial and war propaganda. Drew Pearson, the zealous agent of Wall Street monopolies, is included in this role of infamy."

Long before McCarthyism's weedy growth, Pearson had exposed the Communist spy ring in Canada in February 1946 and had revealed the existence of a Soviet espionage laboratory in a Maryland basement where blueprints of the B-29 were copied.

Although McCarthy's blows had some damaging effects, Pearson fought back effectively. Drew reported that McCarthy was so fearful of being sued for libel because of his charges against Owen Lattimore that the Wisconsin Senator had conferred with experts to make sure he would not suffer financial loss. Several weeks later, Pearson suggested that a special lobbying committee find the answers to the following questions:

> Who pays for Senator McCarthy's secret headquarters in Room 316 in the Congressional Hotel?
>
> Who paid for two hundred long-distance calls from that room?
>
> Who paid four ex-FBI agents who worked for McCarthy and then quit in disgust?

When McCarthy publicly announced that he had the name of "Russia's top espionage agent in the United States," Pearson ruined his sleight-of-words trick by revealing the name McCarthy had was Owen Lattimore. When McCarthy said this top espionage agent had brought "three Communist agents" into this country, Pearson announced that the three men were the "living Buddha" and two Mongolian princes, all with Communist prices on their heads. Pearson further said that Lattimore brought them here so that they could plan resistance to Communists in their native lands.

While concentrating on his high-level attacks on McCarthy, Pearson could not resist peppering him with wry items calculated to embarrass public figures. He wrote: "Senator McCarthy's outcry against sex unfortunates in the State Department is about to backfire against him. While he has been calling the roll on these persons, he has overlooked a member of his own staff who is on the Washington police department secret list. When this man offered to resign after he was arrested by police, believe it or not, McCarthy wouldn't let him, but kept him on the payroll for another three months."

Pearson maintained continual pressure against McCarthy, since the Senator's attacks were relentless. One aspect of McCarthyism's ugliness was the implication that silence was evidence of guilt. And he who testified to someone else's innocence was himself suspected. As a result, the most patriotic of Americans were compelled to intensify and dramatize their patriotism, lest their criticism of McCarthy create the impression they were soft on Communism.

Almost daily, McCarthy employed his immunity from libel to hammer Pearson as a Communist, or a friend of Communists, or a friend of a friend of Communists. Although Pearson retaliated, McCarthy gained several shabby triumphs. In the most unprecedented Senatorial abuse in American history, McCarthy called for a boycott against all newspapers carrying the Pearson column as well as his radio sponsor. At that time, Pearson's sponsor was Adams hats. In the weird melodrama of the McCarthy Era, McCarthy thus brought a hint of subversion to wearing a certain hat. McCarthy's assault against Pearson's sponsor appears ludicrous, yet the sponsor eventually succumbed to the pressure. In addition, McCarthy reprinted, at taxpayers' expense, many of the speeches attacking Pearson; he mailed them, again at taxpayers' expense, to almost two thousand newspapers as part of his campaign to bludgeon editors into dropping Pearson's column. Furthermore, copies of McCarthy's speeches were put in the hands of rival syndicate salesmen for discreet use in efforts to sell rival columns.

While Pearson was McCarthy's major journalistic target, the Senator took on others who were critical of his activities. He smeared newscaster Elmer Davis and subjected New York *Post* editor James Wechsler to an inquisition. Such was the mood of the times that publishers feared issuing books that might alienate

McCarthy. Pearson's associate, Jack Anderson, coauthored a book titled *McCarthy, the Man, the Senator and the Ism*. It was published by Beacon Press, a publishing house affiliated with the Unitarian Church, after other houses had turned down the book. Its publication led to veiled threats and intimidation.

Pearson concedes that "there were some painful and humiliating incidents during the fight with McCarthy." He pauses and adds: "I was able to defend myself. Most of my editors stuck by me loyally, and though I did lose my radio sponsor, a lot of other radio stations and sponsors came to my support."

As the weeks and months passed in the twilight of the Truman Administration, McCarthy's victims piled up. Time and again, Drew cited the tragic casualties in his prolonged campaign to jolt the nation out of the McCarthy grip, which, for a time, amounted to a stranglehold. For example, Pearson cited the case of Val Lorwin, a State Department labor adviser. McCarthy drenched him with red. Lorwin was indicted for perjury when he denied he was a Communist. For the next four years, Val Lorwin lived under a cloud: He was unable to clear his name and unable to earn a living. Lorwin managed to exist thanks to the generosity of friends who loaned him money. Eventually—four years after the indictment—the Justice Department went into court and asked that the case be dismissed. There was no evidence on which to base a prosecution. Pearson spoke to Lorwin afterward. He was too shocked to be bitter. He had been through four years of terror, detained in an invisible concentration camp.

Another McCarthy target had been Abraham Crasnow. After twenty years of service in the Navy Department, he was suspended. No charge was placed against him. For one whole year he was unable to learn the cause of the suspension. Finally, Pearson and several Washington newspapers took up his case, and the Navy belatedly restored Crasnow with a formal and public apology.

A touch of violence was added to the Pearson-McCarthy animosity in December 1950. Senator McCarthy was a guest at Washington's posh Sulgrave Club. Evidently fortified with some of the harsher beverages, the Senator spotted Drew Pearson in the men's cloakroom. What followed was a brief bit of mayhem. The versions offered by witnesses varied: Some said the Senator kicked Drew, others insisted the Senator punched him, and a few contended he scratched him. The half-minute violence was quickly ended by then-Senator Richard Nixon.

The newspapers had a field day with the incident. Conflicting descriptions were reported in detail. The brawl drew headlines in several European papers. According to Senator McCarthy: "Pearson said to me, 'McCarthy, if you talk about personal things regarding me on the Senate floor, I'll get you.' So I slapped him on the face, slapped him hard."

Witnesses have since confirmed Pearson's statement that "the Senator kicked me twice in the groin." The suddenness of the attack, the flurry of excitement, and the consequent public commotion, he describes as "one of the most humiliating experiences of my life." Pearson's foes were quite overjoyed. President Truman, who loathed Drew at that time, was gleeful. The incident gave him a big laugh, but Truman later discovered that McCarthy was no laughing matter. Two years later, Truman wrote: "It is one of the tragedies of our time that the security program of the United States has been wickedly used by demagogues and sensational newspapers in an attempt to frighten and mislead the American people."

The fact is that Truman actively sought to impede the spread of McCarthyism early in 1950. He organized a special task force to supply Congressmen and the press with rebuttals to McCarthy's charges. And he used press conferences and speeches to rebuke McCarthy. Unfortunately, the facts never caught up with the falsehoods. As one newspaperman observed during that period: "McCarthy's lies travel halfway around the world while the truth is getting its pants on."

Another anti-Pearsonite, Utah's Senator Watkins, met McCarthy the next day. Watkins remarked: "Joe, the newspapers differ as to where you hit him, but I hope both accounts were right."

In time, the depth and dimension of McCarthyism expanded and deepened. Early in the spring of 1953, Senator McCarthy was riding a dragon and few had the courage to defy him. His fellow Senators, for example, were terrified at the thought that he might invade their areas, pull out a paper, describe them or their associates as Communists, and thus imperil their re-election. There were several Senators who refused to succumb to the terror. A notable exception was Connecticut's Senator William Benton, who drew up a twelve-point indictment accusing McCarthy of unethical and dishonest conduct. McCarthy never answered the charges, but he bombarded the Senate Election Committee investigating him with fiery epithets.

He charged that the committee was engaged in an effort to "discredit and destroy any man who fights Communist subversion," suggested that "several United States Senators have Communists on their staffs," and set his own staff loose on the trail of one of the investigating Senators. McCarthy also challenged Benton to repeat his charges without Senate immunity, which Benton did. McCarthy sued, but later dropped his libel suit.

In retrospect, it is difficult to accept the twisted power of the McCarthy Era. Within a few years it came close to dominating a nation. In the spring of 1954 the Gallup Poll reported that less than 30 percent of the country's adults disapproved of the Wisconsin Senator's tactics.

McCarthyism reduced some very brave men to silence. John F. Kennedy, then the junior Senator from Massachusetts, was vigorously outspoken on many sensitive issues. But he remained mum on McCarthy, never referring publicly to the stormy activities of his colleague. Of course, Robert Kennedy was a member of McCarthy's committee.

Another man who sought to appease McCarthy was President Eisenhower. In an effort to take some of the thunder from McCarthy's blasts, the White House announced on October 23, 1953, that 1,456 government employees had been dismissed or had resigned under Eisenhower's security program. The Administration played the numbers game too. Within a few months it raised the figure to 2,200, then 6,926, and finally offered a statistical blockbuster with the figure of 9,600. Newspapermen requested names and the explanations for the firings and resignations. Were they native Reds? Communist spies? Fellow travelers? The White House and State Department failed to enlighten them. The State Department announced 306 employees had been released for security reasons. Later, State Department officials informed the House Appropriations Subcommittee that only eleven had been dropped for loyalty reasons, and no active Communist had been detected.

The entire security program was criticized by Pearson, Joseph and Stewart Alsop, Richard Rovere, and several other Washington reporters. The Alsops denounced it as "security-firing fakery" and asserted: "The privately admitted purpose of these 'security firings' has been to grab the Commie issue away from Senator McCarthy."

The White House countered by complaining that the press was "building up McCarthy." The Alsops responded: "Senator Joseph McCarthy was still continuously increasing his political power, by the rather simple system of continuously forcing the Administration into new appeasements and humiliations. The White House was angrily complaining that the press 'was building up McCarthy'—which was nonsense, for the simple reason that any man is news who can regularly blackmail the President of the United States. Meanwhile, it also seemed to be the policy to make McCarthyism respectable by proving that the American government could be quite as unscrupulous as the celebrated Senator from Wisconsin. This was the first exposé of the sleazy 'numbers racket,' uncovered by the younger member of our partnership. It was published, remember, at a time when the Bricker amendment to forbid the United States from having any foreign policy very nearly passed the Senate. Such was the contemporary atmosphere."

As was to be expected, the Eisenhower appeasement of McCarthyism failed. On November 24, 1953, McCarthy said that "Eisenhower was doing more than Truman in ousting security risks, but there were many cases ignored by the White House." In addition, McCarthy denounced the Administration's foreign policy and charged that while we had a mutual assistance pact with Britain, the British traded with Communist China. Secretary of State Dulles replied to McCarthy, but Eisenhower remained silent. He simply told the press that "to coerce our Allies would be the mark of an imperialist rather than a leader."

McCarthy's fervent supporter in his attack against Eisenhower's foreign policy was Westbrook Pegler, one of the more colorful columnists of the period. Inevitably, Pegler's defense of McCarthy resulted in a clash with the Senator's major journalistic opponent—

Drew Pearson. In attacking Pearson, Westbrook Pegler pulled all the stops. He came raging out of the cave to cry damnation. As the Devil's angriest man, a prophet of wrath, he screamed "false reporter" and "smearer" at Pearson. Not many masters of invective have surpassed the vigor of Pegler's epithets.

Pearson eventually filed a token $25,000 libel suit. He later withdrew his suit after an exchange of letters. In a long letter to Pearson, Westbrook Pegler pleaded "for bygones to be bygones." He concluded: "My feelings were hurt, too, but time is a pretty good healer and they are all right again. Now, if yours are cured, how about a drink?" Pearson's full reply was brief and cool: "Dear Peg: I appreciate the spirit of your letter and agree that columnists have more important battles to fight than among themselves. I am therefore asking my attorney to withdraw the suit. This will be a good way to start the new year."

However, as the McCarthy controversy spiraled, Pegler was unable to accept the truce. As some men are driven by conscience, Pegler was dominated by his spleen. He not only sought to mutilate Pearson as a man and a newspaperman, he also abused his friends and associates. His malice sometimes verged on parody. Any individual criticized or exposed by Pearson was publicly embraced by Pegler. Thus he became McCarthy's working ally. He joined McCarthy in launching an assault against Pearson's economic lines. His radio sponsor felt the sting. In a way, it was a Kafkaesque nightmare—blind alleys and phantom charges electrified the atmosphere. Pegler was joined in his anti-Pearson diatribes by newscaster Fulton Lewis, Jr. Among other things, Pegler accused Pearson of being responsible for the suicide of Defense Secretary James Forrestal. He lashed Pearson with the guilt again and again.

Inevitably, the hate mail flooded into Pearson's office. Typical was the following:

> Mr. Drew Pearson: The people of the United States understand you very well. They are kept well informed by a real American, Westbrook Pegler.
>
> It ill behooves a smear artist of your type to question the accuracy of Senator McCarthy's allegations about the slimy

> Communist rats in the State Department. Senator McCarthy is a real man and a patriot in every sense of the word.
>
> Thank the Lord also that we have some patriots like Westbrook Pegler who can place you in the corner where you belong with the rest of the slimy rats.
>
> You were not fooling anyone when you ended your broadcast over WXYZ Sunday evening, November 4, with your fake plea for the preservation of democracy and private enterprise in the United States. Most Americans know where their sympathies are, including many to whom I talk each day.
>
> The general consensus of opinion is that there is no room in the United States for traitors to our country. . . .

It was signed "America, first, last and always."

The truth is that Pegler's untamed attempt to pin the Forrestal tragedy on Pearson represented an ironic absurdity. When FDR was ailing en route from Yalta, Pegler cruelly described him as "a feeble Fuehrer with one foot in the grave." After Roosevelt died, his column coldly noted, "Some Democrats say it is a terrible thing to say such things about a crook because the crook is dead."

Pegler intensified his gin-mill abuse as he swaggered and roared from column to column. Drew retaliated with legal action. This time it was far from a token libel suit. Pearson's professional life was at stake. He sued for a quarter-million dollars and syndicated his libel suit. Individual suits were directed against many of the newspapers that published Pegler.

The syndicated libel suit helped disenchant the Hearst brass with their bad boy. More and more, Hearst editors deleted entire Pegler columns. "I'm writing for the wastebasket," Pegler roared. Later, the Hearst chiefs made a private peace settlement with Pearson. They agreed to imprison Pegler's fury. In addition, Hearst papers in Baltimore, Milwaukee, San Antonio, and Albany began publishing the Pearson column. To add injury to the insulter, on some papers Pegler was dropped and replaced by Pearson.

Pegler's furious descent into oblivion was accelerated by his losing struggle with Pearson. As far as Drew was concerned, it was a policing job that had to be finished. It had been an unpleasant and infuriating ordeal. In the end, he was hardly exhilarated by his triumph. What he gained was not as significant as what he might have lost. It is noteworthy that while Pegler devoted literally dozens of columns to Pearson, his opponent discussed Pegler in just two columns. The disparity was due to Drew's conviction that it was not worth a major journalistic campaign.

Pearson's biggest guns were directed at McCarthyism. His battle reached a turning point late in 1953 and later merged with a new force that marked the beginning of the end for McCarthyism. On December 22, 1953, the Pearson column reported that Gerard David Schine, a former McCarthy investigator, was the object of favoritism after being drafted into the Army at Fort Dix, New Jersey. "Two or three times a week," Pearson noted, "Roy Cohn, counsel for McCarthy's Committee, has called the commanding officer to ask how Gerard David was getting along. 'The Senator,' said Cohn ominously, 'wants to know.' "

In time, General Cornelius Ryan, Commander of the 19th Infantry Division, lost patience with this form of badgering. He contacted Secretary of the Army Robert Stevens, explained the constant interference of McCarthy's counsel, and urged remedial action. Stevens told him "this is one you've got to handle yourself."

Harassment by Cohn continued, and on February 15, 1954, Pearson reported how Schine "led a charmed life in the Army" and how "though only a private, superior officers almost bow and scrape before him." One officer who refused to bend, the Commander of the Provost Marshal's School at Camp Gordon, Georgia, Colonel Francis Kreidel, protested against Schine's assignment to the Provost Marshal's School and was subsequently transferred to Tokyo. Further, Pearson detailed McCarthy's intervention to have Schine transferred from basic training at Fort Dix direct to the Provost Marshal's School—in direct violation of Army regulations.

The Pearson column continued to stack the evidence: McCarthy forced the Army to give Schine weekend holidays to come to Washington; Roy Cohn protested when Schine was detailed at the Provost Marshal's School to learning traffic directions. Cohn was so upset by Schine's duties, he phoned Secretary Stevens and demanded Schine be spared such onerous details. Moreover, he warned that if Schine was not spared he would see to it "that the Secretary of the Army is fired." McCarthy blamed the Pearson columns on Army "leaks." He retaliated by launching an investigation of the United States Army.

The other decisive blow against McCarthyism, the aforementioned "new force," was television. It emerged as a powerful instrument of communications in the 1940's, inflicted heavy damage on the power of radio, and expanded its impact. Unfortunately, its impact was generally confined to billboarding and entertainment. Until 1954 it was a weak journalistic tool. Since television officials had an obsessive fear of "controversy," newscasts were devoted to readings of bland news agency bulletins. In addition, McCarthyism had infected the industry. Blacklists were common—advertising agencies and television stations consulted them before hiring anyone. No question about it, McCarthyism terrified television. Consequently, the medium sought to avoid anything that was unpleasant or disturbing.

One man was disturbed by television's fear of being disturbed: Edward R. Murrow. He was the most respected and popular newscaster of that era. In March 1954 he decided it was time for a candid look at McCarthyism. He prepared a half-hour portrait of Joe McCarthy, sketched with his own pictures and words. The Murrow touch was provided by the newscaster setting the record straight. McCarthy's tirades were familiar to television viewers, but this was the first time his statements were corrected. The cumulative effect of McCarthy's charges and Murrow's corrections resulted in a dramatically impressive and revealing half hour.

Murrow concluded the program by stating: "This is no time for men who oppose Senator McCarthy's methods to remain silent, or for those who approve. We can deny our heritage and our history, but we cannot escape responsibility for its result. There is no way for a citizen of a republic to abdicate his responsibilities. As a nation we have come into our full inheritance at a tender age. We proclaim ourselves—as indeed we are—the defenders of freedom, what's left of it, but we cannot defend freedom abroad by deserting it at home. The actions of the junior Senator from Wisconsin have caused alarm and dismay amongst our allies abroad and given considerable comfort to our enemies, and whose fault is that? Not really his. He didn't create this situation of fear, he merely exploited it, and rather successfully. Cassius was right: 'The fault, dear Brutus, is not in our stars but in ourselves.' Good night and good luck."

The reaction was predictable. Such anti-McCarthy papers as the Washington *Post* praised Murrow, and such pro-McCarthy papers as Hearst's New York *Journal-American* damned him. Senator McCarthy's reaction was predictable too. On the Fulton Lewis, Jr., radio newscast he called Murrow a liar. Later, Murrow's CBS network gave McCarthy equal time to reply. McCarthy's response was written by columnist George Sokolsky. He accused Murrow of giving comfort to our enemies and proclaimed he would not be discouraged by "the Murrows, the Communist *Daily Worker*, or the Communist Party itself."

Following Murrow's exposé of McCarthy, the St. Louis *Post-Dispatch* reported the story under an optimistic headline: "When Television Comes of Age." The truth is that Murrow's broadcast was an isolated incident. Unhappily, his clash with McCarthy damaged his career as a newscaster, and he never again attained the pinnacle he gained in March 1954. As a matter of fact, in October 1958, Ed Murrow offered a bitter indictment of television journalism in a speech delivered before the Radio and Television News Directors' Association in Chicago. Murrow stated in part: "We are currently wealthy, fit, comfortable, and complacent. We have a currently built-in allergy to disturbing information. Our mass media reflect this. But unless we get up off our fat surpluses and recognize that television in the main is being used to distract, delude, amuse, and insult us, then television and those who finance it, those who look at it, and those who work at it, may see a totally different picture too late." By and large, the same criticism is applicable to contemporary television.

Nevertheless, in 1954 television played a major role in the downfall of Senator McCarthy. Its role may have been inadvertent, but it was effective. For two months, beginning April 22, the American people had a front-seat look at the televised Army-McCarthy hearings.

Drunk with power, McCarthy attacked the United States Army early in 1954. He investigated what he described as a "disturbing situation" at Fort Monmouth, New Jersey, and had a two-month headline orgy of espionage charges. When Secretary of the Army Stevens announced after the two-month probe that it had revealed "no evidence of current espionage," McCarthy bullied him into editing his statement to say that the War Department "had no proof of espionage."

McCarthy then reached for something else. He learned that Irving Peress, a New York dentist with left-wing affiliations, had been commissioned a captain in October 1952, despite his refusal to answer questions about his political background. A year later Peress was promoted to major pursuant to provisions of the Doctor Draft Law. As a consequence of McCarthy's disclosures, the Army decided to discharge Peress.

The Senator was not satisfied. He demanded that Peress be court-martialed. Despite his demand, Peress was honorably discharged at Camp Kilmer—and McCarthy went wild. He attacked Secretary Stevens' promise to investigate the case as "Communist jargon" and ordered Brigadier General Ralph W. Zwicker, commanding officer at Camp Kilmer, to appear before his committee. When General Zwicker testified, Senator McCarthy castigated him for "shielding traitors and Communist conspirators." After being flogged by McCarthy, General Zwicker informed Chief of Staff Matthew Ridgway about the ordeal and Ridgway prevailed upon Stevens to intervene. The Secretary of War ordered General Zwicker to refuse to testify again and added, "I cannot permit loyal officers of our Armed Forces to be subjected to such unwarranted treatment." Several days later, after a secret meeting between Senators McCarthy, Dirksen, Mundt, and Potter, Secretary Stevens surrendered to McCarthy and agreed to give him everything he wanted. Within a fortnight, Stevens reversed his position. He released a chronology of events in which he accused McCarthy of persecuting the Army because the Army had refused to give McCarthy's investigator, David Schine, a commission before he was drafted and preferential treatment after his induction.

McCarthy fired back with forty-six charges, accusing the Army of "coddling Communists." The result of the charges and countercharges was an overwhelming demand by the press for an investigation to determine their accuracy. Within days, the Senate subcommittee voted to investigate the Army-McCarthy charges, with Karl Mundt temporarily replacing McCarthy as the chairman. During this period, while the investigation was incubating, Pearson exposed the behind-the-scenes maneuvering in column after column.

He published the details of secret Senate meetings on the McCarthy problem and the Senatorial attempts to whitewash McCarthy. When the Senate finally voted to publicly investigate the controversy, the investigating committee chose one Samuel Sears as its chief attorney. The next day Drew revealed Sears was one of McCarthy's ardent admirers. He was replaced by Ray H. Jenkins.

When McCarthy learned that Pearson was preparing a devastating review of his Senate record for a television newscast, the Senator employed a diversionary tactic. He publicly charged Pearson had violated the Espionage Act and that one of the columnist's assistants blackmailed a Pentagon official. Drew reported the background of the story:

> The Pentagon official to whom McCarthy refers was Don Murray, an assistant to the Chairman of the Munitions Board, whose job it was to handle press relations. As such he frequently saw one of my assistants, Fred Bluementhal, but at no time did Fred threaten, blackmail, or try to intimidate Mr. Murray. Fred is a friendly guy who just doesn't operate that way, and I would fire him if I had the slightest suspicion that he did. However, to make absolutely sure, I talked with both Murray and Bluementhal after McCarthy circulated this rumor last summer, and I am convinced no such thing happened.
>
> It is a fact, as McCarthy states, that some production figures were discussed by Murray with Bluementhal, but as McCarthy also admits, they were not published. It is not uncommon—in fact, it is almost a daily occurrence—for Government officials to discuss confidential matters with responsible newsmen. But this obviously does not constitute a violation of the Espionage Act. If it did, almost every newspaperman in Washington would be in for trouble. Mc-

> Carthy's intimation that the figures were "used for other purposes" is absurd and untrue.
>
> McCarthy's claims that a Justice Department official named Murray called me in and gave me all the facts on an espionage case just doesn't make sense. I never heard of the official in question, nor of any such case. However, it should be noted that even if McCarthy's piece of fiction had happened, it is no violation of the Espionage Act for a newspaperman to receive information from a Government official. The American Society of Newspaper Editors at this very moment is fighting for a broadening of this right of the press for freer information.

During the Truman Administration, when Roy Cohn, the McCarthy counsel, was a member of the Justice Department, he processed a case against Pearson based on the aforementioned information and he urged superiors to approve. They ruled there was no case. When Attorney General Brownell took over the Justice Department, McCarthy demanded that he review the case again. It was reviewed, and the Justice Department officials came to the same conclusion—no case. However, when Vice President Nixon and Deputy Attorney General Rogers met with McCarthy in Miami in order to persuade him to grant immunity to the Eisenhower Administration, he renewed his demand that Pearson be prosecuted. It was reported to Pearson later that McCarthy was told the Justice Department stlil believed there was no case, but to please him the matter would be put before a Grand Jury. As far as Pearson knows, it was never put before a Grand Jury, though personally he believed it would be an excellent idea.

Meanwhile, Pearson publicly suggested to Senator McCarthy that he ask the same Grand Jury to consider various allegations that he violated the Espionage Act and the Corrupt Practices Act as follows:

> 1. The Army publicly stated, September 11, 1953, that McCarthy violated the Espionage Act when he published a 75-page restricted Army Intelligence report on Siberia. On the outside of the document was clearly stamped: "This document contains information affecting the National De-

fense of the United States within the meaning of the Espionage Laws, Title 18, U.S.C., Sec. 793 and 794. The transmission or the revelation of its contents in any manner to an unauthorized person is prohibited by law." Yet despite this, McCarthy made the document public.

2. Senator McCarthy also violated the Espionage Act in a speech January 22, 1951, in which he made public "Document No. 3019 dated December 15, 1950," this being a military report radioed from Korea. Revelation of the date of a radioed coded message makes it easier for a foreign power to break the code.

3. McCarthy collected $10,000 from Congressman and Mrs. Alvin Bentley for the express purpose of fighting Communism. According to an official Senate report, he used the money not to fight Communism but to speculate on the soybean market.

4. During four years as a Senator, McCarthy deposited $172,623 in the Riggs Bank—a lot of money for a Senator with a salary of $12,500. The Senate Report that details his finances states that $19,000 was deposited in cash from unidentified sources; $40,562 in checks from unidentified sources. If these were campaign contributions, McCarthy is required by law to report them. If not, he has other obligations.

5. McCarthy's assistant, Ray Kiermas, deposited another $92,921 at the Riggs Bank, of which $29,230 was in cash. Not many people deal in cash these days, especially huge chunks of cash, and the Senate Committee that reported these interesting finances wanted to know why.

Since Attorney General Brownell came into office, the Justice Department has done absolutely nothing about the Senate Report on McCarthy. If the Senator has nothing to hide, he might join me in urging that the whole matter go before a Grand Jury.

For once, McCarthy failed to respond to Pearson. He was concentrating on his clash with the Army, which was destined to become a struggle for his political life. The gist of the Army charges against McCarthy: From July 8, 1953, to February 16, 1954, the

Senator and two of his associates had "sought by improper means to obtain preferential treatment for one Pvt. G. David Schine." The Army document contained twenty-nine instances of misconduct on the part of McCarthy and his aides. Special counsel for the Army was Joseph N. Welch, a senior member of a distinguished Boston law firm. He was sixty-three, a tall and tweedy man, always conservatively dressed with dark bow tie and vest.

The Caucus Room of the Senate Office Building was transformed into a television studio. For the next thirty-six days over twenty million television viewers witnessed a remarkable spectacle. Tragedy, comedy, melodrama. It was described by one reporter as "the national business, the national pastime, and the national disgrace." The disgrace was provided by McCarthy, who came out roaring, making his customary charges, some more reckless than usual. He smeared while he accused others of smearing. He jeered, scowled, and constantly interrupted the proceedings. McCarthy's published comments helped his buildup. But the menacing sight of McCarthyism in action helped tear him down. Wittingly or unwittingly, the television cameras pointed at the Senator were a firing squad. As the hearings ground on, McCarthy's popular support was weakened by his tactics. When he demanded the records of privileged conversations in the White House, the President refused and forcefully stated those rights "cannot be usurped by any individual who may set himself above the laws of the land." President Eisenhower was now actively fighting McCarthy, Joseph Welch was fighting McCarthy, and McCarthy was fighting McCarthy. As the days passed, he became more desperate, more vicious—and the television cameras caught every backhanded thrust, every ugly mood. Even President Eisenhower and the Republicans were included in McCarthy's soft-on-Communism charges. He spoke about "the evidence of treason that has been growing up over twenty-one years."

In full view of the television audience, McCarthy then displayed the dark, destructive power he represented. It was capsuled in a single dramatic incident. McCarthy bitterly attacked a member of Joseph Welch's law firm for once having belonged to the Lawyer's Guild, "which was named, oh, years and years ago, as the legal bulwark of the Communist party."

Welch listened to the attack, his face turning rigid with anger. Then he replied: "Until this moment, Senator, I think I never really gauged your cruelty or your recklessness. . . . Little did I dream that you could be so reckless and so cruel as to do injury to that lad. . . . I feel he shall always bear a scar needlessly inflicted by you. If it were in my power to forgive your reckless cruelty, I would do so. I like to think I am a gentleman, but your forgiveness will have to come from someone other than me."

McCarthy attempted to interrupt, but Welch continued with controlled fury: "Let us not assassinate this lad further, Senator. You have done enough. Have you no sense of decency?" McCarthy again sought to interrupt, to ask additional questions. Welch refused to listen. He concluded: "Mr. McCarthy, I will not discuss this with you further. . . . If there is a God in Heaven, it will do neither you nor your cause any good."

After Welch completed his statement, a stunned silence pervaded the room. Then spontaneous applause exploded. At that moment, McCarthy changed from a roaring bully into a forlorn figure. He said: "What did I do wrong?" McCarthy did not know what he had done wrong, but millions of television viewers knew. They could see, hear, feel. The walls tumbled around McCarthy. Within two weeks after the hearings began, the Gallup Poll disclosed the sudden erosion of McCarthy's popularity.

McCarthyism, which appeared to be hard-muscled ruthlessness, turned into jelly within weeks. The Senator's "Point of order!" interruptions became a theme for comedy material. McCarthyism took on the sorry aspects of a melancholy farce. Several minutes before the hearings were gaveled to an end, Mr. Welch said: "Would you, Mr. Chairman, hear a personal note? I alone, I alone came into this room from deep obscurity. I alone will return to obscurity. As it folds about me, softly as I hope it does quickly, the lady who listened and is called Judith Lyndon Welch will hear from me a long sigh of relief. I am sorry that this play had to take place in the fretful lightning and the ominous roll of noises from Indochina and around the world. It saddens me to think that my life has been lived so largely either in wars or turmoil. I allow myself to hope that soon there will come a day when there will, in this lovely land of ours, be more simple laughter."

Thus a spectacle that began on a note of raw fear concluded with hope. Within ninety days the committee found McCarthy guilty of improper conduct and the Senate recommended that he be censured. On December 2, 1954, the Senate voted to "condemn" McCarthy for contempt of the Elections subcommittee, abuse of its members, and insults to the Senate during the censure proceedings. All forty-four Democrats voted for the condemnation. The Republicans were evenly split. The stark fact was that McCarthy was politically dead.

Surprisingly, newspapers offered few editorial comments on McCarthy's political demise. In a way, he was no longer news. You never find reporters in the loser's dressing room.

However, there were some journalistic reactions, both thoughtful and emotional. Cabell Phillips, *The New York Times* Washington correspondent, later wrote: "From early 1950 through most of 1954, Joe McCarthy dominated the political life of this country as no demagogue had done before him. He scraped the raw nerve of the nation's anxiety and turned it into a neurosis. He spit in the eye of constituted authority, undermined public confidence in the government and its leaders, and tore at the nation's foreign policy. He used lies, slander, innuendo to smash his opponents and to build his own image of invincibility. He made cowards of all but a handful of his fellow Senators, and he kept two Presidents angrily and helplessly on the defensive in nearly everything they did. It is lucky for the nation that Joe McCarthy was at heart a street fighter rather than a zealot. If he had more guile and genius he might have wrecked the government."

Newscaster Eric Sevareid depicted McCarthyism as "a sudden rocket in the sky, enrapturing some, frightening others, catching millions in a kind of spell that dissipated only when the rocket itself, as a rocket must, spluttered, went cold, and fell."

National Review, a conservative journal, saw McCarthy as a powerful symbol of anti-Communism and "the very essence of Western civilization," a fighter for truth and justice. *Commonweal*, a Catholic periodical, concluded that McCarthy's cause was "an essentially know-nothing attempt to gain personal power by playing on the very real fears of his fellow citizens." *New Republic*, a liberal publication, feared that "if the Republicans won in 1956, McCarthy would be back in business." The general newspaper reaction to the fall of McCarthy fell in the category of good-riddance by the anti-McCarthy press, and the Communist-victim theory by the pro-McCarthy journalists.

Joe McCarthy's name virtually vanished from the press after 1955. He made the front pages in May 1957 when he died. *The Nation*, a liberal periodical, carried the following obituary: "Senator Joseph McCarthy is dead. So quickly does malevolence rise and vanish in American life that news of his death, which would have incited sensational interest two years ago, may now be noted in a paragraph, sealing as it does a verdict then returned. The junior Senator from Wisconsin left a squalid political estate with few legatees or claimants. His single contribution was the addition of the word McCarthyism to the American language. The best that can be said of him was that his idea of American patriotism, which we hope he was sincere about, is not one that the Nation shared while he was living and could, of course, never accept now that he is dead."

Pearson's post-mortem was rather casual. He admitted the McCarthy interlude was "one of the most painful of my life," and added, "I was mainly concerned with the damage McCarthyism inflicted on the country." The fact is that newspapermen rarely have time for historic reflections. Events move swiftly. The pressure is constant and the daily deadlines are relentless. For Drew Pearson, the story of McCarthyism was followed by a sensational exposé involving President Eisenhower's leading adviser.

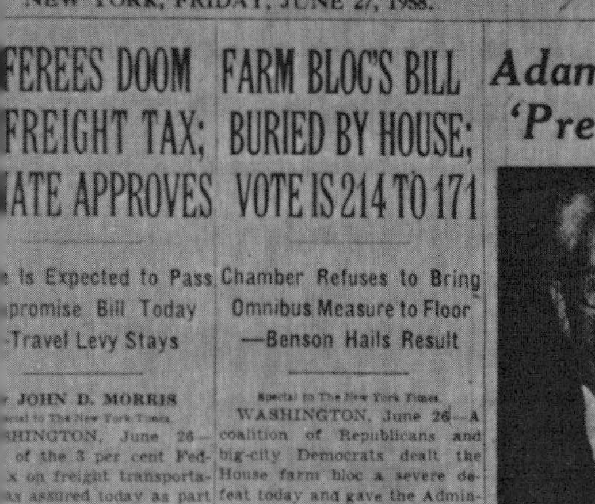

New York Times.

NEW YORK, FRIDAY, JUNE 27, 1958. FIVE CENTS

Mostly fair today; fair tonight. Fair and pleasant tomorrow. Temp. range: 74—60. Yesterday: 66.5—67

[CON]FEREES DOOM FREIGHT TAX; [SEN]ATE APPROVES

[Hous]e Is Expected to Pass [Com]promise Bill Today [—]Travel Levy Stays

By JOHN D. MORRIS

Special to The New York Times.

[WAS]HINGTON, June 26— [Repeal] of the 3 per cent Fed[eral ta]x on freight transporta[tion w]as assured today as part

FARM BLOC'S BILL BURIED BY HOUSE; VOTE IS 214 TO 171

Chamber Refuses to Bring Omnibus Measure to Floor —Benson Hails Result

Special to The New York Times.

WASHINGTON, June 26—A coalition of Republicans and big-city Democrats dealt the House farm bloc a severe defeat today and gave the Admin[istration a victory.]

Adams Calls Fox Charges 'Preposterous, Malicious'

FOX TELLS INQU[IRY] GOLDFINE BOAS[TED] OF AID BY AD[AMS]

Swears Industrialist[...] Official Would 'Tak[e...] of F. T. C. Trou[ble]

LINK TO MILLS CHA[...]

Ex-Publisher Asserts[...] President's Assist[ant] Has 'Some Intere[st]'

Excerpts from Fox test[imony] and Adams' reply, Pag[e...]

By WILLIAM M. BL[...]

[F]RIENDLY MR. GOLDFINE, [G]ENEROUS TO A FAULT

[The mo]st surprising character in the case of Sherman [Adams a]nd the vicuña was a man who until last week was [virtually] unknown outside New England. Bernie Goldfine, [a d]apper and Russian-born, spent a penniless youth [in Bosto]n, then started selling wool remnants. In time [he bough]t a mill of his own, then several. Now 67, he [says] 'I'm worth $5 million. But I won't say how much [more.' A]s he acquired his wealth Goldfine also acquired [friends l]ike the influential politicians shown at right. And [he] genuinely liked politicians; indeed he seemed to [take pri]de in just knowing important men, aside from [what the]y might do for him. "I never put a rope around [anybody's] neck," he says, "and I never will." But the hotel [bill show]n below suggested that Goldfine had a friend [who allo]wed him to carry generous friendship too far.

ADAMS, M/M SHERMAN 2/50.0
TILDEN ST NW WASHINGTON,D.C.
W 9/21 NL/IP CE 26289

	Date	Explanation	Charges	Bal Due
1	SEP21 57	RESTR —	• 41.80	• 41.80
2	SEP21 57	ROOM ••••	• 50.00	• 91.80
3	SEP22 57	RESTR —	• 5.47	• 97.27
4	SEP22 57	RESTR —	• 8.63	• 105.90
5	SEP22 57	ROOM ••••	• 50.00	• 155.90
6	SEP23 57	RESTR —	• 5.21	• 161.11
7	SEP23 57	— PdOut GAR	• 4.50	• 165.61
8	SEP23 57	VALET —	• 6.25	• 171.86
9	SEP23 57	LREST —	• 0.72	• 172.58
10	SEP23 57	LNDRY —	• 1.82	• 174.40
11	SEP23 57	ROOM ••••	• 50.00	• 224.40
12	SEP24 57	RESTR —	• 4.21	• 228.61
13	SEP24 57	VALET —	• 2.75	• 231.36
14	SEP24 57	— PdOut GAR	• 2.50	• 233.86
15	SEP24 57	ROOM ••••	• 50.00	• 283.86
16	SEP24 57	RESTR ••••	• 0.50	• 284.36
17	SEP25 57	RESTR —	• 6.97	• 291.33
18	SEP25 57	LNDRY —	• 3.32	• 294.65
19	SEP25 57	ROOM ••••	• 50.00	• 344.65
20	SEP26 57	— PdOut GAR	• 4.50	• 349.15
21	SEP26 57	RESTR —	• 6.76	• 355.91
22	SEP26 57	PHONE —	• 5.22	• 361.13
23				

SEP 25 '57

SHERMAN ADAMS RESIG[NS]; SEES 'VILIFICATION' DRI[VE]; PRESIDENT VOICES SADN[ESS]

AIDE GOES O[N AIR]

Tells Nation He[...] Innocent of Wr[ongdoing] in Goldfine Ca[se]

Texts of Adams speech[...] President's letter, Page[...]

By RUSSELL BAKE[R]

Special to The New York Times.

WASHINGTON, Sept. [22]—Sherman Adams resigned [his] White House post today [under] heavy political pressure.

Mr. Adams, the Assista[nt to] the President since early [1953], told a national radio and tel[evi]sion audience that the deci[sion] had been forced upon [him] through a "campaign of vilif[ica]tion" calculated to destroy [him] and embarrass President Ei[sen]hower and his Administrat[ion].

Rather than let this h[a]ppen and endanger Republi[can] chances for gaining control [of] Congress this November, M[r.] Adams said, he decided to qu[it].

Resignation Accepted

[SIL]ENCE IN NEWPORT: President Eisenhower [accompan]ies Sherman Adams to helicopter after talk at [Summer W]hite House. The Assistant to the President had [flown ther]e early yesterday to confer on his resignation.

Associated Press Wirephoto

[Co]ntrol Rule [...] Physicians [C]ertify No[...]

REPUBLICANS SEE GOVERNMENT [...]

8

OF POLITICS AND VICUNAS

President Eisenhower used the Army staff system of administration. He delegated a great deal of authority to subordinates. Among those he entrusted with unusual power was Presidential Assistant Sherman Adams and Press Secretary James Hagerty. The power exercised by his press secretary represented a marked departure in White House press relations. Never before—or since—has a press secretary been as influential as Hagerty. Some of his power resulted from his unquestionable gift for public relations; the rest resulted from the power vacuum created by the President.

Eisenhower's attitude toward the press corps was in direct contrast with both Truman and FDR. The latter Presidents mostly ran the news show themselves, albeit they received major assists from press secretaries (respectively, Stephen Early and Charles Ross). However, James Hagerty was the White House news producer, director, and writer. He not only conveyed White House policy, but the wide latitude he enjoyed in disseminating information enabled him to help formulate Presidential policy. His job was made easier and his authority wider by two factors. One was the widespread support Eisenhower had among U.S. publishers. After some twenty-years of Democrats in the White House, the publishers had a President who echoed their Republican sympathies. The other was the phenomenal proliferation of the government's public relations structure.

FDR launched the growth of publicists within the government.

At the start of Roosevelt's fourth term, the Executive branch had about 1,200 employees engaged in press agentry. Frequently, their roles were disguised by seemingly innocuous titles, the most popular being "Administrative Assistant" or "Executive Assistant to the Assistant Secretary." Under one title or another, the publicists in the Federal branch mushroomed during the Truman Administration. Without much public notice, they had sprouted to a small propaganda army of more than 3,000. During that period, one Congressman noted: "During the recent session of Congress our Federal bureaucracy revealed itself as the most powerful and potentially the most dangerous lobby of all. It fought, bureau by bureau, every Congressional move to curb its innate desire to expand. It is backed by its vast tax-supported propaganda machine." Several months later, Senator Byrd endeavored to cut the Federal information services. He argued that the cut would lead to "more news and less bull from the Federal publicity mill." But nothing was done about the expanding publicity structure. It continued growing. During Eisenhower's first term, the number of Federal publicists were close to 7,000.

Equipped with a massive government propaganda machine, supported by the great majority of publishers, aided by Eisenhower's winning personality and the genuine affection of the public, Jim Hagerty successfully merchandised the Presidency and practically overwhelmed the Washington press corps, particularly during Eisenhower's first four years. Of course, the President was a military hero and he was well aware of image-building maneuvers. Besides, his magnetic personality enchanted the people. One Washington correspondent wrote: "The public loves Ike. The less he does the more they love him. That, probably, is the secret. Here is a man who doesn't rock the boat."

Political euphoria and the immense personal affection the people had for Eisenhower were aided and abetted by Hagerty's propaganda ploys. Some of these were transparent to Washington correspondents, but all were effective. For example, Hagerty decided which news stories should involve the President. When the Army had good news to announce, it was announced by the White House. When there was bad news, it was released by the Army. During

Eisenhower's frequent vacations, Hagerty avoided the possibility of criticism by making them appear to be working holidays. During his vacation, the White House press secretary would announce Presidential appointments or other news tidbits, calculated to create the impression the President was working, although the appointment may have been made weeks before Eisenhower began his vacation.

The problem correspondents had of countering Hagerty's astute news management was explained by Russell Baker of *The New York Times*: "Hagerty's enduring contribution to the White House was his demonstration of how to exploit the weakness of the American newsgathering system for the promotion of his boss. . . . If editors demanded a Presidential story a day, it follows that reporters will be bound to satisfy them one way or another. On days when there is no news, they will poke around darkened rooms, look under the carpet, or start staring at the west wall and adding two and two in the news stories. When that sort of thing happens, the White House is in trouble. Hagerty prevented this by seeing to it that there was rarely a newsless day. If there was no news, he made a little."

Another Washington reporter conceded, "Jim Hagerty holds a lens ground to his own prescription over the White House—and outsiders have little choice but to look through it."

The Hagerty publicity style was detailed by *Time* magazine: "Hagerty struggled valiantly and, to a point, successfully in stressing work over play. He took with him on trips briefcases full of executive orders, and parceled them out daily to make news under the Augusta and Gettysburg dateline. He encouraged feature stories on the Army Signal Corps' elaborate setup to keep Ike in close touch with Washington. He produced Cabinet members in wholesale lots. (Does Hagerty really call for Cabinet members? Says he: "Maybe sometimes I do.") He did anything and everything, in short, to keep the subjects of golf and fishing far down in the daily stories about the President.

Incidentally, *Time* magazine noted that "by every standard, Jim Hagerty was the best—and most powerful—White House press secretary in U. S. history. . . . Hagerty is the authentic voice of the White House."

One of Hagerty's major publicity coups was a journalistic innovation. He added television to press conferences, although the conference was on film and it was edited by Hagerty before being released to the networks. Eisenhower was an immediate television star. The intimate view of the President under questioning and his electric smile made the people forget both the questions and answers. The Eisenhower personality came through with warm and powerful impact. One Washington correspondent cracked, "To a political Confucius like Hagerty, the TV picture is worth all the 4,000 printed words of the conference."

During his first term, most correspondents seemed to be awed by Eisenhower. Their questions during press conferences were generally polite. They made it a point to avoid the barbed queries that had characterized the Roosevelt-Truman press conferences. Among the few exceptions to the rule was a White House newspaperwoman named Sarah McClendon, who covered Washington for a string of Texas papers. She peppered the President with aggressive questions. She riled him with queries about his golf game. Another newspaperwoman, Doris Fleeson of the Chicago *Daily News*, was more gentle in her scolding. She spoofed the President's bland news conferences and his cautious commentaries by writing a version of the Gettysburg Address in Eisenhower style. Sample excerpt: "I haven't checked these figures, but 87 years ago, I think it was, a number of individuals organized a governmental setup here in this country. I believe it covered certain Eastern areas, with this idea they were following up based on a sort of national independence arrangement and the program that every individual is just as good as every other individual."

Among the small minority of Washington press critics of the Administration was Drew Pearson. He was more trenchant than most. He brought to light several conflict-of-interest cases. Peter Strobel, who was in charge of public buildings for the General Services Administration, approached the Army engineers on behalf of his own firm while he was working for the Government; Carl O. Hansen conducted a wool-buying business while working for the Farmers Home Administration. Both were fired. Another Pearson story involved Richard Mack, a member of the Federal Communications Commission. He accepted money from an interested party in the award of a Miami television license. Mack resigned, too. Several other scandals in the Eisenhower Administration were exposed by *The New York Times,* the New York *Herald Tribune,* and the Chattanooga *Times*. None aroused public uproar or resulted in tainting the Eisenhower prestige. Hagerty blunted the power of exposé by releasing front-page stories at the same time as a diversionary tactic.

The Hagerty touch was most evident when Eisenhower suffered a heart attack in 1955. The Press Secretary instituted a candid publicity campaign. He held numerous press conferences and issued medical bulletins for every edition. He invited heart specialist Dr. Paul Dudley White to brief reporters on medical details. Hagerty kept the nation constantly informed and probably averted public hysteria. Only a few days after Eisenhower was stricken, Hagerty brought every Cabinet member to the hospital for alleged conferences with the President. The impression was conveyed that Eisenhower was working despite his illness. Hagerty's public relations methods in this case were as unprecedented as they were effective. Previous Presidents hit by serious illnesses preferred secrecy. For a year and a half of President Wilson's term the public was unaware he was recovering from near-fatal paralysis. The press did not learn of President Cleveland's surgery for mouth cancer until a quarter-century after it had taken place.

Following Eisenhower's recovery from the heart attack, Pearson confidently predicted that he would not run for a second term. The President had privately assured Pearson he would be a one-term President. The columnist's personal relationship with the President was generally cool, but polite. It was markedly different from Pearson's love-hate relationship with Truman and FDR.

Politically, Eisenhower and Pearson were far apart. Washington correspondent William L. Rivers has quoted another reporter's statement that "during the Eisenhower Presidency, you could count on Pearson attacking the President every other day—sometimes with facts." Rivers adds that "Pearson's fancies included a long, fuzzy column on an imaginary Eisenhower 'relapse' after an illness and a fantastic report asserting that Vice President Nixon had tried to seize the reins of government while the President was ill (the very last action Nixon could take and hope to succeed Eisenhower in the Presidency). During the Kennedy Era, Pearson reminisced in a column on Presidential news management about the time when Eisenhower's press secretary, James Hagerty, managed the headlines in 1954 by rushing out an announcement 'that Mr. Eisenhower planned to launch a satellite into outer space.' This would be three years before the first satellite was launched."

Pearson's rebuttal: "Hagerty did make the announcement of the new satellite three years before it was launched. This was the whole point. Harold Talbot had been exposed as having a conflict of interest. Talbot was Secretary of the Air Force and as a Cabinet member it was a very serious scandal. The plans to launch a satellite were a long way from being ready, but Hagerty jumped the gun three years early in order to take the headlines away from the conflict of interest case in the Eisenhower Cabinet."

He also added: "Actually Nixon was entirely capable of this and I am quite sure, despite his denials, he did discuss with his friends the idea of taking over the presidency not publicly or officially but quietly and factually while Eisenhower was first stricken. My story told how Nixon held late midnight conferences with some of his dearest friends asking their advice as to whether he should quietly begin making major decisions regarding affairs of state. After about two days he was quickly shunted aside by Secretary of the Treasury George Humphrey and Sherman Adams, who disliked Nixon and were jealous of their and Ike's authority."

The columnist's record on the subject of space and the Middle East crisis during the Eisenhower Administration represented notable illustrations of vigilant journalism.

Starting in 1951, Drew Pearson published a series of columns stressing Russian progress in the development of new weapons—specifically, space-age weapons. Pearson continued his reports of Russian accomplishments in rocketry until 1957 when his warnings were confirmed. Russia crossed the frontier of the Space Age by successfully launching the first earth satellite. The Eisenhower Administration accepted the electrifying events with detached calm. The President said "the satellite itself does not raise my apprehensions, not one iota." Other Administration spokesmen dismissed it as "a neat technical trick," and Presidential aide Sherman Adams shrugged it off with an uncharacteristic display of humor by referring to the satellite as "an outer-space basketball game."

However, Pearson quoted Democratic Senate Majority Leader Lyndon Johnson's comment: "The Roman Empire controlled the world because it could build roads. Later—when men moved to the sea—the British Empire was dominant because it had ships. Now the Communists have established a foothold in outer space. It is not very reassuring to be told that next year we will put a 'better' satellite in the air. Perhaps it will even have chrome trim—and automatic windshield wipers."

"Eventually," as columnist Joe Alsop later reported, "the Administration was rescued from the worst sort of trouble by Vice President Nixon, who spoke out about the Sputnik on his own initiative, with a bold sobriety and honesty."

The year the Space Age opened, Pearson returned from a tour of the Middle East and reported a "Kremlin timetable" for revolutions in Arab nations. Within days after his report, it was disclosed that Egypt and Syria had accepted military and economic aid from the Soviet Union, and other Arab nations were similarly inclined. President Eisenhower acted swiftly. At his request, Congress declared that the United States was prepared to use force to protect the Middle East against armed aggression by international Communism, and appropriated $200 million for military and economic aid to all Middle Eastern states willing to receive it. Some time later, British and American forces were sent to the Middle East to support friendly governments in Lebanon and Jordan.

Following Eisenhower's re-election, Jim Hagerty's news management expanded and intensified. Administration investigators tapped wires of officials when they spoke to newspapermen. Then they called them in and played back the tape. Obviously, fear was rampant in government agencies. Some officials maintained furtive contacts with reporters, only speaking to them in corridors or on street corners to avoid having their conversations recorded. This form of heavy-handed suppression infuriated columnist Joe Alsop, who wrote: "This reporter's official acquaintances and friends are subjected to the most shameful harassment. . . . The real object is not to locate the reporter's source, but simply to strike at the reporter through the men he knows in the government."

Some of the Hagerty-tamed correspondents began showing their claws in 1957. An economic recession helped tarnish the era of good feeling between Eisenhower and correspondents. Some of the news conference questions became blunter. The dignified courtesy that seemed to pervade conferences during the Administration's first term diminished significantly. Eisenhower, who had eagerly replied to all questions in the past, more and more used the "no comment" evasion. Occasionally he lost his temper with reporters. When one correspondent asked him about charges in Congress that his plan to reorganize the Defense Department might make it possible for him to set up a personal army, the President literally sputtered with rage and snapped: "I've got one question to ask you. Have you read the law?"

Despite the altered attitude of Washington correspondents, the clashes between the press and the President took place rather infrequently. On balance—until 1958—Hagerty's projection of the Presidency as efficient, well-organized and dynamic, shaped public opinion. During this period, Correspondent Frederick Collins of the Providence *Journal* observed, "Except in rare instances, no outsider knows who in the White House or in the government at large is responsible for a given decision, however diligent his inquiry." Reporters had the feeling that they were being briefed. Hagerty created a great deal of news about Eisenhower, but very little hard information.

A turning point in the Administration's relations with the press was marked by the Sherman Adams case. Officially, Adams was a Presidential Assistant. But the power he enjoyed caused a reporter to crack, "Adams is the best President this country never had." As much as the President himself, Adams reflected the collective character of the Administration, which was rooted in personal probity. He was a craggy New Englander who deplored smoking in White House corridors and outlawed office gossip and feet on office desks. He was sharp, cold, tough—always in command of situations. Passion seemed as foreign to Adams as snow in the Sahara. He was a man without personal or oratorical flourishes, a man who worked long and hard. He considered it a waste of time and energy to say hello or goodbye on the phone. Dour and faithful, Adams was a no-nonsense get-to-the-point personality. Consequently, he was often demanding and brusque. In Cabinet sessions the President expressed his gratitude to Adams. As he later declared publicly, Eisenhower would frequently state privately, "I need Sherman Adams."

Newsmen described Adams as "The Iceberg," "The Abominable No-Man," and "The Granite Politician." His speeches conveyed a sense of bitter partisanship. Time and again he continued to blast "the Truman mess." He scorned and excoriated members of the Truman Administration who were involved in corruption or were derelict in their duties. He was stern and unforgiving.

For some time Pearson and Jack Anderson had been tracking down reports of a strange friendship between Sherman Adams and Bernard Goldfine, a New England industrialist for whom Adams was reported to have done favors. It was a difficult story to confirm. White House news sources were blocked. Pearson suspected that Congressman Orin Harris, chairman of the House Commerce Committee, who was then supposed to be investigating conflicts of interest in the regulatory agencies, was not eager to probe Sherman Adams' activities. A lack of enthusiasm dictated by his ambition to become a federal judge. Adams, as No. 2 man in the White House, could block that appointment. Pearson was about to leave for Europe. But the day he departed, he and Anderson conferred about the final details of the Adams-Goldfine story. On May 13 Anderson shook the Eisenhower Administration. "Now that the public clamor has died down," he reported, "Congressman Orin Harris has quietly called off the investigation of the second most powerful man in the government—President Eisenhower's crisp, curt little overseer, Sherman Adams."

Once before, Adams had been accused of exerting pressure on this Congressional committee. After Dr. Bernard Schwartz was ousted as the committee's chief counsel, he accused Adams of bringing White House pressure on various regulatory agencies. After

Sherman Adams.

James C. Hagerty, Presidential Press Secretary.

Congressman Harris took charge of the investigation, he ignored two letters Adams wrote to Vice President Nixon's campaign manager, Murray Chotiner, in behalf of North American Airlines. The firm had hired Chotiner to help solve its problems with the Civil Aeronautics Board.

The column then listed some of the suppressed facts:

> Federal Trade Commission records show that Adams intervened to help textile tycoon Bernard Goldfine, who got into trouble with Uncle Sam for mislabeling wool products. After Adams poked his sharply chiseled nose into the case, Goldfine was excused from further investigation with the admonition not to violate the law again.
>
> But in less than nine months he was caught pulling the same old tricks. This time the FTC attorney in the case, Charles Canavan, recommended criminal proceedings for "willful and deliberate flouting of the law."
>
> Again Adams came to the rescue with a phone call to FTC Chairman Edward Howroy, asking him to see Goldfine. The textile baron and his son, Horst, showed up in Hagerty's office in April 14, 1955, for a confidential conference. At the end of the meeting, Goldfine blurted: "Please get Sherman Adams on the phone for me."
>
> Then, in front of FTC officials, he made a great show of his friendship with the assistant president.
>
> "I'm over at the FTC," Goldfine boomed, "I have been treated very well over here. Thanks for arranging the appointment."
>
> His friendship with Goldfine has been something of a mystery. It is known that Goldfine contributed to Adams' past political campaigns for governor and congressman in New Hampshire. Most of Adams' neat, gray suits are also made in Goldfine's mills.
>
> The most startling description of their relationship, however, was given by John Fox, former publisher of the Boston *Post*, who charged in Federal Court last month that Goldfine embezzled $6,788,819 from the Boston Post Development Corporation because Sherman Adams was in his pocket. "I asked Mr. Goldfine how it was possible to keep on embezzling, which he admitted he was doing, and how it was

possible for him, how he dared to do this in the face of the regulations of the United States Securities and Exchange Commission," Fox told the court. "He told me that as long as he had Sherman Adams in his pocket he could do it."

Yet Congressman Harris, who is supposed to be investigating both the FTC and the SEC, has instructed his investigators to lay off Adams.

One week after Jack Anderson's story appeared, the New York *Herald Tribune* and the St. Louis *Post-Dispatch* confirmed the Adams-Goldfine scandal. Pearson continued the barrage.

From June 15 to June 20 his columns were packed with the subject. *Item*: Adams received $2,000 of free hotel hospitality at the Sheraton Plaza in Boston. The tab was picked up by Goldfine. *Item*: Adams arranged a quick Goldfine interview with President Eisenhower at a time when Senators and Congressmen were kept waiting for months to see Ike. *Item*: Goldfine paid for most of Adams' clothes. Moreover, he presented Adams with an expensive vicuna coat. The column carried a quip: "What would happen if Sherman Adams died and Eisenhower became President?"

On July 20, 1955, Pearson reported Sinclair Armstrong, Chairman of the Securities and Exchange Commission, swore under oath before the Kefauver committee that Adams had phoned him asking that he postpone SEC hearings on Dixon-Yates because the House of Representatives was considering an appropriation bill on Dixon-Yates. The SEC hearings would have revealed that Adolphe Wenzell was planted inside the Budget Bureau to put across the Dixon-Yates deal. Obviously Adams did not want this to come out before Congress voted. On February 5, 1955, Adams held a meeting in his office of Republican Congressmen from the northwest, regarding the competition between Northwest Airlines and Pan American Airways for the great circle route over the Arctic to Japan. The Department of Commerce had demanded that Pan American get a duplicate route, but Adams intervened and the decision went to Northwest. Whether right or wrong, his actions in February 1955 conflicted with his sworn testimony later.

In June 1955, ex-Senator Harry Cain, a Republican member of

the Subversive Activities Control Board, made an impassioned public plea for tolerance in handling allleged security risks. His speech had been sent to the White House in advance, but apparently none of Adams' staff had bothered to read it. Adams thereupon intervened directly in the affairs of the independent Subversive Activities Control Board: He ordered Cain to report to his office and reprimanded him. Later he made certain that Cain was not reappointed, though he had been a fervent Eisenhower supporter.

In the spring of 1955, Pat McGinnis of the New Haven Railroad wanted to take over the Boston and Maine. A group of New England bankers sought to block the merger and to that end wanted the Interstate Commerce Commission to investigate, prior to a B&M stockholders' meeting, in order to discourage the merger. The ICC, however, declined to investigate. ICC Chairman Richard Mitchell told Senator Saltonstall of Massachusetts that Governor Christian Herter of Massachusetts said there would be no investigation. The ICC, he said, could not stage an investigation when it got a formal request from one of the railroads. However, Commissioner Oren Clark, a close friend of Sherman Adams, was summoned to the White House. Thereafter, an ICC investigation was ordered. The ICC is completely independent, just as the Federal Trade Commission is supposed to be independent. However, both came to heel in a hurry when Sherman Adams intervened.

Jim Hagerty sought to conquer Drew Pearson's fact-finding by a series of maneuvers. First, he used the claim of "executive privilege" in an effort to cloak Sherman Adams. "Executive privilege" is the right to withhold any information in the executive departments if the President believes it to be "in the national interest." This brazen attempt at suppression resulted in an editorial uproar, and the White House rescinded its "executive privilege." Then Hagerty called a press conference and lamely explained there was nothing improper in Sherman Adams' three calls to Federal agencies on behalf of his friend Mr. Goldfine, adding that "Adams would do the same for anyone." One reporter commented, "He's sure going to get a big mail." Hagerty then accused those who exposed Adams of "trying to smear him."

Some of Hagerty's best journalistic allies expressed shock and dismay. *Life* magazine's editorial comment, in part: "It was Adams, more than any other Presidential adviser, who dispelled the easier moral atmosphere of the smoke-filled room, who personified Ike's often stated principle that honesty and integrity are the essentials of good government. Adams hammered away at the Truman Administration's marked tendency to reward friends and disfavor enemies. He was always ready to brush aside clumsy defenses that the ever-increasing freezers and mink coats were just the accruals of old friendships (the same defense, ironically, which Hagerty made for Adams). No man to cushion his neighbor's feelings if he could avoid it, Adams has taken the lead in forcing the resignations of Administration officials with the slightest suspicion of irregularity in their political or business dealings."

Editorial pages from Washington to Kokomo expressed surprise and indignation. *Newsweek*'s reaction was typical: "It was inconceivable. It was the sort of thing that could not happen, it could not happen to this sort of man. Certainly, the President did not believe it could. The tragic, unbelievable essence of the matter was this: Possibly the most important non-elected official of the United States Government had accepted favors from a pleader before Federal agencies whose duty it is to regulate business practices. The official was Sherman Adams."

The national shock spiraled when Pearson reported that President Eisenhower had been given a gift by Goldfine, a vicuna coat. Jim Hagerty promptly issued a qualified denial of the story and attacked Pearson. However, Hagerty never publicly mentioned that in the past he had phoned Pearson twice and privately conceded he had been wrong in blasting Pearson's stories. One editor called Pearson and said that Hagerty's denial sounded like someone alibiing: "I didn't blow up the safe. I knew the combination." Actually, Pearson had checked his facts carefully. He had gone over them point by point, again and again—with a member of Goldfine's staff.

Pearson learned the behind-the-scenes story. It offered a rather dismal illustration of men and politics. When the Goldfine story began popping, Adams was hardly the soul of candor with the President. On the contrary, he privately denied the charges, apparently hoping the developing storm would vanish if he ignored it. In his private conversations with Eisenhower, Adams minimized the gifts from Goldfine. As a consequence, Eisenhower suggested that Adams go before the House Legislative Oversight Subcommittee and tell his story: "I'm certain everything will be all right after you explain," the President confidently stated.

Adams, however, was a reluctant explainer. For about four days he resisted pressures from Republican Senators and Congressmen and Republican Chairman Meade Alcorn. They put it to him bluntly: Explain or resign. In addition, there was a series of White House staff meetings during which such Administration stalwarts as Thomas Dewey and Herbert Brownell were consulted. Finally Adams yielded.

On June 21, 1958, Pearson wrote a personal and confidential letter to his editors:

> When Hagerty went to Adams and asked him about the vicuna coat, Adams replied that "the old man" got one too. He even described it as a three-quarter length coat. You will recall that Hagerty came back and told newsmen at the time that he couldn't comment. He continued to be evasive and on Monday, June 16, even when he received a direct question from the correspondent of the Manchester, N.H., *Union* as to whether Goldfine had "offered some suits to the President," Hagerty replied, "I have no knowledge of that."
>
> This, of course, was untrue. Hagerty had known the facts for three days. It was not until the next morning, June 17, that Hagerty, faced with my categoric statement that Ike had sent a letter to Goldfine thanking him for the coat and that the letter had been seen by others, finally admitted that at least some vicuna cloth had been received and accepted.
>
> Since Hagerty issued a series of detailed denials, those denials have been checked once again, and I am convinced that the original story is accurate. Take, for instance, the matter of Goldfine liquor which I reported was sometimes given to Adams. The fact is that Goldfine has a small storehouse in the rear of his home in Boston well stocked with liquor, and on one occasion Adams' station wagon hauled

> away approximately twenty cases. Adams denied that he had received other rugs from Goldfine. He called them "mats." His statement that the $2,400 Oriental rug was "borrowed" was made after Internal Revenue in Boston started a check on Goldfine's income taxes. Among other things, they are checking on whether gift taxes were paid on presents to Adams or whether they were business deductions. A gift tax would not be paid on a "borrowed" rug. Adams held a three-hour session with Goldfine while he was reported on that "fishing trip" in New England.

Incidentally, while the Adams scandal was splattering the front pages, history again demonstrated it was not above cruel little jokes. The Eisenhower Administration, which had come to office with the promise to clean up the "mess in Washington," spurred the prosecution of the Truman Administration's Matthew Connolly and Lamar Caudle. The same week that the newspapers carried a brief, buried note reporting Connolly and Caudle went to jail, page one was the scene for the Eisenhower Administration's "Goldfine Follies."

In an effort to stem the tide of headlines and outraged editorials, President Eisenhower conceded that "what Sherman Adams did was imprudent, but I need him."* Hagerty and other Administration leaders desperately concentrated on striving to convince the public that Adams was the victim of a smear. This time, the Hagerty forces were repulsed. Pearson and other columnists and editorialists continued fanning the flames. Moreover, Eisenhower was caught in an embarrassing contradiction. His decision to stand behind Adams imposed an intolerable double standard on Administration ethics. Further, GOP leaders were feeling the pressure of political consequences.

Late in August, Vice President Nixon bluntly informed the President that Adams was a political liability. Republican Senate and House nominees insisted Adams' presence in the White House was ruining them. In addition, a top secret survey of Republican sentiment concluded that "Adams must go." Hagerty and Eisenhower

* When Pearson's associate, Jack Anderson, was caught with a bugging device at the Carlton Hotel in Washington, D.C., Pearson coolly commented, "What he did was imprudent, but I need him."

were informed that some Republican leaders in Congress were planning to publicly demand Adams' ouster if the President refused to take action. Consequently, Hagerty arranged for a radio-television broadcast wherein Sherman Adams would explain his position. This was Hagerty's final public relations attempt to save what was left of Adams' reputation.

The stage was set when Adams, accompanied by Hagerty, held a lengthy conference with Eisenhower at the President's vacation office in Newport, Rhode Island. Hagerty then called a press conference and announced: "I have asked the radio and television networks to furnish time this evening for Sherman Adams to make a statement in connection with the controversy concerning himself. Others have expressed themselves through the media of national circulation and Mr. Adams now wishes to have a similar opportunity. This request is being made with the knowledge and approval of the President and that's all I have to say to you gentlemen."

One reporter asked: "Has he resigned, Jim?" Hagerty replied: "All I have is the statement I have just read you."

Sherman Adams' radio-television appearance was dramatic news. On September 22 he announced the resignation of his White House post under heavy political pressure. Adams said the decision was forced upon him "through a campaign of vilification calculated to destroy him and embarrass President Eisenhower." Adams depicted himself as the innocent victim of elements engaged in a plan to ruin him. Although Eisenhower had conceded there might have been imprudence in his relationship with Goldfine, Adams made no such concession. "I have done no wrong," he insisted.

Eisenhower accepted Adams' resignation with "sadness." A letter from the President was made public as soon as the Adams radio-television program began. The letter to Adams stated in part, "Your service has been of the highest possible order." The President hailed him as "brilliant and unselfish" and added "you will be sorely missed."

Following the speech, correspondent James Reston wrote: "In a dignified resignation, Sherman Adams said he would stay on long enough to permit an orderly transition of his duties to somebody else. This will not be an easy transition. He and he alone knew the full range of his duties. The White House staff while owing primary allegiance to the President was essentially an Adams staff."

A handful of Republican papers and several GOP leaders continued to stress that Adams was a smear victim. The overwhelming majority of the press concurred with *The New York Times* editorial position: "The resignation of Sherman Adams from his post as assistant to the President comes in belated deference to the fact that he failed to meet the highest standards of official conduct demanded by the American public and frequently proclaimed by both him and the President. . . .

"Both the President and Mr. Adams ought to have recognized the impropriety of his position long ago; but through a curious form of astigmatism they do not seem to recognize it yet. It was only after the Maine election, in which the Goldfine case contributed prominently to the disastrous rout of the Republican Party, that the political pressures from the GOP have been so strong as to lead to Mr. Adams' tardy resignation. And we have yet to hear a word of moral condemnation from the President of Mr. Adams' disregard of the proper standards of government service. In saying this, one more thing ought to be said for the thousandth time; members of Congress themselves are every day involved in conflicts of interest far more glaring than those that led to Mr. Adams' downfall. Yet Congress has failed to enact any kind of effective legislation in this regard, or to adopt for itself the kind of conflict-of-interest regulations that it rightly requires of other Government officers."

The Sherman Adams scandal damaged Eisenhower's prestige. All the king's horses and Hagerty's men never again could restore its original luster, albeit Adams' departure from the White House revived the vitality of Eisenhower's leadership. Correspondent Cabell Phillips noted in August 1959: "Eisenhower got tough with Congress where he used to be wishy-washy. He has come to grips with the substance of many big issues before him, whereas it had often seemed he was familiar with the form only. He has acquired a new sense of the institutional quality of the Presidential office and a new respect for its prerogatives." More and more the business of the Presidency received Eisenhower's personal attention. Congressmen and party leaders found it easier to reach the President. Before that, they were unable to get past Sherman Adams.

An examination of the coverage of the Sherman Adams scandal in over thirty newspapers revealed that not a single paper gave Pearson credit for the prominent role he played in the case. When this was mentioned to Pearson, he shrugged. Envy among newspapermen is not news.

New York World-Telegram and The Sun

Local Forecast: Mostly cloudy, with some rain tonight and tomorrow. Weather Forecast on Page 2.

NEW YORK, SATURDAY, MAY 7, 1960 — TEN CENTS

SPORTS FINAL — Feature Section

EDITION: BROOKLYN EDITION

Khrushchev's 'Amazing' Story!

Downed U.S. Flier Is Alive, Admits Spying, Reds Say

'Incidents' Risk H-Bomb Reprisal, Premier Hints

By HENRY SHAPIRO

MOSCOW, May 7.—Premier Nikita Khrushchev said today the pilot of a United States plane shot down 1300 miles inside Russia May 1 was alive and would be tried on spy charges. He warned that such incidents could result, under the worst circumstances, in immediate retaliation with a hydrogen bomb.

Khrushchev referred to a U.S. State Department statement that the pilot may have suffered giddiness and drifted across the border because of an oxygen failure and said:

H-Bomb Warning.

"In this case one could recall the statement of the Soviet government to the effect that a similar adven-

---

York Times.

LATE CITY EDITION

Partly cloudy today, mostly cloudy tonight. Mostly fair tomorrow.

MONDAY, AUGUST 7, 1961. — FIVE CENTS

IET ASTRONAUT DOWN SAFELY
ER ORBITING EARTH 17 TIMES;
RCISED, ATE AND SLEPT ALOFT

"All the News That's Fit to Print"

The New York Times.

LATE CITY EDIT

VOL. CX. No. 37,804. — NEW YORK, WEDNESDAY, JULY 26, 1961. — FIVE CEN

MAYOR ENDORSED BY LEHMAN GROUP; GETS PRIMARY AID

Committee for Democratic Voters Says Its Choice in Party Fight Is Clear

MOVE SWINGS 39 CLUBS

Their Members Will Provide Manpower for Petitions—Wagner Acts on Stark

By CLAYTON KNOWLES

It's 92 in Fifth Day Of Heat Wave Here

U.S. SEEKS VOICE IN TRUSTEESHIP FOR NEW HAVEN

Proposes Ex-Governor of Rhode Island for Post—Judge May Act Today

KENNEDY CALLS FOR 217,000 MEN AND 3.4 BILLION FUND TO MEET 'WORLD-WIDE' THREAT BY SOVIE

DRAFT RISE IS SET

Conventional Arms Stressed in Order on Build-Up

By JACK RAYMOND

WASHINGTON, July 25—

NO NEW TAX

207 Million Is So for Civil Defense Speech on Berl

Rendezvous With Destiny: 25 Russian Ships

—SEE STORY BELOW—

NEW YORK Herald Tribune

Established 122 Years Ago. A European Edition Is Published Daily in Paris

WEATHER
Today: Partly cloudy, breezy and cold.
Tomorrow: Fair and seasonably cold.
Reports and Maps—Page 21

THE LATE CITY

VOL. CXXII No. 42,329 — WEDNESDAY, OCTOBER 24, 1962 — FIVE CENTS

IN THE NEWS THIS MORNING

TOPIC A: THE CUBAN CRISIS—

Momentous alert. As a tense world grimly considered the war or peace prospects of the gravest crisis to confront the nuclear age, President Kennedy signed the proclamation establishing (at 10 a. m. today) the blockade of Soviet Cuba. How near the brink? U. S. warships were ready to intercept, search, and sink if necessary, 25 Soviet ships presumed to be carrying rockets and atomic warheads to Cuba. *The delay in the blockade's timing was a forewarning to Moscow—an 11th hour chance to avert a showdown.* Defense Secretary McNamara ordered all Navy and Marine Corps personnel kept on active duty.

The Communists. The Soviets canceled all troop leaves.

Zero Hour—10 A. M.; A World in Suspense

MOTOR POOL

LAUNCH PADS

Proclamation By President—

9

MR. RUSSIA MEETS THE PRESS

To join the diplomatic corps was one of Pearson's youthful aspirations. In common with all young dreams, it was lit by candlelight. Consequently he derives pride from his efforts in the diplomatic field. The Friendship Train was an outstanding quasi-diplomatic accomplishment. There have been others. On January 3, 1948, Pearson broadcast a suggestion from Milan, Italy, urging Americans of Italian descent to write their friends and relatives in Italy regarding the peaceful intentions of the American people and the advantages of our non-Communist system. His idea was promoted by Italian-language newspapers in the United States. From New York alone over one million letters were sent to Italy. Pearson also organized an overseas radio contest for the best letter written by an Italian on how to make democracy live. During the next Italian election, the Communists received an unexpected setback, and some American diplomats gave Pearson credit for helping turn the tide.

It was Pearson's idea to send balloons with friendship messages across the Iron Curtain to Czechs, Poles, Hungarians, and others in the satellite nations. Pearson proposed the balloon idea in 1948, but it was not until 1951 that the first ones were launched. The delay was caused by State Department opposition and lack of money. Ed Barrett, Assistant Secretary of State, overcame State Department reluctance, but stipulated that Pearson organize a committee of Europeans who would sign the leaflets. The Crusade for Freedom donated the money. Pearson went to Europe in 1951 and was surprised to discover the French, British, Italians, and Turks were reluctant to participate in the friendship balloon campaign. They feared it would antagonize Russia.

Only the Yugoslavs and some West German officials were willing to cooperate. Pearson managed to secure the help of the Federation of Women's Clubs (which has branches in a score of countries), the American Federation of Labor, the CIO affiliates in Canada and Cuba; the International Federation of Free Journalists signed the first friendship pamphlets. These were carried over the German border into Czechoslovakia in August 1951.

Pearson later reported: "Since then, more than 200 million pieces of literature have floated down on the Czech, Polish, and Hungarian people. The Crusade for Freedom has done a tremendous job of accelerating the idea. Judging from the bitter protests of Communist governments, the program has had some impact."

A more direct Pearson diplomatic effort was exemplified by his role in securing Cardinal Stepinac's release from a Yugoslav jail. He persuaded the Yugoslav Ambassador in Washington that freeing Stepinac would enhance American-Yugoslav relations. Pearson offered to swap the Cardinal's freedom for printing any statement Marshal Tito cared to issue. Upon the Ambassador's recommendation, Tito accepted the terms and freed Stepinac. The Yugoslav leader explained his action in a letter that Pearson duly published. Then came an unexpected problem. Everyone had acted in good faith, but Tito's letter was so lengthy that several newspapers cut it. Although such cutting of a column by syndicate editors is routine, in this case it caused Tito to accuse Pearson of bad faith. Nevertheless, relations between Pearson and Tito remained cordial. The Yugoslav dictator granted Drew an exclusive interview—one of the few he has given in latter years—in the summer of 1962. He also entertained Pearson at his summer island, Brioni, and when he came to the United States the next year, he invited Pearson to breakfast at the Waldorf-Astoria, the only newspaperman to receive such an invitation.

This doubtless inspired the accusation by Congressman Michael Feighan that Pearson was a paid agent of Tito. Feighan demanded the expulsion of Pearson from the House Press Gallery. Drew requested that the Standing Committee of Correspondents investigate the charge. They did and held that the Feighan accusation was completely without basis of fact. The charge may have had its origin in Pearson's work in Yugoslavia after World War I. From 1919 to 1921 he directed the American Friends Service Committee. Pearson contributed his own time at a salary of $10-a-month, plus more than a million dollars worth of supplies and labor, while rebuilding bombed-out Serbian villages and settling Montenegran refugees on the land.

At one time, Pearson challenged Communist Hungary. He learned that the man who had drugged Cardinal Mindszenty was Dr. Emil Weil, then serving in Washington as the Hungarian Minister. In addition to administering the drug, Dr. Weil had taken a direct hand in the Cardinal's torture both before and during his Budapest "trial." Pearson's forces were quickly mobilized. He exposed and attacked Weil in a series of columns. Not long after, Weil was recalled.

In May 1958, Pearson served as a diplomat-journalist by attending a meeting of the Union of Rumanian Journalists behind the Iron Curtain. He later wrote about his experiences in a personal and confidential letter to his editors. Pearson stated in part:

> The Union of Rumanian Journalists meeting was a three-day session for which I arrived late, attending only the last day. For the most part it was a conglomeration of either out-and-out Communists or fellow travelers. There were a few Western or pro-Western journalists. The speeches by some of the satellite journalists were most revealing. One Rumanian made a long speech about the idea of not disturbing the public by reporting train wrecks and airplane accidents. He said that under no circumstances would he bring anguish to the relatives of the injured. I discovered later that train wrecks, airplane accidents, disturbances of this kind are never reported in the satellite countries. They reflect on the efficiency of the regime.
>
> In my speech I tried to emphasize the importance of the press conference and the role the press frequently plays in criticizing government operations. I tried to point out that

> the press does not necessarily accept government statements or official handouts, but tries to serve as a watchdog for the public. I don't know whether any of this sank in or not, but they listened very carefully and there was excellent instantaneous translation into Rumanian, Russian, Chinese, French, Spanish, and I believe Korean.
>
> At the end of the session, a resolution was adopted urging that newspapermen work for peace. I had the feeling that this had political connotations, but since I had been harping on this for many years and also quoted American newspapers as being for peace, I couldn't very well be the lone objector. During the two days before I arrived, they had elected me to an executive committee, and, faced with this *fait accompli*, I accepted. After all, having made a trip halfway around the world to see how this kind of journalistic outfit operates, I figured I might just as well be on the inside. Actually, there wasn't anything very revealing about being on the inside except that we got a little extra brandy and salami sandwiches. I also got a chance to get acquainted with the Russian who was a member of the same committee. He and I frequently found ourselves in opposition to the satellites.

Whether overseas or in Washington, Pearson has an unmatched record of exclusive diplomatic stories. They fall in his column like ripe apples. For example, during the 1960 Presidential campaign, he reported that if John F. Kennedy was elected President, Russian Premier Khrushchev would make two gestures to ease East-West tension. He would release the RB-47 fliers who crashed in the Arctic and would free Francis Gary Powers, the U-2 pilot shot down over Russia. Following Kennedy's election, Pearson's story was corroborated.

The foregoing hardly lifts the eyebrows of Pearson's friends. He has pipelines into every embassy, including the Russian. Over the years he has carried on spirited debates with Russian ambassadors, notably Troyanovsky and Oumansky. Often, the discussions have taken place during dinner parties in Pearson's home. He has argued the case of the United States and expressed dismay over the Communist suppression of human rights. Nevertheless, he is fervent in his belief that the United States and Russia can exist in peace—uneasy as that peace might be—since the alternative is global annihilation.

In the summer of 1961, Premier Khrushchev put the world on the brink of war. The building of the Berlin wall and Russian threats against West Germany and other Western powers made a nuclear holocaust imminent. On July 25, 1961, President Kennedy alerted the American people to prepare for war. "We do not want to fight," the President said in an emotion-packed voice, "but we have fought before. . . . It would be a mistake for others to look upon Berlin, because of its location, as a tempting target." Further, Kennedy grimly spoke of expanding civil defense air raid shelters and the horrendous consequence of nuclear fallout.

Such was the background for an historic Pearson scoop, probably unparalleled in journalistic records. The significance is difficult to evaluate. Nonetheless, its substantial influence is beyond doubt, since it came at a time when the world was on the verge of life-or-death decisions for civilization in general.

It began when Mrs. Eugene Meyer, the Washington *Post* publisher, invited Mr. and Mrs. Pearson to join her on a chartered boat to tour the Norwegian fjords. The Pearsons were enjoying a carefree holiday when the Berlin crisis reached a critical state. Pearson decided to plan a side trip. Accompanied by Mrs. Pearson, he headed for Russia via Stockholm. His prime objective was to obtain an interview with Khrushchev.

After the Pearsons landed at the Moscow airport, Drew contacted Yuri Zhukov, chairman of the committee for cultural exchange, and Danul Kraminev, coeditor of the Russian magazine *Abroad*. It required several days and repeated phone calls to reach them. During the wait between calls, Pearson considered leaving Russia as a result of the slow-motion progress. Finally the editor called, and several days later called again and said he was arranging a luncheon for the Pearsons with prominent Russian newspapermen. Among the newsmen present at the luncheon were Aleksei Adzhubei, Khrushchev's son-in-law and editor of *Izvestia,* and Pavel Satiukev, editor of *Pravda*. They spoke English, and their discussion with the Pearsons was both lively and enlightening.

Among other topics, Aleksei Adzhubei expressed outrage about a front-page story in *The New York Times* concerning letters President Kennedy had received on ways to solve the Berlin problem. Some of the letters suggested that he "poison Khrushchev." The Russian Premier's son-in-law used this incident as an illustration of factors disrupting Russo-American relations.

The Pearsons remembered that issue of the *Times* and pointed out that the same issue carried a story about the John Birch Society contest on why Chief Justice Warren should be impeached. They told Adzhubei that they had been with the Chief Justice in Norway when he read this story, and he had laughed. Two days after the luncheon, Yuri Zhukov informed the Pearsons that an interview with Khrushchev had been arranged.

Mr. and Mrs. Pearson spent two days with the Soviet leader at his summer home on the Black Sea discussing Russo-American relations. Apparently, Khrushchev shared Pearson's apprehension that the Berlin crisis might trigger World War III. Equally apparent was his reason for agreeing to an interview: It would give him an opportunity to make new proposals through an informal meeting, and possibly help ease the tension.

Initially, Khrushchev's mood was abrasive, but as they talked he mellowed considerably. He punctuated his comments with a chuckle or a robust laugh. Even his interpreter and his two secretaries, who took notes, occasionally smiled. After four hours of conversation, Khrushchev invited the columnist and Mrs. Pearson to join him in the swimming pool and later to be his guest at dinner. The Russian leader also extended an invitation to the Pearsons to spend the night at his adjacent guest house. There was a Soviet official in the guest house, and Khrushchev told him: "You have been living like a wolf all alone down there. I have company for you."

The dacha or villa where Pearson interviewed Khrushchev was built for the benefit of holidaying Soviet officials. Comfortable but not ornate, it offered such luxurious knickknacks as a pushbutton glass partition that enclosed the pool for cold-weather use, and a huge veranda where the Khrushchev family dined. The veranda offered a breathtaking view of the Black Sea, stretching off to Turkey, Bulgaria, and Rumania.

The Eisenhowers and the Khrushchevs.

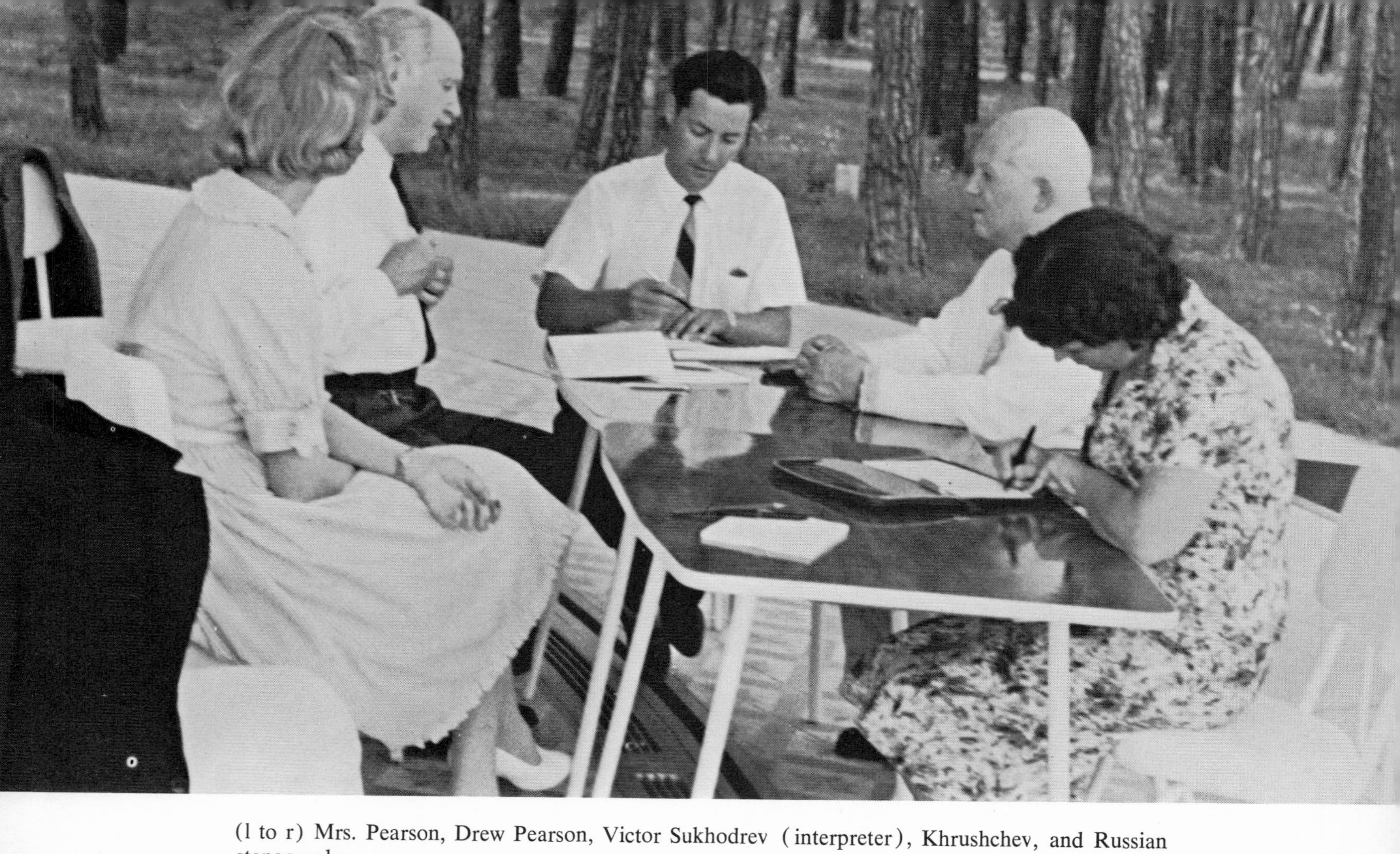

(l to r) Mrs. Pearson, Drew Pearson, Victor Sukhodrev (interpreter), Khrushchev, and Russian stenographer.

On the pebble-dappled beach there were several unpretentious bathhouses for the Khrushchev family and their staff. The Russian leader confided to Pearson as they sloshed into the water: "I can't swim very well. The only water I knew as a miner in the Ukraine was surface water in the mines."

Throughout his conversations with the columnist, Khrushchev reiterated the Kremlin's arguments over the desirability and necessity of signing peace treaties with Germany—and its determination to act alone if the Western Powers would not go along. But he also made specific proposals on Russia's willingness to help enforce all necessary safeguards for maintenance of West Berlin's freedom and independence as a "free city."

The second day of interviewing took place during breakfast, lunch, and dinner. Along with the Pearsons, the others present included one Cabinet member and his interpreter. Throughout the give-and-take, Khrushchev was generally in a relaxed, easy-does-it mood.

Pearson told Khrushchev that he suspected President Kennedy was almost more concerned over the Soviet reversal of its stand on nuclear testing at the Geneva nuclear bomb tests talks than he was over Berlin. The columnist asked why the Soviet Union had reversed its more reasonable stand of the previous year. The Russian leader emitted a deep sigh and emphasized his words as if fastening them down with thumbtacks: "A lot of time has passed, during which France was testing the atom bomb. There was no longer a monopoly among us. Perhaps tomorrow there will be others testing the bomb. So the Geneva talks are of no value now. We are interested in the much broader problem of overall disarmament."

"Would you demand the troika inspection system for general disarmament?" Pearson asked, referring to the new Soviet inspection plan devised at Geneva whereby the Soviet would have a veto over inspection.

"No, we would not," replied Khrushchev. "There would be no veto. If we had inspection for nuclear testing only, the inspectors might be agents spying on other forms of arms. But if there is total disarmament then we are not worried about inspection. We would welcome it. . . . We propose that nuclear arms be destroyed and nuclear war be banished forever—and the world agrees to us."

Khrushchev had an elephantine memory of almost every prominent American who came to Moscow in recent years. He liked Hubert Humphrey, but they did not talk the full eight hours Humphrey boasted about. "It included lunch and dinner," Khrushchev said. "I remember Kefauver. He impressed me as a strong man. I find Ambassador Thompson very intelligent and wise. And I found Ambassador Harriman a reasonable man. He and I once joked about becoming my economic adviser," Khrushchev said. "What kind of a job could you do for us?" I asked him.

"How much would you pay me? Would you give me a dacha?" Harriman asked, referring to the Russian country house. "If so, I'll take this one."

" 'OK, it's yours,' I said. 'Let's sign a contract.' I'm still waiting for him to come to work."

Khrushchev subjected Pearson to some good-natured ribbing about the benefits of Communism over Capitalism. Pearson told him his new twenty-year plan was imitating some of the things we had already achieved in the United States—good roads, more cars, shopping centers, free lunches for school children.

"We are glad to take from you," he cracked back. "We profit from your mistakes and your good points. We admit you have some. Capitalism is the father of Communism. And when I say your grandchildren will live under Communism, I want to emphasize that that does not mean war. That means healthy competition. Competition is a good thing for all of us. We intend giving you what-for, but we won't give you any black eye. We'll have a wrestling match. This we can do and yet live in peace."

Pearson asked Khrushchev about his new program of developing virgin soil in Asiatic Russia and whether he was not making a mistake in growing too much corn. "If a good capitalist can give you a suggestion," the columnist added, "why don't you try sorghum which doesn't require as much rainfall as corn, yet is excellent for feeding cattle."

"Maybe we should try it," he said. "Send me some samples. Meanwhile, I can recommend a crop to you. A new type of bean we have developed in the Ukraine. The Kavoun Collective Farm recently raised two tons to the acre. It has a short growing season and puts ninety-two kilos of nitrogen back in the soil per hectare. Also, it's a good crop to precede wheat and is an excellent weed killer. I'll send you some seed."

Following his interview, Pearson sent a private memo to his Washington staff:

> The most striking personal impression I carried away from the talks was regarding K's esteem of Eisenhower and his feeling that Ike let him down with the U-2 incident. Actually, he didn't blame Eisenhower for this. He was certain Ike didn't know about it. But he did blame him for letting it appear that he knew about it.
>
> K's personal regard for Eisenhower stemmed from two things—their talks at Camp David and Eisenhower's role in the war. Khrushchev talked at great length of the Stalingrad and Kursk fronts.
>
> During parts of our conversations I tried to explain American politics; the effect of his speeches on the U.S. public opinion; the fact that every time he got belligerent it fed the American warmongers whom he, Khrushchev, criticizes, and made Kennedy's position re Berlin more difficult. In the end, he seemed to understand this—though he is mercurial and I'm not sure he'll remember it.
>
> I must say that after the first two hours of our conversation he was most congenial, and when I said goodbye he gave me a little speech about the fact that if Russia and the United States could stand together nobody could ever start a war. I had the very definite feeling that he meant it.
>
> One other important point; from various talks with individual Russians, I gathered that the Russian people are, first, genuinely worried; second, considerably puzzled over the talk of war. They get only one point of view, of course, and they all repeat the same party line on the mistakes of the West. However, they shudder at the idea of war. I think they will support their government if war should come, but I feel sure the Kremlin realizes it will not be a happy course.
>
> I got the impression, partly from the talks with Khru-

shchev, partly from other sources, including those around him, that the time may be ripe for quiet negotiations on a diplomatic level regarding Berlin.

The rolling Black Sea was lacquered with sunlight as the tall, lanky columnist bade farewell to the short, stubby Russian leader. "Before I left," Pearson reports, "Khrushchev expressed interest in the coverage of the interview in American newspapers. Several members of his staff expressed doubt the American papers would publish it at all." The interview with Khrushchev was published in every major American newspaper and later gained worldwide coverage. As a matter of fact, after Pearson returned home he requested editors to send tear sheets. He made them into a scrapbook and sent it to Khrushchev to demonstrate a free press in action.

At the same time, Pearson wrote to editors: "Khrushchev definitely wants peace. Everything he's planning for the future of the Russian people indicates this. Furthermore, his own war experiences make him shun war." Pearson's optimism was motivated by several factors. The culmination of a sensational scoop contributed to his sense of buoyancy. Moreover, the intoxicant of engaging in high-level diplomacy and the knowledge that he helped ease world tensions helped create a mood of optimism. As a matter of fact, for several months after Pearson returned from Moscow, lesser problems failed to attract his interest. For example, he neglected to criticize Majority Leader John McCormack after Congress blocked Federal aid to education. A reporter for *Newsweek* magazine was surprised by Pearson's silence and requested an explanation. "I've been crusading for aid to education for years," Pearson commented. "The last few months I've been concentrating on how to prevent a war."

Mrs. Pearson shared her husband's zeal for world amity. She wrote an account of her thirty-six hours with Khrushchev for the *Saturday Evening Post*. The informative article was enhanced by a woman's perceptive eye for detail.

She concluded her article: "Perhaps I am naive, but I have talked to no one who has been with Mr. Khrushchev who doesn't like him and believe, as I do, that he is really a man of peace. As strongly as

Napoleon and Hitler wanted war, Khrushchev wants peace. Peace is essential for the development that he wants for his country, and he knows it. I was shocked and horrified on returning to America to find that most of the cartoonists and headline writers were depicting him as another Hitler. He is obviously not a Hitler. Of course, by then he had started testing the bomb, which was deplorable. He told us he had little choice, because America was increasing the arms to West Germany and NATO. He did not mention his own troubles with the Red Chinese.

"My family and friends have accused me of being brainwashed. One friend asked me to leave the house, saying that anyone who could say anything good about that double-crossing s.o.b. who started the Korean War was not welcome. Before leaving the house I proved via the Encyclopedia Britannica that Stalin was alive, kicking, and in command at the time of Korea. I began to feel that one first-class controversial character in the family is enough. Drew's fan mail after he merely reported what Khrushchev told him was so vitriolic I couldn't read it. So it was really against my better judgment that I was persuaded to write this report. I hope it will lead to better understanding and no controversy."

Mrs. Pearson's hope was quickly shattered. Her magazine piece was followed by a brief controversial comment: "Note: The skeptical editors of the *Post* do not share Mrs. Pearson's estimate of Mr. Khrushchev's peaceful intent. We do share her hope for 'better understanding.' "

Newspaper reaction to the Khrushchev interview was mixed. Some were quite critical. A paper in Wilmington, California, called Pearson a Communist. Pearson sued for libel—and won. Editors generally seemed to feel that what Khrushchev said should be examined and studied. On the whole, eastern editors were more favorable than those in the rest of the country. Two years after his interview with Khrushchev, Drew Pearson was in Europe visiting countries behind and in front of the Iron Curtain. In a confidential letter to editors, he wrote in part: "Two years ago, I stuck my neck out by reporting that Khrushchev was potentially a man of peace. I am now going to stick my neck out further by reporting that the Russian people, plus many of the satellite people, are ripe for the warmest kind of friendship with the United States—if we want it and if we meet them 40 percent of the way."

During this visit to Europe, Pearson had his second interview with Khrushchev—on August 16, 1963, at his summer home on the Black Sea. When Pearson arrived, Khrushchev and his son-in-law, the editor of *Izvestia*, were standing in front of the swimming pool waiting to greet him. The first thing Pearson noticed as he strolled up to the dacha was that the Russian leader had neglected to follow Mrs. Pearson's gardening counsel. (During the first visit they had exchanged gardening tips.) The grass around the house had not been mowed for weeks. This time the preparations for the interview were casual but adequate. The meeting included just one interpreter who took his own notes on a pad of paper. Pearson was interested in trying to ascertain whether Khrushchev's health was reasonably good and whether he had aged since the interview two years before. The physical change was minimal.

Following the interview, Pearson toured southern Russia. He came away impressed with the tourist activity. "The beaches in this area were jam-packed. Some of our party tried to swim at one beach, but you couldn't even sit down on the sand. There were too many people. Finally, our folks were taken to a more distant and restricted beach. The Russians operate a hydroplane service between Sochi and Gargi, and these planes, also packed with tourists, skim over the water every hour on the hour. The airplanes between Sochi and Moscow were booked solid for weeks, and the Sochi airport was crowded. Trains ran frequently through Sochi, some of them with cars marked 'Moscow to Batumi.' The rolling stock was practically new, and the trains looked more modern than most of those in Europe. I mention these things because they are indicative of the relaxed atmosphere of the Soviet world and the fact that Communists are enjoying their vacations just as much as we are and are demanding a higher standard of living."

The second Khrushchev interview was accepted with relative calm compared with the uproar evoked by the first. This was hardly surprising, since the first interview came at a time when the Russian leader had incited a grave world crisis. The anger initially directed at Pearson by many editorialists and readers is understandable. At the time, the national mood was generally querulous and uneasy. It was difficult to accept Pearson's portrait of Khrushchev as a peace-lover at a time when his threats and actions had driven civilization to the brink of nuclear war. Besides, the first Khrushchev interview posed the problems created by journalists who dabble in diplomacy.

Over the years, some of the leading Washington newspapermen have had mixed opinions on the subject. *New York Times* columnist Arthur Krock once summarized the conflicts: "Our obligations are merely those in deciding whether to go into print with information: Is it true? Has it been legitimately acquired? Is it fit to print—public property or a private matter? These satisfactorily settled, the facts are ready for their bath of printer's ink. But the statesman has other considerations. Is it premature? Will publication make the going more difficult? Will publication tend to confuse, rather than clarify, the popular mind? These are some of the problems before him, particularly if he is the President of the United States in a catastrophic hour, forcing the innnermost fibers of his body and the full resources of his spirit into his colossal task."

Walter Lippmann recognized the problem during his seventieth birthday speech before the National Press Club: "Is it not absurd that anyone should think he knows enough to write so much about so many things? You write about foreign policy. Do you see the cables which pour into the State Department every day from all parts of the world? Do you attend the staff meetings of the Secretary of State and his advisers? Are you a member of the National Security Council? And what about all those other countries you write about? Do you have the run of No. 10 Downing Street, and how do you listen in on the deliberations of the Presidium in the Kremlin? Why don't you admit that you are an outsider and are therefore by definition an ignoramus?"

On the other hand, columnist Joe Alsop has argued: "Tell the people the truth about their situation, and people will respond to any challenge that the truth offers. That is the fundamental rule of democratic society. If you do not believe it, you do not believe in democracy. And it is a reporter's job to see that the truth is told. In the American democracy, moreover, the reporter has a very much more important role than in other Western democracies. No government in history, alas, has ever voluntarily told the whole truth, or anything like the whole truth, in its official statements, its approved discourses, and its organized press conferences. The whole truth is only revealed or approximated by long public debate; the realistic estimate is only reached after viewpoint has been tested against viewpoint, and all the facts, pro and con, have been weighed against each other. And in the United States, the debate about the nation's situation and the nation's policy is mainly carried on in the press."

Pearson tends to agree with Alsop's view. He knows that officials often attempt to conceal or distort. It is the reporter's job to get the facts and stimulate public debate. Too, he can serve as a channel for concepts and policies that provide healthy democratic controversies. The Khrushchev interview enabled Pearson to function as a diplomatic broker, albeit critics accused him of operating as a mouthpiece for Communist propaganda. Actually, the function of newspapermen as middlemen on all levels of government represents an essential contribution to a free society. For the alternative is to allow the government to decide what the people shall know—and that is tyranny.

Pearson rode out the storm caused by the initial Khrushchev interview serene in the knowledge he had played a constructive role. Years later, in recalling the Khrushchev story, he proudly stated: "It probably helped to lead to the test-ban treaty, more East-West trade, and the present coexistence period." Whether his journalistic coup had such sweeping historical consequences is questionable, but it is undeniable that it had an impact on the course of events. And it is equally undeniable that the Khrushchev interview was a scoop of the first magnitude.

e New York Times

LATE CITY EDITI

Weather: Fair, windy and co
day and tonight; milder tom
Temp. range: today 55-38;
51-37, Full U. S. report on Pa

NEW YORK, FRIDAY, APRIL 28, 1967

10 CE

rson Sued $5 Million

CHADWICK

ON (AP) — Sen. odd has answered ew Pearson's and on's charges of filing a $5 million d libel suit against d in U.S. District

attorney, accuses the columnists of falsely picturing the Connecticut Democrat as unfit to be a senator, as an agent of foreign interests, as interfering with the award of government contracts in return for bribes, and as unlawfully diverting campaign funds for his personal

Among other things, Dodd denies in the suit that he had made a trip to West Germany in 1964 to help Chicago public relations man Julius Klein "hang onto his clients," that he had ever made any Senate speeches written for him by Klein, or that

CENSURE OF DODD IS ASKED IN ETHICS PANEL'S REPORT FOR 'DISHONOR' OF SENAT

VOTE UNANIMO

Diversion of Campai Funds for Persona Use Is Assailed

Are LBJ Press Conferences 'White House Snow Jobs'?

By ERWIN KNOLL
FROM THE PRESS WASHINGTON BUREAU

The White House is pleading "not guilty" to a professional journalism society's charge that President Johnson has downgraded the presidential press conference in an effort to produce a "snow job."

George Christian, Johnson's press secretary, produced statistics showing that the President has held 113 news conferences in his four years in office—an average of better than one session with reporters every two weeks.

That record, Christian noted, compares favorably with the frequency of news conferences in previous administrations.

But the record also shows that the number of news conferences has declined within the past year, while the administration has increasingly been ... for fostering a "credibility ... g the American people.

RITICISM of the President's ... ce came over the weekend ... Freedom of Information Com... Sigma Delta Chi, the national ... society.

...mittee said in its annual re... some of the administration's ...ficials have been "deliberate... ing the public, the press and ...ss through flat lies, through ... s and through clever use of ... that distort."

...rt singled out as particularly ... Johnson's refusal to conduct ...ferences with "reasonable ad...ce," and added:

...e of press conferences makes ...ble for any but the White ...ulars to be present, and it ...nlikely that he will face any ... consistent hard questioning ...bject.

• • •

AS IT well organized for a ...use snow job,' even though it ... if he is as successful in ac... ng his purpose as he was a ...ore ago."

...sked to comment on the re... ...ristian told White House cor... ...are better

Of the 113 conferences Johnson has held since entering the White House, Christian noted, 25 have been carried "live" by one or more of the television networks, and 22 have been filmed or taped for TV. The remainder have been attended only by the writing press.

Most of the latter have been "... promptu" sessions when regular Wh... House reporters were summoned w... little or no advance notice.

Figures for the current year, f... nished by Christian at a reporter's ... quest, show that there have been ... news conferences for the writing pr... only, and seven before the cameras. ... the seven, however, at least two we... held away from the White House a... attended only by the reporters who re... ularly cover the President—one on th... island of Guam and one in a hang... at the LBJ ranch in Texas.

• • •

ALTHOUGH Johnson as well as h... press spokesmen have pledged on ... number of occasions to hold at lea... one pre-scheduled televised news co... ference a month, the President allowe... a period of more than five months ... elapse this year—from early March u... til late August—without such a pre... conference.

Johnson's aides have made no secre... of the President's distaste for the larg... televised news conferences. They sa... he must carefully weigh every word h... utters at such sessions, and is require... to spend too much time being "briefed... on topics that might come up.

The President himself has confide... that he much prefers the informal an... impromptu gathering of White Hous... correspondents around his desk in th... oval office.

He knows most of these "regulars" by name, and in the absence of th... cameras does not hesitate to brush aside an unwelcome question, or even to rebuke a reporter for asking it.

• • •

THE READINESS with which the President can avoid questions he prefers not to answer is one of the major criticisms leveled at these informal sessions. Another is the fact that they pro... vide no opportunity for the "specialists" ... press corps — the

L

The New York Times

Published every day by The New York Times Company

ADOLPH S. OCHS, Publisher 1896-1935
ORVIL E. DRYFOOS, Publisher 1961-1963

re for Dodd

...rtisan committee has reached the expected ...dgment on the conduct of Senator Thomas ... Connecticut. Although Mr. Dodd ...e censure verdict as "harsh," the co... ...could not in conscience have done le... ...ver aspects of this case are the resp... ... Justice Department and the courts. ...o decide whether Mr. Dodd's diver... ... dinner funds to his own use con... ... evasion.

...he censure is voted, Mr. Dodd's ef... ... member of the Senate will be at ... ... do better to withdraw to private li... ... a political ghost in the pathetic l... ...n" in the 1970 election.

...d case has frequently been compar... ...dam Clayton Powell. There are sig... ... as well as similarities. They are ... ... misconduct is deserving of censu... ...s the courts find them guilty of a... ...ould be expelled.

...ell's misuse of public funds as a com... however, was a more clear-cut offen... ... shuffling of campaign funds. Mo... ... has been virtually a fugitive from ...rk because of the contempt-of-court ...g against him. It is for this latter ...gh the House should recognize Mr. ... elected member, we believe it shoul... ... to stand aside until he purges him...

... Mansfield, the majority leader, a... ...nocrats have an obligation to emula... ...nocrats and strip Mr. Dodd of his sen... ... conduct "is contrary to accepted m... ...the public trust expected of a Senato... ...ing the Senate into dishonor and disre... ...e grotesque to continue him as chairm... ...mmittee on Juvenile Delinquency and ... of the Subcommittee on Internal Sec... ...mittee report mildly rebukes Senator D... ...ployes for rifling his files to obtain ... ...vidence of his activities. Yet it is dif... ... Mr. Dodd's misdeeds could have be... ...erwise. These former employes acted ... ...rivate gain and, indeed, have suffere... ...tive. They deserve approbation, as d... ...rew Pearson and Jack Anderson, wh... ... the documents, acted in accord wit... ... of crusading journalism.

...ercover acquisition of this evidence w... ...ot have been necessary if Congress ... an independent board to which these ... employes could have complained.

REAGAN REBUTTED ON AIDES' OUSTER

Homosexuality Was Reason, Press Secretary Admitted

By TOM WICKER
Special to The New York Times

WASHINGTON, Nov. 4—Although Gov. Ronald Reagan of California publicly has denied that Lyn Nofziger, his press secretary, told reporters that two Reagan staff members had been dismissed as homosexuals, The New York Times has learned that Mr. Nofziger did make such a statement on several occasions.

Mr. Nofziger gave that explanation of the dismissals to at least three reporters aboard the S.S. Independence, as it sailed to the Virgin Islands last month with the 1967 National Governors Conference aboard.

Mr. Nofziger, reached by telephone at the Santa Monica Airport, said:

"This is a closed subject and I don't have any comment to make."

The three reporters were Paul Hope of The Washington Evening Star, David Broder of The Washington Post and Karl Fleming of the Los Angeles bureau of Newsweek magazine.

None of the three would allow himself to be quoted for publication.

Before that, Mr. Nofziger made the same allegation to three West Coast reporters, Carl Greenberg of The Los Angeles Times, Jack McDowell of The San Francisco Examiner, and Bill Ames of the Columbia Broadcasting System.

None of them would comment publicly, either.

Mr. Nofziger made his com...

Continued on Page 78, Column 3

Gen. Westy Rips Pearso 'Feud' Repo

By KEYES BEECH

HONOLULU (CDN) — William C. Westmoreland ... that a report by syndicat... umnist Drew Pearson tha... at odds with his civilian ... in Washington is a "vicio... licious smear, complete... leading, completely d... and completely wrong."

The general made a bi... rebuttal of Pearson's ... before he left for Was... to report to President J...

Pearson reported on ... that Westmoreland wa... fire in Washington fo... thing "from playing te... ery afternoon while hi... sweat it out in the ... jungle" to harboring ... ambitions.

Asked if he had poli... bitions, a recurrin... Westmoreland said: ... swer is an emphatic ...

About Tennis

On his tennis play... you know, I spend th... days a week in the fi... times, when I was in ... went to play tenn... Sports Club during ... —I had a sandwich a...

"Not long ago I ... my new headquarte... Son Hut (near Saigo... so I resigned from ... Club. I still play te... can, during my lun... court less than fi...

REAGAN REBUTTED ON AIDES' OUSTER

...ntinued From Page 1, Col. 1

...nts to these reporters long ...r the men in question had ... the Reagan staff. There... ... the reporters considered ... incident closed and none of ... wrote or broadcast ...t it.

...st week, however, the col... ...st Drew Pearson alleged in ... ...ndicated article that two ...sexuals had been dis... ...d from the staff and that ... Nofziger had told this to ...ers aboard the Independ...

... Reagan then held a news

news conference, raised his hand and said, "Confirmed."

The two statements together constituted apparent denials that neither Mr. Nofziger nor Mr. Reagan had told reporters aboard the Independence that two staff men had been dismissed as homosexuals.

The New York Times has learned, however, that one reporter asked Mr. Nofziger directly why a former member of the Reagan staff had left. The press secretary replied with the allegation that the man in question was a homosexual.

The reporter asked Mr. Nofziger why he would give out such information.

Mr. Nofziger replied that the deposed aide had been spreading the word that he was still influential with Governor Reagan. Therefore, Mr. Nofziger ...

months in getting rid of the offenders" and Mr. Nofziger "belatedly sought to create the impression that the Governor had acted promptly."

"I'm quite convinced that Governor Reagan has lied regarding his knowledge of homosexuals in his government," Mr. Pearson said.

Asked to comment on Mr. Pearson's assertion, Mr. Nofziger, reached by telephone in Sacramento, said:

"We are just not discussing it."

The Governor himself was not available for questioning.

In a column, Mr. Pearson had charged that a homosexual ring involved two persons on Mr. Reagan's staff and that the ring had included ...

glad to ... Lynch.

When M... to invest... pointees ... ministration ... re's elec... said, he w...

Mr. Pear... no threats ... been made ... before or a... of his column...

However, ... been inform... call from o... foremost pu... eminent Reaga... an agreement ... pers not to p...

Governor R... that he did th...

10

WASHINGTON, VIETNAM, AND HELL

The relationship between the press and President is influenced primarily by political exigencies, the course of events, and the Chief Executive's personality. By and large, the methodology is as individual as fingerprints. Thus, President Kennedy made extensive use of televised press conferences. Articulate, witty, and handsome, he was the perfect camera subject. His television performances enchanted the nation; he was a star as well as a President. President Johnson, on the other hand, believed the informal press conference was his milieu. During his first few months in office, he held off-the-cuff conferences whenever the mood was upon him. They took place on the White House lawn and beside haystacks at his Texas ranch. His random press meetings inspired the Baltimore *Sun* to comment: "Will the next conference be tonight, tomorrow, or next week? Will it be held on horseback? In the White House swimming pool? Will the public be invited and the press excluded?"

Of course, no President governs for long without clashing with some members of the press. John F. Kennedy made a massive effort to befriend journalists. He socialized with many of them, sought their counsel, and offered the utmost in cooperation. Nevertheless, after his first year in office, Kennedy's honeymoon with the press lost much of its romantic glow. As Kennedy's involvement and responsibilities in controversial issues expanded, he became the focus of criticism. The Washington *Post*'s Carroll Kilpatrick scolded Kennedy: "He has neglected his opportunities to use the forum of the

Presidency as an educational institution." Walter Winchell charged JFK with dictatorial tactics. James Reston regretted Kennedy "never really exploited his considerable gifts as a public educator." Drew Pearson criticized him for escalating the war in Vietnam. *Look* magazine listed the indignities suffered by Washington newspapermen as a result of high-handed tactics by the Kennedy Administration. It inspired JFK's comment to reporters, "This is the best example of paranoia I have seen from those fellows yet."

Inevitably, Kennedy's detachment and objectivity gradually diminished and the element of self-justification became paramount. Consequently, the New York *Herald Tribune*'s criticism of the Kennedy Administration provoked the President to bar the paper from the White House. Later, some newspapers and columnists accused his Administration of "managing the news." As his difficulties with the press increased, Kennedy became, according to his aide, Theodore Sorensen, convinced of the truth of Oscar Wilde's observation, "In America, the President reigns for four years, but Journalists govern forever."

Inevitably, Kennedy's successor was confronted with the general accuracy of Wilde's aphorism. Following the customary brief press euphoria, journalistic hostility erupted. The President conveyed his dismay to James Reston, who reported: "Johnson said he wanted to do only one thing as President of the United States: 'I want to unify this country.' But he doubted whether he could do so because of the antagonism of some elements of the press. There was in this country, he went on, a group of papers and writers determined to make him look like 'an irresponsible hick.' I tried to interrupt, but he wouldn't let me. He really wondered, he said sadly, whether we were 'far enough from Appomattox' for a Southern President to be able to unify the country. I was so disturbed by this that I finally managed to blurt out that he had problems with the press, but nobody was trying to cut him up because he was a Southerner, and we had enough problems in the South without imagining things that weren't true. No, he concluded, it was true, and maybe we were talking about the wrong question."

President Johnson is not always quietly melancholy in dealing with journalistic opposition. More often than not, he functions best privately—and he operates like a whirlwind. Ted Lewis, the New York *Daily News* Washington correspondent, once described Johnson in action: "He is formidably ingratiating—in private or semi-private gatherings. He easily dominates any group where he can look a man in the eye, grab lapels, poke chests, and talk about what happens to be on his mind." Another Washington journalist, Stewart Alsop, was a prime subject of the Johnson method. Alsop was called in and listened to a two-hour appeal by Johnson as a result of something he wrote in a magazine. Johnson explained, cajoled, pleaded, and thundered—and finally escorted the dazed reporter out of his office with an arm around his shoulder. Johnson's objection was evoked by two sentences in Alsop's lengthy magazine piece.

Late in 1967, Pearson opined that Johnson had adopted a more benign attitude toward the press: "The President has become philosophical about the press. He is still sensitive to criticism, but far less so than Kennedy or Eisenhower or even Franklin Roosevelt. No longer does he argue with newspapermen as he did during his first two years in office." Several weeks later, Max Frankel, *The New York Times* White House correspondent, offered a conflicting opinion: "The President openly taunts the reporters around the White House by explaining some imprecise answer as his way of making sure he will not appear 'incredible.' He regularly berates the columnists for dissecting his policies without asking to hear his justifications. He monitors the television newscasts, three screens at a time, and begs to know why one or another action is ascribed to him when he has barely begun to think of the matter. He hurls newspapers at visitors, pleading to be told why two rude dissenters in an audience are able to steal headlines from his Secretary of State." In November 1967, the Wall Street Journal reported that FBI agents were diverted from their duties to investigate "leaks" of non-military news that the President planned to announce on his own time.

President Johnson's fury reaches tantrum proportions when journalists bare his secrets. When Bill Moyers was the White House Press Secretary, he explained the President's view: "It is important for a President to maintain up to the moment of decision his options, and for someone to speculate for days or weeks in advance that he's going to do thus and thus is to deny the President the time he needs in order to make, in the light of existing circumstances, the best possible decision." In some circumstances this is true. But not in every circumstance. And therein lies the dilemma between the press and the President.

More important than personality—and more significant in the course of Johnson press relations—has been history. In this case the tragedy of Vietnam was the major factor in the President's press problems. This difficult, tortuous struggle eventually aroused bitter condemnations in and out of the press. Later, the White House was accused of creating "a credibility gap."

The President, while ascribing to the principle of dissent, made public his anger with critics, journalistic and otherwise. He argued: "Put away all the childish divisive things if you want the maturity and the unity that is the mortar of a nation's greatness. I do not think that those men who are out there fighting for us think we should enjoy the luxury of fighting each other back home. . . . The road ahead is going to be difficult. There will be some nervous Nellies and some who will become frustrated and bothered and break ranks under the strain and turn on their own leaders, their own country, their own fighting men. If you are too busy or not inclined to help, please count ten before you hurt. Because we have no doubt today about the determination of the American men wearing American uniforms . . . trying to protect your liberty. These men are not going to fail us. Now the real question is: Are we going to fail them? Our staying power is what counts in the long and dangerous months ahead. The Communists expect us to lose heart. . . . They believe that the political disagreements in Washington, the confusion and doubt in the United States, will hand them a victory on a silver platter in Southeast Asia."

The sharpest response to Johnson's oration was made by columnist Walter Lippmann, a prime critic of the Administration's Vietnam policies. Lippmann wrote: "If the President's version of history is correct, it follows that when there is an issue of war and peace, the only safe and patriotic course is to suspend debate and rally around the President. It amounts to saying that debate on the vital issues of war and peace gives aid and comfort to the enemy. Under such a rule, the American people would have had no right to debate the momentous question of whether in 1917 and 1939 they should emerge from the isolationism which they had practiced since Washington's Farewell Address and the Declaration of the Monroe Doctrine. This is an impossible course for a free people. . . . How else but by debate are the great questions of war and peace—of isolation and intervention and of military expansion onto the Asian continent —to be decided?"

Lippmann later broke relations with the Johnson Administration by exiling himself from Washington and migrating to New York.

Strangely, another battle-scarred veteran of Presidential wars has generally maintained cordial relations with the White House: Drew Pearson, of all people.

Pearson and Lyndon Johnson crossed paths when Johnson was a young Congressman from Texas. They often met at the home of Charles Marsh, a newspaper publisher who owned a string of papers in Texas. Marsh played a major role in financing Johnson's campaign for the House of Representatives and later for the Senate. The publisher was a bona fide New Dealer and his friends included Henry Wallace, then Secretary of Agriculture, Claude Pepper, Senator from Florida and Creekmore Fath, a young Texas liberal who was then counsel for a Senate committee. It was with the Marsh group that Lyndon absorbed his political liberalism.

From that time, Pearson and Johnson have liked each other, sometimes fought with each other, but always maintained a mutual respect. When Johnson was running for Senator from Texas and faced a bitter battle with Governor Coke Stevenson, it was Pearson's pointed question at a Stevenson press conference which tipped the balance in Johnson's favor. He won by a mere eighty-seven votes.

The controversy over the Taft-Hartley Act was a crucial factor in the election. Johnson was anti-Taft-Hartley while Governor Stevenson remained mum on the subject, albeit he privately assured labor leaders in Texas he would support it. Thus Stevenson was in the position of gaining the support of those who supported the Taft-Hartley Act as well as the labor leaders who opposed it.

When Stevenson came to Washington and held a press conference, Pearson confronted him with a point-blank question: Was he for or against the Taft-Hartley Act? Stevenson was compelled to confess his opposition. The headlines in Texas papers cost Stevenson many votes. The result was Johnson's narrow victory.

Johnson was temporarily grateful to Pearson. Some time later, he tangled with Pearson in 1956 when as Senator from Texas, Johnson pushed the Natural Gas Act, which would have permitted gas companies to be exempt from Federal Power Commission regulation. Pearson retaliated by exposing some of the lobbying connected with this legislation, including that of John Connally, Lyndon's one-time administrative assistant, who operated brazenly for the gas companies and later was to become Governor of Texas. The exposés infuriated Johnson. He countered by phoning every one of Pearson's papers in Texas and demanded that they cancel the column. About half of them did.

Earlier, in January 1950, Pearson and Johnson clashed over Senator Joe McCarthy. Drew visited Johnson, then Senate Minority Leader, and informed him that McCarthy planned a one-hour anti-Pearson speech on the Senate floor the following day. Aware that McCarthy would call him a Communist, Pearson said "it would be helpful if one of my friends stood up and defended me."

Johnson gave Pearson an icy stare: "You've been writing some unkind things about me lately," he said, closing the subject.

Johnson did not defend Pearson on the Senate floor the next day and Pearson did not defend Johnson for some time thereafter. He went back to his files and collected the items he had written about Johnson since he arrived in Washington. The tabulation showed Pearson comments were 99 per cent pro-Johnson. He sent the score to the Senator from Texas without comment.

Another event which marred the Johnson-Pearson relationship was the attempt of the Senate subcommittee of the Rules Committee to report on Joe McCarthy's shocking financial transactions. The committee, under the chairmanship of Senator Tom Hennings of Missouri, did an effective job of uncovering the enormous sums of money McCarthy received from the public to investigate Communists, but which he used to speculate on soy beans and various other commodities on the Chicago Board of Trade. McCarthy had used over $100,000 for such speculative purposes. The subcommittee collected the facts and prepared a detailed report that was to be issued in December 1952. Time was a crucial factor. It was doubtful whether it would be published after January 1, 1953. In early December, Senator Tom Hennings disappeared. Hennings was an outstanding Senator when sober. Pearson had known Hennings since he arrived in Washington and had helped him survive his alcoholic bouts as well as an unfortunate marriage.

Hennings' disappearance meant the McCarthy report might die aborning. Pearson eventually located the chairman of the subcommittee in the Plaza Hotel in New York in the company of the daughter of a Congressman. Hennings was persuaded to return and dined with Pearson soon after he came to Washington. He went back to work the following morning and did a masterful job, completing the McCarthy report and preparing it for publication.

Johnson was not opposed to the Hennings report, nor was he enthusiastic. At the time, he had no firm convictions about McCarthy or McCarthyism. Most of his Texas constituents, especially his campaign contributors, were in McCarthy's corner and Johnson was walking a political tightwire. Hence it was embarrassing for him when Pearson urged him privately to support a move to bar McCarthy from being seated on the ground that he had misappropriated public funds. Johnson flatly refused. Pearson did his best to rally a handful of Senators and received sympathetic support from a small band: Senators Margaret Chase Smith, George Aiken, Irving Ives and Wayne Morse. The report on McCarthy's financial affairs was published, but played down by most papers. At the time, McCarthyism was riding high, Senator McCarthy had helped elect Eisenhower and the newspapers of the nation, 80 percent Republican, did not consider the report big news.

The small group of Senators Pearson had enlisted did make a vain effort to prevent McCarthy from being seated. They were swept aside by the power of the Republican majority combined with the Senator from Texas, who led the Democratic minority. It follows that for some months thereafter, Johnson and Pearson were not on the best of terms. Nor were their relations aided by Pearson's revelations that during FDR's Administration, Congressman Lyndon Johnson helped the Brown and Root construction company when they were in serious tax trouble. The company contributed $100,000 to the Democratic campaign in Texas and then sought to deduct it as a business expense. Pearson told in detail how Lyndon had gone to the White House and persuaded President Roosevelt to countermand Secretary of the Treasury Henry Morgenthau's order to prosecute Brown and Root.

The two men resumed diplomatic relations after Johnson played a major role in pushing through the first Civil Rights Bill in 83 years. To Pearson, this was a heartening reminder that Johnson had reverted to his New Deal liberalism. This was buttressed by other pieces of legislation promoted by Johnson. Times had changed. The Natural Gas Bill was dead, Joe McCarthy had been censured. Many of the policies involving the oil barons and McCarthyism, which had split Johnson and Pearson, were now historic landmarks.

Pearson dropped his term "Lying Down Lyndon" and wrote a column highlighting the liberal policies which made him "Likeable Lyndon." The two men then joined forces to defeat Admiral Lewis Strauss, former chairman of the Atomic Energy Committee, who was nominated by Eisenhower for Secretary of Commerce. Pearson explains: "Strauss had fallen for McCarthyism and staged a trial of Dr. Robert Oppenheimer, father of the A-bomb, which ended in Oppenheimer being purged from the government altogether. I went to bat vigorously for Oppenheimer during his trial and felt that it was only poetic justice that Strauss, the man who persecuted Oppenheimer, get his just desserts when he came up for Senate confirmation. I argued that Strauss had been mixed up in the Dixon-Yates conflict of interest case, had not told the truth in the Senate during this investigation, and that any man who did not tell the truth to the Senate was not worthy of confirmation. Senator Clinton Anderson, who had dealt with Strauss in detail on atomic matters, vigorously agreed, as did Senator Warren Magnuson, chairman of the Senate Commerce Committee, before whom Strauss came for confirmation. At a dinner meeting in my home, it was decided to make the fight against Strauss. Lyndon Johnson, then majority leader of the Senate, masterminded the drive. Strauss was defeated. It was only the fifth time in American history that a President had been denied confirmation of a member of his Cabinet."

Since then, Pearson and Johnson have remained reasonably good friends, although Pearson reserves the right to disagree. After supporting Johnson against John F. Kennedy at the Democratic convention in Los Angeles and later writing a series of flattering columns about the Vice-Presidential candidate, Pearson wrote a scathing report on Lyndon's attempt to dominate the Senate after he became Vice President. Shortly after Pearson denounced Johnson's power grab, there was a New Year's Day reception at the home of Congressman Hale Boggs. The host showed Pearson and the Vice President into separate rooms. "Lyndon is in the other room," said Boggs to Drew. "You stay in this room."

Pearson was in Dallas on the black day in November 1963 when John F. Kennedy was assassinated. He did not see the new President on that day. They got together at dinner approximately a week later and Pearson learned at first hand the trials and tribulations the new President faced. Since that time, he has differed with the President on some things and supported him on others.

Some of Pearson's columns about Luci and Lynda Bird have riled the President. He defended Lynda when she went to Greece in September 1964 as an official representative of the United States for the wedding of King Constantine. Some of the Greek papers were critical, but Drew reported in detail how hard she worked, the visits she made to hospitals, servicemen's clubs and universities. On the other hand, when she went to Spain in the summer of 1966 with eight Secret Servicemen, at a time when her father urged foreign travel restrictions, Pearson wrote a column that caused pain at the White House. He also wrote critically of Luci's wedding. While thousands of families were burdened by the sacrifices of the Vietnam war, he stressed the contrast offered by Luci's wedding extravaganza. The President was furious. The mail flooded Pearson's office in general approval.

On a political level, Pearson has differed with the President on the dispatch of troops to the Dominican Republic and some Vietnam policies, such as bombing the north. On the constructive side, Pearson sent a vital message to Johnson (after he interviewed Khrushchev in 1964) involving relations with Cuba. He has also counselled the President from time to time on Pan-American relations, Russian policies, and on various consumer projects.

At one time, the President remarked: "I can always tell when I'm up or when I'm down, according to what Drew writes. When I am down, Drew goes to my defense. When I am up, Drew takes a nick at me." Pearson's sympathy for Lyndon Johnson stems partially from his advocacy of the Administration's Great Society aspirations—an extension of the New Deal. Additionally, although Pearson is not a supporter of Johnson's Vietnam policies, his criticism has been tempered by his earnest opinion that in the Vietnam quagmire the President has been a victim of historical forces. Pearson's position in this case is activated by his knowledge of backstage history.

It is a history replete with the vagaries of contemporary events as well as the dramatically distinct human elements. Yet, through the complicated fabric of Vietnam, there is a single bloody thread. It began in 1946 when the French army became embroiled in Indochina's guerrilla war. For the next eight years the United States expended about $4 billion in aid to the French army. In 1953 United States Lieutenant General John W. O'Daniel submitted a secret report to the Pentagon suggesting the creation of a Vietnamese army. In the spring of 1954 he was dispatched to Saigon. The French were uncooperative. Jealous of their sovereignty, they banned United States military activity in Indochina, although they permitted Americans to inscribe requisition blanks for additional United States supplies. Meanwhile, a power struggle was brewing between the Pentagon and the White House.

The Pentagon favored direct American intervention in Indochina. President Eisenhower and Army Chief of Staff Matthew Ridgway were vigorously opposed. Secretary of State John Foster Dulles vacillated. Early in 1954, President Eisenhower privately informed Pearson, "I'm not going to get American boys bogged down in the swampland of the Asian mainland." Nevertheless, Eisenhower was continually pressured to change his mind by Admiral Radford, Chairman of the Joint Chiefs of Staff. The Admiral urged American air strikes in Indochina plus the dispatch of four American Army divisions. The President flatly rejected the proposal.

August 1964: Humphrey, Johnson, and Senator Dodd.

However, behind-the-scene pressures on Eisenhower remained constant. Vice President Nixon, as well as Admiral Radford, led the interventionists. Eventually—in January 1954—Secretary Dulles, who had been indecisive on the issue, publicly proclaimed his doctrine of "instant retaliation at times and places of our own choosing." It was assumed he was referring to Indochina. Nevertheless, one month later, Eisenhower declared all-out American intervention in Indochina would be a tragedy. Several weeks later the President learned French forces in Indochina were on the verge of defeat. Accordingly, Eisenhower changed his tune, and on March 24 he informed the American people that Indochina was of "transcendent importance" to the United States.

On April 16, in an off-the-record talk to the American Society of Newspaper Editors, Vice President Nixon stated that the United States was considering sending troops to Indochina. The *London Daily Telegraph*, not bound by the off-the-record pledge, published Nixon's statement. It created a headline splash on both sides of the Atlantic. At this point, Admiral Radford took an unprecedented action. With the tacit approval of Nixon, he went to London to enlist Winston Churchill's support. Churchill, Pearson later learned, supported the concept of a united allied front against Communist expansion in the Far East, but he feared direct intervention in Indochina would endanger Britain's Hong Kong. Further, Foreign Minister Anthony Eden bluntly informed Washington via transatlantic phone that if the United States intervened in Indochina "it would fight without allies."

Late in April 1954 the beleaguered French made a desperate plea for direct British-American intervention. Foreign Minister Eden flew to Geneva to report that the British government opposed even moral support for intervention. At the same time, Eisenhower called a meeting of Congressional leaders. Richard Russell, the Chairman of the Senate Armed Services Committee, and Lyndon Johnson, the Majority Leader of the Senate at the time, agreed that Vietnam was not vital to the security interests of the United States and expressed firm opposition to intervention by American military forces. Consequently, the United States failed to buttress the Nixon-Dulles tough-talk with action. Another reason for Washington inaction was a secret Congressional poll by the Administration. It showed only five Congressmen willing to approve a war. Thus, the French turned to Russia's Foreign Minister Molotov, who intervened with the Red Chinese, bailed out the French, and dictated the terms of an Indochina settlement. The fateful settlement consisted of carving Indochina into North and South Vietnam, Laos, and Cambodia. North Vietnam was controlled by the Communists and South Vietnam was presumed to be independent. At this point, Eisenhower decided to send 1,000 American troops to Vietnam as advisers. His decision was partly influenced by die-hard interventionists at the Pentagon and State Department and partially because of Cardinal Spellman, head of the New York Roman Catholic archdiocese.

Cardinal Spellman's interest in Vietnam was understandable. The carving of Vietnam into Communist North and non-Communist South created a major problem. Over one million Catholics resided in the north and thousands decided to migrate south. This required social readjustments and money. In December 1954, Cardinal Spellman went to Saigon and announced a gift of $100,000 to aid Catholic refugees. This was followed by a contribution of more than $20 million by the United States.

From December 1954 to late in 1961, American policy in Vietnam was inconclusive. In the fall of 1961, President Kennedy sent Walt Rostow, his foreign affairs adviser, and General Maxwell Taylor, his military adviser, to South Vietnam to examine the problems of the small war. Rostow studied the situation, retreated to Baguio, the Philippine summer resort, and wrote a report recommending that Kennedy order a full division to South Vietnam. At that time there were about 1,500 Americans there. Rostow urged an increase to about 18,000. General Taylor signed the report. President Kennedy, shaken by the Bay of Pigs fiasco and anxious to recoup his prestige, subsequently sent 18,000 troops. Later he raised the number to 30,000. In Pearson's judgment, Kennedy was consistently hawkish. In 1954 when John Foster Dulles shook his fist at North Vietnam, the then-Senator Kennedy supported Dulles and added, "If necessary, the United States will take the ultimate step—it is war." Further, as President, his military build-up in South Vietnam caused the International Control Commission on June 25, 1962, to officially cite South Vietnam for violating the 1954 Geneva agreement by making "a factual military alliance with the United States."

Thus, on the basis of historical evidence, the columnist believes President Johnson inherited an insoluble war. Consequently, Pearson's position is something of a paradox. He deplores the war, debunks the hawks—yet refuses to be harshly critical of Lyndon Johnson. One striking example of his debunking campaign was offered in a column dated February 28, 1965: "We contend that we are in South Vietnam at the request of the popular government. This is pure bunk. The government in South Vietnam has changed so often that no one can keep track of whether Big Minh, Little Minh, or Minnie Mouse is in power. There have been fourteen changes of government since January 30, 1964, which is an average of one government per month. Government in South Vietnam is of the military, by the military, and for the military, and Vietnamese civilians have no illusions about it."

In Pearson's opinion, the best long-range hope for the United States in Indochina is Titoism. "Ho Chi Minh," he writes, "could be another Tito if we don't drive him into the hands of the Chinese as we have been doing. It is important to remember that the Thais, the Vietnamese, and Burmese have hated and feared the Chinese for centuries. If given a chance for independence they don't want to come under the domination of the Chinese dragon."

Pearson's compassionate perspective of Johnson's role in the Vietnam crisis includes the lush landscape of his Administration's domestic achievements. The columnist believes Lyndon Johnson's home-front accomplishments exceed those of Franklin Roosevelt, although they may be jeopardized by the war in Vietnam and all that goes with it—inflation, high interest rates, and the drop in political popularity. The Pearson rationale is interesting: He holds President Johnson's advisers primarily responsible for escalating the war. The main culprit, in Pearson's judgment, is Walt Rostow, his chief foreign affairs adviser. Incidentally, it was Lyndon Johnson who elevated Rostow from the State Department to the White House.

"Johnson," contends Pearson, "is a prisoner of the State Department and of men like Rostow, promoted from the State Department. The State Department has a habit of looking not at the long-range problems of the Presidency but a day-to-day international bureaucracy. Franklin Roosevelt spent much of his three terms bucking the State Department. His pupil, Lyndon Johnson, has gone along with the State Department. Nevertheless, Johnson knows that he must get peace in Vietnam or endanger all his great domestic accomplishments. And he has tried. He has tried much more than the American public realizes." Time and again, Johnson has sent emissaries to Russia and to other Communist and neutral nations in a persistent effort to gain a reasonable peace settlement with North Vietnam leaders. He has been constantly rebuffed.

All in all, it is Pearson's earnest contention that the enormous achievements of Lyndon Johnson's domestic program far outweigh the failures of his foreign affairs advisers. In international affairs, he depicts the President as a slave of history, manacled by the State Department, carrying on a war he never wanted.

In 1967, Pearson was publicly critical of Johnson's Vietnam policies on several occasions. On March 23, Pearson told reporter Susan Corey of the Newport News (Va.) *Times-Herald* that President Johnson could have ended the war immediately after he was elected and had erred in not doing so. Concomitantly, he declared Johnson is sincerely making an effort for peace, but wants to find a way to withdraw from Southeast Asia with honor. Pearson then added: "He's not going to find it and we just can't stay there forever."

In November 1967, Pearson declared that Johnson's biggest mistake in the war dated back to the summer of 1964 when United Nations Secretary-General Thant advised him that North Vietnam was ready to talk peace. This opinion, Pearson added, was backed up by the Canadian ambassador to North Vietnam. "But Johnson was in the midst of campaigning against Goldwater," Pearson stated, "and it turned out he waited too long."

In October 1967, Pearson charged Johnson with a tragic blunder: "Another mistake was made by Johnson in February 1965 when he started bombing North Vietnam. There were less than 30,000 U.S. troops in South Vietnam and the rate of Communist troop infiltration south was about 2,000 a month. Today we have 465,000. From 22,000 North Vietnamese troops in the south in

1965, the number has gone up to 297,000. And the end is not in sight."

Until late in 1967, Pearson's sympathy for Johnson had been shared by a majority of American editorialists. Despite the bitter controversy generated by Vietnam, most editorial pages supported the President's Vietnam policies. But at that time there was a subtle —although meaningful—change in their editorial attitudes. The Los Angeles *Times*, for example, made it clear it would oppose any extension of the war through invasion of North Vietnam or through bombing or blocking the port of Haiphong.

The Washington *Post* commented: "The President's speech and other Administration pronouncements are beginning to be colored by a fixidity and rigidity that does not encourage belief that the strategy and tactics of diminishing the scale of the effort always get full examination."

The Atlanta *Journal:* "Evidence continues to mount that the bombing does not now do, and never has done, what its strongest advocates have argued it might do. Bombings have been a serious inconvenience for North Vietnam's efforts in the South, but virtually every reliable observer has reported that they also have been a mighty factor in building morale there. . . . The spectacle of the world's most powerful nation becoming obsessed with the destruction of a relatively insignificant Asian country, for whatever reason, is unseemly. It is foolish, too."

The Miami *Herald:* "Politically, militarily, and most important, honorably, the time for change has come. The alternative is to fight the war on the terms dictated by the terrain, climate, and enemy methods. This would probably require an invasion of North Vietnam and the deployment of tens of thousands of fresh troops from the U.S."

The Richmond *Times-Dispatch:* "There must be a better way to carry on this war and bring it to an honorable conclusion. As things are going now, it will never end and the U.S. will be bled white. It has become obvious that little progress is being made, despite the presence of 500,000 U.S. soldiers in Vietnam."

Although Vietnam dominated the headlines in 1966, another story attracted front-page attention throughout the year. It was the

Dodd Case, which began as the result of a series of Pearson columns.

Ironically, the leading domestic political story of 1966 was greeted by some editors with indifference or outright rejection. Pearson says privately: "During the first weeks, the Dodd conflict of interest crusade almost failed."

The Washington *Post* did not publish the first Dodd column. Several other papers either omitted the early columns or complained about them.

The initial columns detailed the relationship between Senator Dodd and General Julius Klein, a lobbyist for West Germany, and the part both Klein and Dodd played in expanding West Germany industry in direct contradiction with the peace treaty between the United States and Germany. Dodd was Klein's messenger during one trip to Europe, and inserted various speeches and statements in the Congressional Record on behalf of West German leaders. In fact, Klein and Dodd were actually molding the foreign policy of the United States. However, the story, though extremely important, was complicated, and many editors and readers failed to grasp its significance.

Less important, but more easily understood, was the long list of gifts which Dodd received, and the testimonial dinners which he staged, the funds from which went to pay his personal expenses. This was in violation of the law, since these funds were supposed to be used for his reelection. Only after the publication of these columns did the Dodd story generate momentum. On January 24, 1966, Pearson charged that Senator Dodd had received "things of value" from Julius Klein, a public relations man, for traveling to West Germany in April 1964 and interceding with Klein's clients, including the West German Government. On February 23, Senator Dodd asked the Senate Foreign Relations Committee to conduct a thorough investigation, and promised he would make his records available. On June 6 the committee decided to develop its own evidence and conduct hearings.

The charges on both the Klein relationship and the use of campaign funds and testimonial proceeds were based on more than 4,000 documents taken from the Senator's files in the summer of 1965 by three former employees acting in concert with a person who was still employed at that time by Senator Dodd. They had turned the documents over to Pearson for copying and then returned them to the files.

Pearson says: "The Dodd employees did not come to us, we went to them. I had suspected for years that Dodd was on the take and had written some stories about him, particularly about his being paid by Guatemala as a foreign agent. There was nothing illegal about this, since he was registered. After Jack Anderson heard about the Dodd employees being disgruntled, we decided to seize the opportunity."

The former employees were James P. Boyd, Jr., who had been administrative assistant; Mrs. Marjorie Carpenter, a private secretary, and Terry Golden, a secretary. The fourth person involved was Michael V. O'Hare, office manager and bookkeeper. Senator Dodd dismissed Mrs. Carpenter and Mr. Boyd in December 1964, but then kept Boyd on until May 15, 1965. Miss Golden was discharged in October 1965; Mr. O'Hare stayed until January 31, 1966.

The committee held hearings on the Senator's financial affairs for five days beginning March 13, 1967. The crux of the issue over Dodd's use of the proceeds from the dinners was the intent of those who bought the $100-a-plate tickets. Dodd and his counsel, John F. Sonnett, insisted the purchasers intended to make a "gift" to the Senator to use as he "saw fit," and that therefore the proceeds were not taxable income. Seven Democratic politicians, all close friends of Dodd who were connected with the fund-raising affairs, testified that they regarded the purpose of the testimonials to be the raising of money for the Senator's "personal use."

Furthermore, the Senator submitted affidavits from about 400 of the approximately 2,300 persons who attended the affair stating that they intended the price of the tickets as a gift and not a political contribution. The committee received the affidavits "for the record," but noted that their language had been "prepared by his office" and that they had been distributed by Edward P. Sullivan, in charge of Dodd's Hartford office. As for the testimony of those who helped organize the affairs, the committee noted that the solicitation letter from the November 1961 dinner represented the event as "a testimonial dinner" without stating its further purpose. But the solicitation letters for all other affairs represented them as being "for political campaign purposes."

In conclusion, the committee said: "Not one solicitation letter, invitation, ticket, program, or other written communication informed the public that the funds were to be used for personal purposes. Senator Dodd used part of the proceeds from these political testimonials and part of the contributions from his political campaign of 1964 for his personal benefit."

Among the personal uses, it said, were payments of Federal income taxes ($28,588), improvements on his home in North Stonington ($9,480), "transfers" to his son, Jeremy ($4,900), "and certain other transportation, hotel, restaurant, and other expenses incurred by the Senator outside Connecticut or by members of his family or his representatives of the political campaign period."

At the end of the 1964 campaign, a total of $94,896—representing what was left from his campaign contributions and dinner proceeds—was transferred to the Senator's personal account. Out of this, the Senator used $81,788 to retire personal loans, including those made to pay income tax. The committee also said that Dodd had been reimbursed by both the Senate and private organizations for seven "official" trips from 1961 to 1965, and that on six other "nonofficial" trips he had been reimbursed by both a private organization and his campaign fund.

The Dodd scandal was a front page story in 1966 and 1967. During the period, Pearson continued to unearth additional shocking evidence. The case inspired an editorial deluge. Following is a cross section:

Washington *Post:* "Senator Thomas J. Dodd's testimonial dinner, former Senator Richard Nixon's expense funds, Senator Ralph Yarborough's radio fund—and other curious devices by which many Senators and Representatives augment their public income by private and often secret gratuities are all of one piece. In varying degrees of vulnerability they are all open to the objection that they put the office-holders who are paid for serving the whole public under peculiar and special obligations to a select group of citizens. Campaign contributions are bad enough—and worse when they slop over from the campaign period into private coffers of office seekers.

. . . Congress may not be ready or able to deal with the campaign expenditures. But it ought to be able to forbid by explicity and definite enactment the solicitation or acceptance of other contributions. . . . In effect, they [the present laws] put a premium on concealment. They ought to at least put a premium on disclosures and require the regular publication of any such contributions."

St. Petersburg *Times:* "Drew Pearson has done it again. His persistent reporting of the curious relationship between Connecticut's Democratic Sen. Thomas J. Dodd and Gen. Julius Klein, has become a national story too big for Pearson's syndicated column. . . . The question raised by Pearson's disclosures is whether this is proper conduct for a United States Senator. But that basic issue has been lost in the furor. The feeling in Washington is that the columnist and the Senator are on a collision course which is certain to hurt one of them. Knowing Pearson's talent, we're betting it won't be the columnist and that the sidetracked Dodd case will return to the central issue raised by Pearson before it ends."

St. Louis *Post-Dispatch:* "The Senate Committee on Standards and Conduct ought to be encouraged to get to the bottom of what it has termed 'charges of misconduct' against Senator Dodd of Connecticut. . . . What is disturbing about the case is that the Federal Bureau of Investigation and Attorney General Katzenbach apparently are questioning some of Mr. Pearson's sources to determine how they obtained the information used by Mr. Pearson in his columns. Since Mr. Dodd has powerful friends in the White House and federal agencies there is bound to be ugly suspicion that someone is trying to discredit Mr. Pearson's case by showing he obtained the evidence in an irregular manner. The point here is not how Mr. Pearson obtained his information, but whether his charges stand up. That is what the Senate Committee is honor bound to determine. Any other inquiry is out of order at this time."

Los Angeles *Times:* "Grave charges of misconduct in office have been levelled against Senator Thomas J. Dodd (D-Conn.) by columnist Drew Pearson. Some of these accusations go far beyond alleged unethical practices. They involve charges that Dodd siphoned political campaign funds into his private bank account. With obvious reluctance, the Senate's Permanent Select Committee on

Standards and Conduct, established in the wake of the Bobby Baker scandals, has undertaken a probe of these accusations. Their problem, say Washington observers, is compounded by the fact that the committee as yet hasn't even drawn up a yardstick for measuring misconduct. This strikes us as a weak alibi, in the Dodd case, for not pressing vigorously ahead with their investigation. If true, Pearson's charges against the Senator go beyond any borderline aspects of unethical conduct."

Boston *Herald:* "Congress will sometimes investigate a fellow Congressman. But it is who and how thoroughly they investigate that counts, and the record of Congress in this respect is not good. . . . We hope Congress conducts a thorough investigation of Dodd and then gets around to the real problem: the adoption of a strong code of ethics and the machinery to enforce the code."

New Haven, Connecticut, *Register:* "Pending official Senate action on the charges—and this action should not be delayed in any way—it is probably inevitable that a great deal of political interplay will develop in Connecticut and in Washington. The issues, however, are too serious—for the principals and for the process of representative government—to be exploited in partisan terms. What is most needed now is an impartial determination of any truth."

New York *Post:* "In recent days, there has been audible lament in Washington that Senators' salaries, now $30,000, may be too low. This is a legitimate subject for inquiry; raises may be necessary. But the complaints and the continuing resistance to financial disclosure provide ground for the suspicion that some Senators may have so much to disclose that they prefer concealment."

Durham, North Carolina, *Herald:* "One need not have a very vivid imagination to sense the hazard in having important Senators dependent on the proceeds of appreciation dinners to make their personal ends meet. . . . The practice is no less pernicious when it is limited to a Nixon or a Dodd. And if the Senate Ethics Committee's reaction is just to commiserate with Senator Dodd because that bad man, Drew Pearson, has been picking on him, it will, indeed, stir new questions about the general ethics of the Senate."

As the months passed, the evidence against Dodd dominated Pearson's columns. During a six-month period he devoted more than thirty columns to the subject. Senator Dodd countered with a series of denials. One June 13, 1967, the Senator offered a prolonged and emotional plea of innocence on the Senate floor. He concluded his defense by stating: "A question at issue is whether freedom of the press involves the right of muck-raking columnists * to conspire to steal the files of any public official or any private citizen they dislike. Let no one say that the means do not matter. I submit that my case cannot be fairly judged if it is not considered in its full context and in all its implications. . . . I do not ask for mercy, I ask for justice."

Washington columnist William S. White voiced the case for Senator Dodd: "The four disgruntled ex-employees who betrayed the trust of their employer and friend, Sen. Thomas J. Dodd of Connecticut, to filch private papers from his office and so to put him through the ordeal of public trial by his colleagues have at last gone too far. . . . Reasonably fair men would have supposed that their original accusations would have been quite enough to content them. Now, however, they are leaking yet more of the same. The pursuit of Dodd began in the shallow 'moral indignation' of people who discovered that he was a bad fellow only after three of them had been fired by him long before there ever was 'a Dodd case' and for reasons which, in charity to them, the Senator has never trumpeted. Now, to venom has been added a tireless vindictiveness."

William F. Buckley, Jr., politician, columnist, and conservative crusader for the upperdog, chimed in with: "It is of course Pearson who has done more than any man in recent times to sanctify the violation of privacy—by trafficking, endlessly, in documents stolen from the private files of a United States Senator by thieves who did not cavil even at the removal of the Senator's correspondence with his children."

Washington correspondent Joseph Kraft adopted an historical perspective: "The old politics lie at the very center of the case of

* Late in 1967, Pearson told Chicago's Headline Club that he takes pride in being a muckraker. He added: "There is always the danger of libel suits in muckraking. One must be cautious and obtain air-tight evidence before one accuses." Incidentally, Pearson and his staff worked nine months to collect the evidence in the Dodd case.

Sen. Thomas Dodd of Connecticut. . . . Two major historical events combined to produce the old politics. First, there was the depression with the political premium it put on support for New Deal measures. Next there was the post-war period with the premium it put on breast-beating hostility to communism. . . . As a pure product of the old politics, Sen. Dodd had a burning faith in the principles bred out of the depression and the post-war era. And he is in trouble now mainly because he clung to that faith long after it ceased to have political impact or even much relevance. Dodd's fidelity to the depression experience, for example, went beyond continuing support for social security and laws favorable to labor and minority groups. Unlike most of his colleagues in the Senate who adjusted to prosperity by developing interests in law firms or family properties, Dodd tried to live on in the old way of the New Deal bureaucrat—on his salary. He fell, in consequence, badly in debt. And that is how he came to be draining off funds meant for political and official business to his personal account."

A perceptive analysis of press coverage in the Dodd case was written by Robert H. Yoakum for the *Columbia School of Journalism Review:*

"There are more than 1,400 correspondents milling around Washington, several hundred of them bona fide employees of wire services, newspapers, magazines, and broadcasting companies paid to relay tidings of interest to readers, listeners, and viewers throughout the nation. It must be assumed that a corrupt Senator is a tiding of interest, i.e., news. But in the three months from the first Pearson-Anderson column on January 24, 1966, until the Ethics Committee announced hearings on April 29, 1966, the Dodd employees were interviewed by only two people: Sarah McClendon representing some Texas newspapers, and James Canan of the Gannett Newspapers which take in the Hartford *Times.* The wire services were no more energetic than the newspapers. The AP stories were normally based on leads developed by others, and the UPI's dispatches often sounded as though they had been processed in Dodd's office. ('For eight years, he has been one of the most respected members of the Senate,' a UPI background story reported inaccurately in April 1966, compounding the error later in the piece by referring to Dodd as '. . . a man respected for his views on foreign affairs.') So much for our huge, probing, restless, truth-seeking news agencies. A Senator was up to his clavicle in ill-gained dollars, but the wire services were unable to spring even one of their 141 Washington reporters to interview the ex-employees who had the story."

In addition, Robert H. Yoakum offered a revealing examination of the home-state coverage. In general, Connecticut newspapers ignored the story. One exception was Charles B. Lenahan, publisher of the Hamden *Chronicle,* who wrote a column titled "Connecticut's Silent Press." Lenahan had just returned from a visit to Saigon, and he reported: "Senator Dodd was spread all over the front pages of such disparate papers as the Bangkok *World,* the Saigon *Post,* the Hong Kong *South China Post,* and the Tokyo *Asahi Evening News.* This was a bigger story in the English language press of the Far East than it evidently was in the Connecticut press. This is the condition that has existed from the beginning of the Dodd revelations. . . . There is no doubt that the [Connecticut] state press has held back on the Dodd story. The question is why. . . . Whatever the reason, the newspaper reading public of the state has been subjected to a remarkable example of non-reporting, of quite self-conscious evasion of an important public matter."

Yoakum phoned many Connecticut editors in an effort to determine why they failed to adequately cover the Dodd case. He received no satisfaction. He had assumed, he wrote, that "When editors learned of the serious charges against Dodd, they would have peppered Washington correspondents, stringers, or wire services with queries; begun an investigation of Dodd's office in Hartford; obtained interviews with the disillusioned ex-employees; found out whether state laws had been violated; written indignant editorials calling for a speedier and broader Senate probe; followed up the fascinating leads that emerged from March 1967 hearings and the April letter of his ex-employees; printed the text of that letter (as the Washington *Post* did), and kept the entire staff alert to one of the biggest political scandals in Connecticut's history in the making."

Concluded Yoakum: "This is an almost precise account of what the Connecticut papers did not do."

What some papers did not do, Pearson and others did. As a

result, on April 27, 1967, the Senate Ethics Committee recommended that Senator Dodd be censured for conduct "contrary to accepted morals" that tended to bring the Senate "into dishonor and disrepute." The Senate supported the recommendation. Dodd became the sixth Senator whose conduct has been censured or condemned by his colleagues. Pearson played a major role in two of them: Senator Joseph McCarthy as well as Dodd.

While Pearson was uncovering information about Dodd, he was investigating the record of Congressman Adam Clayton Powell. Among the many Pearson columns on Powell, perhaps the most sensational was that of September 13, 1965, in which he quoted verbatim the text of the State Department cable to American embassies abroad, instructing them to secure theatre tickets, nightclub reservations, and a yacht for Powell and his two secretaries. Further, Pearson reported in detail on Powell fishing trips, how he had sidetracked the Anti-Poverty Program as the consequence of one fishing holiday and his failure to vote on civil rights legislation as the result of another. On September 1, 1966, Pearson published the details of Mrs. Powell's trip to Washington with her three-year-old son and Powell's refusal to see her. He reported that Mrs. Powell, residing in Puerto Rico, had not received salary checks which Congressional records showed were supposedly paid to her. In addition, Pearson published details of Powell's misuse of air travel cards to Miami en route to his vacation home in Bimini. Subsequently, Adam Clayton Powell had the dubious distinction of being the only Congressman to be expelled from the House of Representatives.

Pearson later said that Powell's plight was in part due to the fact "he was mean to his wife. That made all the women mad. I don't think Powell was half as bad as Dodd in what he did."

The Dodd controversy did not end with censure. Since Pearson and controversy have a magnetic attraction, the Dodd affair resulted in another headlined conflict.

On May 7, 1967, *Newsweek* magazine disclosed that the Pulitzer Prize jury's recommendation of a Pulitzer award for Drew Pearson and Jack Anderson—for their exposure of the Dodd scandal—had been overruled by the Pulitzer Prize Advisory Board in favor of Stanley W. Penn and Monroe W. Karmin of the *Wall Street Journal* for their investigative reporting on the links between organized crime in the United States and gambling in the Bahamas.

Several days later, Paul Sann, executive editor of the New York *Post,* who served as a member of the Pulitzer jury, reported that the jury "never even saw the winning entry." Sann said the jury recommendation had been given in strenuous terms, and he complained that its rejection by the advisory board "tainted the prizes."

When news of the Pulitzer controversy reached Pearson's office, the columnist sighed and said he was "philosophical about not getting the prize." Then he smiled and observed: "The day before the prizes were to be announced, I told Jack Anderson I'd bet him we would not get it. He had some hopes. But I've been around longer than he has."

In November 1967, Pearson again hit the front pages with a shocker involving California Governor Ronald Reagan. "A homosexual ring has been operating in his office," Pearson reported. He added that the homosexual group involved eight men, including two former members of Reagan's staff. The California Governor, the story noted, had been made aware of the facts six months before he dismissed the members of his staff involved in the incident.

Governor Reagan responded to Pearson's story with a twenty-minute press conference in which he denied the Pearson report, called the columnist a "liar" and "scurrilous." In addition, he recalled that President Truman had called Pearson an "s.o.b."

Within forty-eight hours after Reagan issued his flat denial, Pearson's story was confirmed by *The New York Times,* the Boston *Globe,* and rival columnists Rowland Evans and Robert Novak. Governor Reagan then conceded he may have created a credibility gap by repeatedly denying reports that a homosexual ring had been uncovered in his administration. But he said it was for humanitarian reasons.

Incidentally, Reagan's revival of the Truman s.o.b. story offered Pearson an opportunity to write: "I cherish in my files a statement which Mr. Truman gave me, which I have never published, in which he revises his opinion. The statement reads in part: 'In my judgment Pearson is by and large a force for good in the country. He is sincere, fearless, has the courage of his convictions, and hammers away at what he believes is right, however unpopular it may be. He takes the side of the less privileged."

On November 20, 1967, I received a letter from Drew Pearson. "Dear Herman," it read in part, "have you considered the possibility of adding a chapter on recent stories which have molded history, such as the Reagan piece on homosexuals on his staff? I think this has pretty well knocked Reagan out of the box as a Republican candidate and as an attempt by the far right to take over the Republican Party—and the United States—in 1968."

It is evident that as big government becomes bigger and more complex, investigative, crusading journalism becomes more difficult and more urgent. Exposed politicians are professional whiners. And the elements in the press guilty of negligence or downright venality demonstrate the realistic necessity of newspapermen who raise hell and report the facts.

The problem was polarized a long time ago by the comments of two government leaders. In 1787, Thomas Jefferson issued his classic admonition: "The basis of our government being the opinion of the people, the very first object should be to keep that right, and were it left to me to decide whether we should have a government without newspapers, or newspapers without a government, I should not hesitate to choose the latter."

Another point of view was offered in 1920: "Why should freedom of the press and speech be allowed? Why should a government which is doing what it believes to be right allow itself to be criticized? It would not allow opposition by lethal weapons. Ideas are much more fatal than guns. Why should any man be allowed to buy a printing press and disseminate pernicious opinions calculated to embarrass the government?"

The foregoing in an excerpt from a speech made in Moscow by Nikolai Lenin.

HE WALL STREET JOURNA

EASTERN EDITION

WEDNESDAY, MAY 25, 1966

demands be discussed.
hey and the college presi-
t, Dr. Albert Jacobs, were
lly allowed to leave at 8:30
nday night, but most of the
dents stayed in the building,
king entry to all but re-
ters and student sympa-

Most Stay Overnight

hey brought mattresses,
s, hamburgers and text-
s, and most of them spent
night sleeping on desks or
erence tables.
Ve're prepared to stay until
meet our demands," said
Jones, the demonstration
r.
. Jones is president of the
y Association of Negroes,
n includes nearly all of
20 or so nonwhites in the
-man student body of this
l arts college.
is is our commitment, and
proud to have so many
guys with us," said the
r, soft-spoken youth.
Mr. Jones's direction, the
nstrators took care not to
sorderly in the building.
stopped visitors with a
"I'm sorry, sir, but we
et you in."
students demanded that
llege immediately com-
5,000 to a new scholar-
nd for Negroes, giving
nce to high school stu-
from Hartford and New

ew Courses Asked

other $75,000 in the
uld come from a col-
nd now used for such
activities as the stu-

the New Yor
Student Nonv
ing Committee
nationally by
The protest b
noon when ab
gathered arou
front of Low
Columbia U
administrative
the sundial, t
surged up the
Low building
test directly
tration.
The Low bui
however, and
tors were turn
versity securit
the guards s
members of a
stration group
tive-oriented
Free Campus.
The S.D.S.-le
ered around M
umbia's S.D.S.
read a letter
Truman, vice
university, offe
with the group
the McMillan
Columbia camp
The boisterou
down the offer
then marched to
new gymnasium,
and Morningsid
they tore down
chain link fence
being cleared
million gymnasi
moved in, wieldi
and arrested one
Wilson.
The protesters
blocks back to
campus, where M
addressed the gro

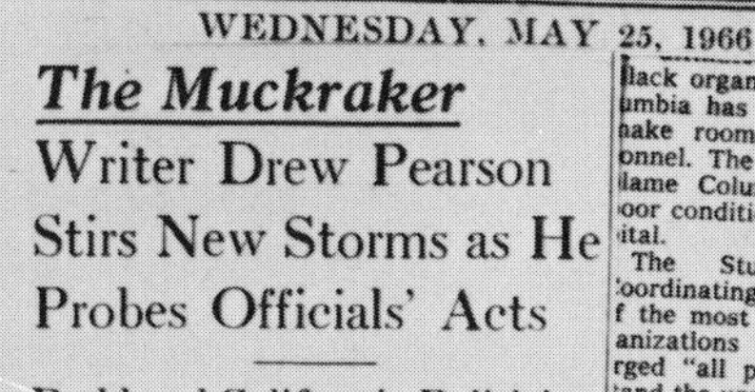

The Muckraker

Writer Drew Pearson Stirs New Storms as He Probes Officials' Acts

Dodd and California Politician Sue, but an Editor Calls Him 'a Real Public Servant'

Selling Manure on the Side

By FREDERICK C. KLEIN
Staff Reporter of THE WALL STREET JOURNAL

WASHINGTON — A new product is due to go on the market this summer. It is to be called "Drew Pearson's Muck," and it's to be billed as "packaged by the best muckraker in the U.S." The seller: Mr. Pearson himself.

The muck, Mr. Pearson says, will come from the bottom of an old canal on his sprawling dairy farm in northwest Maryland, about 18 miles up the Potomac River from here. "The stuff is more than 100 years old—very rich and fine for gardeners and people who have window boxes," he says enthusiastically.

The self-advertising venture certainly is a natural one for Andrew Russell Pearson, the white-mustached news man who has been raking muck in the figurative sense for nearly 40 years. His column, Washington Merry-Go-Round, is a collection of hard news, gossip and prophecy that alternately delights or enrages Washingtonians, depend-

lack organizations charge Columbia has evicted Negroes to make room for hospital personnel. The organizations also blame Columbia for allegedly poor conditions at Harlem Hospital.

The Student Nonviolent Coordinating Committee, one of the most militant black organizations in the country, urged "all people who understand the urgency of this struggle to support t he students, community people and their lies."

"It should be crystal clear at the issue at stake is the control by local people of their community and the institutions within their community, and e right of black people to otest injustices perpetrated on them by institutions such Columbia University," N.C.C. said.

The group's spokesman said t I.D.A. "works on military ojects aimed at the oppression of the people of Vietnam" "develops riot equipment commit mass genocide inst black people here in the ."

Groups Invited

illiam Sales, a 25-year-old mbia graduate student who working on a doctorate in national affairs and who is member of the five-man ring committee leading the est, said all off-campus ps participating in the demonstration had been invited the steering committee, h is composed entirely of ents.

hile demonstrators filled corridors of Hamilton Hall, e playing guitars and others ng blankets and engaging scussions, Mr. Sales summed his feelings about Col-

Remodeled Vessel Sports a Wild Decor in Debut Here

By WERNER BAMBERGER

The American Export Isbrandtsen Lines passenger ship Independence, operated for the last 1
trans-
made
as a
The
pletely
at a c
new
hotel
traditi
amid
The
operat
image
first
Indies
the Fo
The
be
cruises
this y
make
to the
June a
trans-A
operate
Her
pearanc
500-foo
bling an
low an
with ey
mixed
ship fra

Accor
er, exec
America
parent
ship line
vessel w
thing ne
Mr. W

flown
The
design
gade f
turban
said. A
to be
artiller
Bragg,
Baltim

Pearson Pr
Muckraking

CHICAGO—Colum
PEARSON takes pr
called a muckrak
150 members of
Headline Club rece
"There is alway
of libel suits in
One must be cauti
tain air-tight proof
accuses."
For example, h
Senate never would

Drew Pearson

to censure Sen. Th
(D-Conn.) for
funds from political
als if it hadn't bee
closures in the P
Anderson column. Pe
his staff worked nine
get "airtight evidenc
"If it weren't for

PEARSON PREDICTS

OP Front Runners Out In '68

AN COREY
ld Staff Writer
—Veteran Wash-
r and political
Pearson met
orters last night

The widely-known columnist met the press earlier at a party in the Golden Triangle Motel.
His predictions

date, but made it obvious throughout the talk that he likes President Johnson.
Discussing

the Byrd machine is alread
being left

ew March lanned in ouisville

ouisville, Ky. (AP)—Louis-
civil rights leaders, vowing
"escalation" in their drive
an open housing ordinance,
ned to renew their march
tonight and return to the
ndotte Park area, where
earlier were met by rock-
egg-throwing hecklers.
he demonstration would fol-
a Kentucky Derby free
m threatened activities at
rchill Downs, called off by
Martin Luther King as a
ture of good will."
city police follow what has
eared to become a pattern,
will arrest the marchers
ediately if threatened by
crowd of whites.
e nearly 2,000 National
rdsmen pressed into service
eep order at Churchill
ns Saturday have gone
e after a peaceful weekend.
them has gone the slogan
pen housing advocates, "No
sing, No Derby."
e Kentucky Derby is now
ory, and it was undoubtedly
housing advocates' greatest
age to date in their at-

Portrait of Prize-Winners

Post Photo by Del

This year's Albert Einstein Commemorative Award winners (l-r), Sir Isaac Wolfson, for philanthropy; James A. Michener, for humanities; Dr. Andre Lwoff, for science, and Andrew Wyeth, for art, hold medalli bearing likeness of late scientist at Americana presen tion ceremonies.

11

PORTRAIT OF A NEWSPAPERMAN

When Drew Pearson was asked to describe the changes in political journalism over the past decades, he responded succinctly: "The chief change in Washington journalism has been the increase in the number of columns. When I started there were only two columnists. Now—how many are there? Most of these columns are think columns, editorial columns, opinion columns. The second change is that now there is a greater tendency to dig behind the news for the facts. Editors are no longer satisfied with handouts. How have the changes influenced me? Well, they made me work harder. I feel I have influenced the changes because now the AP and UP don't turn down stories; they figure if they don't print it, Drew Pearson will—so they'd better."

Being a reporter in Washington is not much different from being a reporter anywhere else. It is basically an infantry job—lots of shoe leather. You must get around, speak to people in Washington, New York, London, Rome, and Moscow—wherever news is breaking. As Joe Alsop has noted: "If you go out and see what is going on yourself, and talk to a great many people who are responsibly involved in what is going on, you can hardly help doing a good job of reporting."

What Drew Pearson has continued doing is a good—sometimes extraordinary—job of reporting. "I have always tried," says Pearson, "to emphasize the personal side in Washington. I think it's helped make my broader points about clean government more effective." The Dodd case, of course, was his latest effective point. Pearson has inspired younger correspondents to probe beneath the surface of government, and thereby given Washington journalism a unique zest and excitement.

While studying Pearson the newspaperman, it becomes pertinent to examine Pearson the man. He is a principal subscriber to what Bertrand Russell called the Grand Fallacy of the 20th Century, the theory of the superior virtue of the oppressed. On the other hand, he will ruthlessly use his power to extract a story, and woe unto the public servant who does not cooperate.

Pearson is sometimes unorthodox in his methods. Disgruntled employees, grudge settlers, informants, ambitious subordinates attempt, sometimes successfully, to use him as an instrument of revenge. These are not the most reliable sources. Further, the accused, so to speak, not infrequently gets no chance to tell his story before Pearson tells his millions of readers.

His loyalty to false friends has limited his effectiveness as a journalist, for he will excuse in his friends acts which he would tolerate neither in himself nor his enemies. Ironically, he is the victim of some of the most monumental ingratitudes in Washington history. He has kept the handcuffs off some people whose sole recognition of his heroic efforts in their behalf was to punch him on the jaw the second their hands were free.

Pearson's belittlers says he is inaccurate and even a liar. But he turns out seven columns a week, a broadcast, and news letter, and the overwhelming majority of his statements—99.9 percent—are beyond challenge. They are good hard news. His critics have learned what is called the "negative pregnant of the law." Thus, Pearson, for example, might allege that a lobbyist passed X dollars to a legislator in the latter's Chrysler car. The legislator will then retort that he never owned a Chrysler in his life, leaving the complaint still pregnant with the charge that he took the bribe. Some of Drew's best and true stories have been fouled up on a detail of this kind. Despite his critics and his flaws, he has been an outstanding reporter, perhaps the most remarkable in political journalism.

In 1958, before departing for Europe, Pearson dictated a memo for his staff:

> Don't hesitate to admit an error. Double and triple check in order to avoid errors, but if you find you are wrong, say so. It is only fair to the man you have wronged, in addition to which the public will respect you for being fair.
>
> Never bear grudges. If a President or a Senator calls you a name, don't call one back. Because he is puerile or small is no reason for you to sink to his level. Write facts; don't go in for name-calling. Any scrivener can fill a column with abuse. Epithets can be culled from any dollar dictionary, but it takes good journalism to ferret out graft of the backstage doings of diplomats or the income-tax cheaters—and then make what you say stand up in court.
>
> Remember that it is part of your job to right some of the news-wrongs of the Capital. The big newspaper chains can be ruthless, their newsmen are in a hurry. It is your job to probe deeper than the handout or the official statement. You are to pick up where the spot-newsman, rushing for the telephone or grabbing for the headline, leave off. Frequently the best part of the story is after the spot-news cream has been skimmed.
>
> Remember also that ever since politicians became politicians, the thing the public was not supposed to know has taken place in the private lobbies and the smoke-filled rooms. Yet what is hidden from the public is usually what the public is most entitled to know about, and the job of a good newspaperman is to report.
>
> Remember that in our system of government by checks and balances, it is your job to help in the checking. Government is so intricate and detailed today that Congress no longer can do all the checking. Furthermore, Congressmen themselves have to be checked. Most Congressmen themselves are honest and reasonably conscientious, but it is your job to smoke out the Parnell Thomases, the Andy Mays, and the "Doc" Brehems and report the facts about them—even if it means a tough battle.
>
> However, it is also important to remember that the government is neither all good, nor all bad. There are bureau-

> crats who are woefully inefficient, and bureaucrats who are a credit to mankind. It is your job to discriminate.
>
> Government is only as good as the men in it. And since men are human, they are subject to all the frailties that make up mankind—laziness, inefficiency, greed, graft, temptation.
>
> But they are also subject to great effort, sacrifice, inspiration. It is your job as a newspaperman to spur the lazy, watch the weak, expose the corrupt. You must be the eyes, ears, and nose of the American people.
>
> But likewise remember that there are scores of underpaid Government servants dedicated to the cause of good government whom the public never hears of. It is your job to encourage them. It is also your job to let the public know that these men are working for them.
>
> For the public must never lose confidence in its government. Should it ever take seriously the scoldings of some of my competitors and lose confidence in our form of government, then the principle we are fighting for would be no more.
>
> Remember that though the world moves slowly toward its two great goals—peace and the brotherhood of man—it is your job when possible to help accelerate the pace.

Many people have articulated those goals for hundreds of years. Only a few have accelerated the movement toward those aspirations. Drew Pearson is one of them.

INDEX

INDEX